I0834118

EVERY-DAY TOPICS

A

BOOK OF BRIEFS

BY

J. G. HOLLAND

NEW YORK
SCRIBNER, ARMSTRONG AND COMPANY
1876.

B. Hermon Smith, Stereotyper,
The University Press, Ithaca, N. Y.

JOHN F. TROW & SON, PRINTERS,
205-213 EAST 12TH ST., NEW YORK.

PREFACE.

A good many years ago, the author wrote and published a series of familiarly didactic books which won a wide reading and which are still so kindly regarded by the public that they maintain for themselves a constant sale. Many of the articles published during the last five years under the general head of "*Topics of the Time*," in SCRIBNER'S MONTHLY, of which he is the editor, have been recognized by the publishers of these books as cognate with them in subjects and mode of treatment, and they have invited him to select from the large accumulation those which seem adapted to the needs of every time, and prepare them for publication as a companion volume. This work he has undertaken carefully to do, and the result is the book herewith presented.

There is, of course, no opportunity in an editorial to treat any topic exhaustively, but a group of brief papers, upon any general subject, may be relied upon to present many of its more obvious and practically important phases. As these papers, however, were written without reference to each other, or to their collection and presentation in a volume, their division into groups has not been effected without some degree of arbitrariness; but it is believed that the direct or indirect relations of the constituents of each group to its general topic will be readily recognized, and that the classification will be helpful in many ways.

The principal difficulty which the Author has encountered has grown out of the attempt to avoid repetitions which, through forgetfulness and inadvertence, have found their way into articles so widely separated in the dates of their production. The most of these he has been able to suppress, but he has been compelled to retain some of them because of their important relations to the context.

With this explanation, these papers, already familiar to many thousands of readers, are submitted to the public, by its grateful friend,

THE AUTHOR.

CONTENTS.

CULTURE.

LITERATURE AND LITERARY MEN.

CRITICISM.

THE POPULAR LECTURE

PERSONAL DANGERS.

PERSONAL DEVELOPMENT.

PREACHERS AND PREACHING.

CHRISTIANITY AND SCIENCE.

REVIVALS AND REFORMS.

CHRISTIAN PRACTICE.

THE CHURCH OF THE FUTURE.

THE COMMON MORALITIES.

WOMAN.

WOMAN AND HOME.

AMUSEMENTS.

THE TEMPERANCE QUESTION.

SOCIAL INTERCOURSE.

TOWN AND COUNTRY.

THE RICH AND THE POOR.

POLITICS AND POLITICAL MEN.

AMERICAN LIFE AND MANNERS.

EVERY DAY TOPICS.

CULTURE.

The Faults of Culture.

Is it heresy to say that no pursuit can be more selfish than that of culture for its own sake? If there be forgiveness for such a sin, either in this world or the world to come, let us commit it, and so have the pleasure of uttering a very earnest conviction. Any competent observer cannot fail to have noticed that the seeking of that which is most admirable in intellectual finish and furniture, simply for the sake of holding it in possession, has the same degrading effect upon the soul that comes to the miser from hoarding his gold. "The greatest, wisest, meanest of mankind" was a typical devotee of selfish culture; and it is safe to declare that all men and women who pursue culture as an end, failing to devote it to any purpose involving self-surrender, are mean in their degree. So it often happens that as men grow more learned by study, and more skilled in intellectual practice, and more nicely adjusted and finished in their power, and more delicate and exact in their tastes, do they lose their sympathy with the world of common life, and become fastidious, disdainful and cold. They seem able to warm only toward those who praise them or who set an extravagant value upon their possessions, and to hold fellowship with none but those of kindred pursuits.

It is often noticed, with surprise and regret, that as culture comes in, faith goes out. The fact seems strange to those who think that faith, if it is a rational thing in itself, should grow vigorous and far-reaching with the rising power and deepening delicacy of the mind. "Is it only the ignorant who have faith?" they ask; "and must man surrender this divinest of all possessions when culture enters?" Ay, he must, if culture is pursued as an end in itself. Culture thoroughly Christianized—culture pursued for ends of benevolence—strengthens faith; but culture that ends in itself and its possessor is infidel in every tendency. The culture which is pursued for its own sake makes a god of self, and so turns away the soul from its relations—earthly and heavenly—that self becomes the one great fact of the universe. A culture which does not serve God by direct purpose, and with loving and reverent devotion, is the purest type of practical infidelity; and there are notable individual instances, even in so young a civilization as ours, in which constantly ripening culture has been a constantly descending path into Paganism. We fear that any thoughtful American, undertaking to name those in his own country who have carried intellectual culture to the highest point, would be obliged to indicate men and women to whom Christianity has no high meaning, and by whom it wins no victories.

When culture is selfish, all its sympathies are clannish. There is nothing outside of its circle to be either admired or tolerated. Such culture can have no broad aims, except the selfish aim to be broadly recognized. Whatever work it does is done for the few. To contribute by kind and self-adaptive purpose to the wants of the many is what it never does. It is too proud to be useful. It would be glad to command or to lead, but it will not serve. It works away at its own refinement and aggrandizement, but refuses to come down into the dusty ways of life, to point men upwards and to help them bear their burdens. The world all might go to the dogs or the devil for anything that selfish culture would do to prevent it. That work is done, and must always be done, by those who have faith—by the humble who have something better than culture, or the high who have placed their culture under the control of that law of love whose feet stand upon the earth, and whose hands grasp The Throne.

The farmer, in recommending an animal to a purchaser, talks of flesh that is "worked on," in contradistinction to that which is acquired while standing still and feeding. The one acquisition is recognized as possessing qualities of power and endurance which the other does not. It is precisely so with culture. That which is "worked on"—that which comes while its possessor is busy in ministry—is as beautiful as it is valuable. This, indeed, is the only culture that comes to a man as a legitimate, healthful and valuable possession. The florist can show us flowers whose beauty has been won by culture, but it has been won at the fatal cost of their fragrance. There may be much in even a selfish culture to admire, but if there is nothing to inhale, our hearts are still hungry. We are obliged to go near to see that which should come to us on all the wings of the air.

There is a sort of blind worship of culture among the people, which would not be worship were it not blind. If they could comprehend its narrowness of sympathy and its selfishness of purpose; if they could see and measure its greed for praise, and its contempt for them and their acquisitions and pursuits; if they could feel its arrogance and pride, its charms would all disappear. If they could see how, in their earnest coveting of the best gifts, those who possess them had utterly forgotten the "more excellent way," they would shrink from them in terror or in pity. It is sad to think that from the most notable school of personal culture in the country faith long since departed, with limping wings, while devotion to the work of making the world better went out with faith. Men who ministered at the altar have forsaken it; and men who broke bread to the multitude refuse to taste it themselves, even when it is presented to them in the name of Humanity's Highest and Divinity's Best. God save us all from the influence of such a culture as this, and help us to be grateful that it has seen its best or its worst days, and is dying at its root! Christianity must kill it or Christianity must die. It must kill Christianity or it must die. The event is not doubtful.

A culture that is in itself a mistake cannot by any possibility become a bar of sound judgment on any subject. It is not safe to trust it in any question of religion, or morals, or society: much less in any question of art or literature. Its own productions the people have always declined to receive as useful to them in any degree, for they have no relation to their wants.

Sectarian Culture and What Comes of It.

It is not to be denied that that culture which accompanies devotion to sectarian systems and ideas is not admirable. It is equally beyond dispute that the style of personal character which accompanies such culture is not lovable. The limit of sympathy is alike the limit of culture and of lovableness. It is a matter of surprise that men whose Christian honesty, purity, and self-devotedness are conceded on every hand, are often men with whom we do not like to associate—men to whom we do not find ourselves attracted—men with whom we have little that is common. There are clergymen of great power and influence in their own denomination who are so entirely out of place in general society that they never appear in it. Their whole life runs in a sectarian rut, and tends toward, and ends at, a sectarian goal. There are great multitudes of laymen of the same sort, who have no associations outside of their own church. Hugging the thought that they monopolize the truth, they can regard no other sect with hearty toleration and respect. Their sympathies are shortened in every direction, and their culture fails to be admirable, because it is based on one-sided views of truth, and limited by the prescribed tenets of their faith. It is not an answer to this statement to say that true Christianity is never popular, and that even its Founder was not popular. It was the narrow sects that hated Him. It was the Scribes and Pharisees whom He denounced who despised Him. The common people heard Him gladly, and followed Him, and received His society and ministry by thousands.

It is also not to be denied that there are styles of character and culture only indirectly formed by Christian ideas, or influenced by them, that are extremely lovable. There are men and women who have had no conscious Christian experience, whose faith is either a negative or a most indefinite quantity, who make no public profession of piety, who do not even privately count themselves among Christians in name, yet who are nevertheless among the most amiable that we know. Their courtesy, their benevolence, their thorough integrity of character, their hearty good-will manifested in all society, their toleration and charity, make them universal favorites. They ignore all sects and all religious and political differences, and sometimes become social centres for the church itself. Many Christians prefer them for companions to those who are enrolled with them on church-registers, and are puzzled to know why it is that they love them more than they do those who are nominally their brethren.

The most lovable men and women we know are under the control of one of two motives, viz: the sympathy of humanity, or the sympathy of Christianity. Both are alike universal in their bearing and reach, and both produce the finest results on human character that are possible to be achieved. Those who are under the control of the sympathy of humanity know no sect, and they only become unlovely when they single out some class of men as the recipients of their good-will and their good offices. The humanitarian who delivers himself to one idea, and concentrates his sympathies and his charities upon a single class, not only injures his own character but his lovableness and popularity. Precisely as when one concentrates his sympathies and labors upon a sect, does he cease to draw the hearts of all men to him. No matter what faith we receive into our heads, our hearts will love the man who loves all men, whether he loves them as a man or a Christian; and our hearts are right. The man who knows no limit to his human sympathy, and the Christian who knows no limit to his Christian sympathy, are those who hold the hearts of the world, and who, in that sympathy, possess the only solid basis for a broad and catholic culture.

The Christian ought to be the better and the broader man. The Christian of genuinely catholic sympathies is the better and broader man; but, alas! a Christian of this type is exceedingly rare. The whole culture of the Christian church is sectarian, and only here and there do men break through the walls that have been built around them, into that large liberty of sympathy and thought which is every Christian's birthright. We fail everywhere to recognize in our sympathies those whom the Master recognizes; for the Master's love is simply the love of humanity, based on a broader knowledge of its nature, its possibilities, and its destiny. The sympathy of humanity is wholly good so far as it goes, but it falls short of Christianity in that it fails to recognize the immortal in the mortal.

We are led to this exposition by the contemplation of a notorious fact in the literary history of the time. It is a subject of sorrow among the churches of the country that the higher literature of the day is very largely the product of men and women who have little Christian faith, or none at all. Did it ever occur to these churches, or the preachers who represent them, to ask why this is the case? Why is it that these men and women have the culture that makes their productions acceptable to the world? Why is it that they, without any organized schools to help them, or organized bodies to patronize them, produce that which is read by all schools and all bodies, and are the grudgingly acknowledged leaders in literary art? There is some sufficient reason for this, and it is not a reason that redounds to the credit of the type of Christianity which prevails. It is time to look this matter squarely and candidly in the face. These men and women are not base usurpers of a sway which by any fairly-achieved right belongs to others. They rule because they have the power to rule. They prevail because of excellence. The public are not deceived by them, nor is their pre-eminence the result of accident. Either their sympathy of humanity is better, as a basis of culture and an inspirer of thought, than the sympathy of Christianity, or the sympathy of Christianity—pure and large and catholic—does not prevail among the churches. Something is wrong somewhere; and we can find that something nowhere but in the narrowing and dwarfing influence of sectarian culture.

The sympathy of humanity was strong in Shakespeare, and it was given to him to weave at once his own crown and that of the language in which he wrote. It was strong in Dickens, and the whole Christian world turned away from its own fountains to drink at that which his magic pen uncovered. It is strong in the hundred men and women whose brains and hands provide the books which the world is reading to-day. Is there no higher source of inspiration? We believe there is, and that it is that sympathy of Christianity which not only ignores but despises and hates all sectarian bonds and bounds. The Christian who does not embrace all mankind in his Christian regard, with the largest toleration and good-will, and who does not refuse to become the slave of a system and the creature of a creed, can never produce a literature which the world will read. It has been tried in books, in magazines, in newspapers, and on the platform, and it has always failed. We must have a broader church before we get a better literature, and before the present literary powers will be deposed from their sway.

Popular Arts.

There are certain arts in high repute among the people which are so inefficiently taught, and so imperfectly acquired, as to call for some stimulating and suggestive questioning. The amount of money expended upon the teaching of music to the young in this country is enormous; and what are the results? In every ladies' school, among our forty millions of people, the piano is sounding from morning until night. In all the cities and large towns, industrious gentlemen, each with a portfolio under his arm, go from house to house, giving instruction upon this popular instrument, and in forty-nine cases out of every fifty, their pupils stop exactly where they leave them. In how many families in this great city of New York can a girl be found who is capable of going on with her practice alone, and perfecting herself in an art, the rudiments and principles of which she has acquired? Very few, we answer. We do not know of one. The universal testimony is, that the moment instruction ceases, progress ceases. Under the tuition of her teacher, the universal American girl learns her dozen pieces so as to play them fairly, and never goes beyond them. These she plays until they are worn out to her own ear, and the ears of her friends; gradually she loses her power to play these well; and then she drops the piano altogether, especially if she is married. The money paid for her accomplishment, and the precious time she has expended upon it, are a dead loss.

The lessons in drawing, given in the same way, are, as a rule, as poor in results as those given in music. A set of pictures, of various degrees of badness, are manufactured and framed, and that is the end of it, unless the bolstering and spurring of a teacher are called in to keep the pupil to her work; but, beyond the eye of a teacher, the work rarely goes. The average American girl not only has no impulse to perfect herself in the ornamental arts to which she has devoted so much time, but she considers it a hardship to be required to take a single step without assistance. She is just as dependent on a teacher, when she ought to be able to stand and walk alone, as she is when she begins with him.

Now we doubt whether this state of things is owing to something radically wrong in the girl. She has her responsibility in the matter, without question, but it seems to us that there must be something radically wrong in the teaching. A method of teaching which universally produces the result of dependence upon the teacher, stands self-condemned. What would be thought of a teacher of mathematics who, under fair conditions, could not teach his pupils to reason for themselves? What of a teacher of the natural sciences who should uniformly leave his pupils incapable of an independent investigation in geology, or chemistry, or botany? Yet here are two great classes of teachers who uniformly leave the young submitted to their tuition, not only practically helpless, but without the first impulse to go on without help. We know nothing of their business, but we know enough, from the results of it, to know that they are as ignorant as we are of certain very essential departments of it. We know, also, that if they cannot produce better results, the quicker they are out of the way the better.

In the entire conglomerate educational system of America there is no department in which so much time and money are absolutely thrown away as in what are called the ornamental arts. The teachers in this department fail entirely to comprehend the end toward which every lesson they give should drive. It is not for us to point out the remedies for their imperfections, but, in the name of a suffering and disappointed people, to call their attention to those imperfections, and to demand that they shall either be remedied, or the costly farce be withdrawn from the boards.

Oratory is one of the most popular arts in America. The man who can speak well is always popular; and the orator holds the hearts of the people in his hand. Yet, what multitudes of young men are poured out upon the country, year after year, to get their living by public speech, who cannot even read well! When a minister goes before an audience, it is reasonable to ask, and to expect, that he shall be accomplished in the arts of expression—that he shall be a good writer, and a good speaker. It makes little difference that he knows more than his audience—is better than his audience—has the true matter in him—if the art by which he conveys his thought is shabby. It ought not to be shabby, because it is not necessary that it should be. There are plenty of men who can train the voice. There are plenty of men who can so develop it, and so instruct in the arts of oratory, that no man needs to go into the pulpit unaccompanied by the power to impress upon the people all of wisdom that he carries. The art of public speech has been shamefully neglected in all our higher training-schools. It has been held subordinate to everything else, when it is of prime importance.

We believe that more attention is now paid to this matter than formerly. The colleges are training their students better, and there is no danger that too much attention will be devoted to it. The only danger is, that the great majority will learn too late that the art of oratory demands as much study and practice as any other of the higher arts, and that without it they must flounder along through life practically shorn of half the power that is in them, and shut out from a large success.

The Art of Speaking and Writing.

A musician is not accounted an artist who, although thoroughly versed in the science of music, knows nothing practically of the art. It matters very little to the listening world how much he knows, if he can neither play nor sing. A man may talk or write very intelligently of picture and sculpture without the slightest practical skill in either branch of performance. So there are multitudes of men with well-stored minds, who live without access to the public, simply because they are not accomplished in the arts of expression by pen and tongue. These men have been trained for public life. They have expected to obtain a livelihood by public service. All their education has been shaped to this end, yet they lack just that one thing which will enable them to do it. That mode of approach and expression which is essential to their acceptableness as writers and speakers is lacking; and so their lives are failures.

The professorship of rhetoric and elocution has been regarded in most colleges as rather ornamental than useful; and only here and there has its incumbent manifested the disposition and the power to magnify his office, and perform the great duty that is placed in his hands. Slovenly writers and awkward and unattractive speakers are turned out of our colleges every year, almost by thousands, whose failure in public life is assured from the first, because they have acquired no mastery of the arts of expression. Men of inferior knowledge and inferior mental culture surpass them in the strife for public favor and influence, by address and skill. They are disgusted with the public, and charge their failure upon the popular stupidity. "Our honest toil has been in vain," they say; "for the people cannot appreciate what we are, or what we have done. They like the shallow man best."

This is not a just judgment. The brighter and stronger the man, the better the people like him, always provided that he understands the arts of writing and speech. Mr. Beecher, Mr. Phillips, Mr. George W. Curtis, and Mr. Collyer are not shallow men, but they are accepted everywhere, and in all assemblies, as the masters of oratory. Mr. Webster, Mr. Clay, and Mr. S. S. Prentiss, in the old days, were not shallow men, but they were orators, and their power over multitudes was the power of giants. Not one of these men would now be heard of as men of national reputation had they not won the mastery of expression.

There is a quality in all good writing—writing thoroughly adapted to its purpose—which we call "readableness." It is hard to define it, because in different productions it depends on different elements. Wit and humor impart this quality, if they are spontaneous and unobtrusive. Eminent lucidity, gracefulness of structure, epigrammatic terseness and strength, downright moral earnestness, gracefulness and facility of illustration, apposite antithesis, forms of expression and uses of words that are characteristic of individual thought and feeling—each and all of these have their function in imparting readableness to the productions of the pen. We find Carlyle readable through a quality which is Carlyle's own—which he neither borrowed nor has the ability to lend. Emerson and Lowell and Holmes are readable because of their individual flavor. There are ten thousand educated men in America who are fairly capable of comprehending these writers, yet who would render them all unreadable by undertaking to clothe their thoughts and fancies in their own forms of language. When this strong individual flavor is lacking—an element that belongs mainly to genius—art must be more thoroughly cultivated. No man of moderate ability and education can possibly make himself acceptable as a writer without a skill in the arts of expression which can be won alone through patient study and long practice.

We have but few men in the country who designedly write for the few. We all seek to write for the million and to find the largest audience. Readableness, then, must depend very largely upon still another element, which is, perhaps, more important than all—direct, intelligent ministry to the public need. People will not be interested in the discussion of subjects that have no practical relation to their life. Any production, in order to be readable, must be based on a knowledge of the wants of the people and the age. What will amuse, instruct, enlighten, or morally and intellectually interest the people? The writer who is not sufficiently in sympathy with the people and the age to answer this question intelligently to himself, cannot be readable, except by accident. The man who shuts himself up in his library, away from his kind, and refuses to make himself conversant with their wants and with the questions that concern them, has no one to blame but himself if they refuse to read what he writes.

The clergyman, conscious of Christian purpose and of thorough culture, and earnestly believing that he understands the message of his Master, finds with grief that he is not an accepted teacher. Let him learn, if it be not too late, that it is his mode of presenting truth that makes him impotent. Water tastes better from cut-glass than from pewter, and people will go where they are served from crystal. Salt is salt, but what if it have lost its savor? There are very few preachers who fail in knowledge of their message, but there are multitudes who know nothing of the people to whom they deliver it, or of the art of so proclaiming it that men will pause to hear and heed. The art of writing and speaking is both shamefully and fatally neglected. Without it, cultivated to its highest practicable point, the learning of the schools is comparatively useless. Without it, the preacher is utterly unprepared for his work; for the grand, essential thing which will make his knowledge and culture practically available is wanting. The man who cannot say well that which he has to say may safely conclude that he has no call to the pulpit.

There is no editor of a newspaper or a magazine who is not constantly returning manuscripts full of useful and good material, which he cannot publish because it is not readable. The style is turgid, or involved, or affected, or slovenly, or diffuse. If the style happens to be good, the subject is uninteresting, or it is treated for scholars, and lumbered with redundant learning. Of course the editor would not hurt the pride of the writers, and in his politeness he simply says that their productions are not "available." They think the editor stupid, and he is content, so long as they do not accuse him of ill-nature. It is only when they charge him with the purpose of refusing all writing that is better than his own that he loses patience, and regrets that he had not been frank and definite in the statement of his reasons for declining their offerings.

LITERATURE AND LITERARY MEN.

The Literary Class.

In the great world of common and uncommon men and women who are outside of the pale of literary culture, there exist certain prejudices against the literary class, which are little recognized and little talked about, but which are positive and pernicious. There is a feeling that this class is conceited, supercilious, selfish, and, to a very great extent, useless. There is a feeling that it is exclusive; that it arrogates to itself the possession of tastes and powers above the rest of the world, upon which it looks down with contemptuous superiority. There is, undoubtedly, connected with this prejudice a dim conviction that the literary class is really superior to the rest of the world in its acquirements, its tastes, and its sources of pleasure; that culture is better than stocks and bonds; that literary life occupies a higher plane than commercial, manufacturing, and agricultural life, and that it holds a wealth which money cannot buy, and which ordinary values can in no way measure. Much of the unspoken protest that rises against the assumptions of the literary class, and against the arrogance which it is supposed to possess, undoubtedly comes from a feeling of inferiority and impotence—of conscious inability to rise into its atmosphere, and to appropriate its wealth and its satisfactions.

Having said this, it may also be said that the literary class is very largely to blame for this state of things. It has almost uniformly failed to recognize its relations and its duties to the world at large. It has been bound up in itself. It has read for itself, thought for itself, written for itself. It has had respect mainly to its own critical judgments. It has been a kind of close corporation—a mutual admiration society. It has looked for its inspirations mainly within its own circle. It has, in ten thousand ways, nourished the idea that it is not interested in the outside world; that it does not care for the outside world and its opinions; that it owes no duty to it, and has no message for it. Its criticisms and judgments, in their motive and method, are often of the most frivolous character. An author is not judged according to what he has done for the world, but according to what he has done for himself, and for what it is pleased to denominate "literature." To certain, or most uncertain, men of art, or canons of art, or notions of art, it holds itself in allegiance, ignoring the uses of art altogether. It has its end in itself. It is a cat that plays with and swallows its own tail.

Now, it seems to us that if the literary class has any apology for existence, that apology must come from its uses to the world. It entertains a certain contempt for the world, which does not appreciate and will not take its wares, forgetting that it has not endeavored, in any way, to serve the world, by the adaptation of its wares to the world's use. Endeavoring to be true to itself, bowing in devotion and loyalty to its own opinions and notions, it utters its word, and then, because the great outside world will not hear it, complains, and finds its revenge in holding the popular judgment in contempt. It gives the world what it cannot appreciate, what it cannot appropriate; what, in its condition, it does not need—what it turns its back upon—and finds its consolation in inside praise, and a reputation for good work among those who do not need it.

In the best Book we have, there are certain rules of life laid down, that are just as good for the literary as for the moral and religious world. The Son of Man came not to be ministered unto, but to minister. He that would be great must be a servant. If any man has special gifts, and achieves special culture of those gifts, his greatness is brought, by irreversible law and the divine policy, into immediate relation with the want of the world. He is to be a servant, and thus to prove his title to lordship. His true glory is only to be found in ministering. If he do not minister, he has no right to honor. If he will not minister, he holds his gift unworthily, and has no more reason to expect the honor of the world for what he does, than he would if he did nothing. The military and administrative gifts of Washington were, undoubtedly, well known and honored among the military and political classes, but their significance and glory were only brought out in service. He is honored and revered, not because he served his class, but because he served his country. Those eminent gifts of his had no meaning save as they were related to the wants of his time; and their glory is that they served those wants. The glory of Watt, and Fulton, and Stevenson, and Morse, and Howe, is, not that they were ingenious men, but that they placed their ingenuity in the service of the world. The honor we give to Howard and Florence Nightingale is not given to their sympathetic hearts, but to their helpful hands.

Why should the literary class, of all the gifted men and women of the world, alone hold its gifts in service of itself? Why should it refuse to come down into the service of life? There is an audience waiting for every literary man and woman who will speak to it. Why should the world be blamed for not overhearing what literary men and women say to each other? The talk is not meant for them. It has nothing in it for them, and there is a feeling among them—not thoroughly well-defined, perhaps, but real—that they are defrauded. All this feeling of contempt for the non-literary world on one side, and this jealousy of the literary class on the other, will not exist for a moment after the relations between them are practically recognized. When the world is served, it will regard its servant as its benefactor, and the great interest of literature will be prosperous. Book after book falls dead from the press, because, and only because, it is not the medium of service. The world finds nothing in it that it needs. Why should the world buy it? The golden age of American literature can never dawn until the world has learned to look upon the literary class as its helper, its inspirer, its leader in culture and thought; and it can never learn to look thus upon that class until it has been ministered to in all its wants by direct purpose, in simple things as well as in sublime.

Habits of Literary Labor.

When Mr. Pickwick informed Mr. Jingle that his friend Mr. Snodgrass had a strong poetic turn, Mr. Jingle responded:

"So have I—Epic poem—ten thousand lines—revolution of July—composed it on the spot—Mars by day, Apollo by night—bang the field-piece—twang the lyre—fired a musket—fired with an idea—rushed into wine-shop—wrote it down—back again—whiz, bang—another idea—wine-shop again—pen and ink—back again—cut and slash—noble time, sir."

There are other people beside Mr. Pickwick who accept this method of literary production as quite natural and legitimate. We remember seeing, some years ago, a sketch by an extravagant humorist of a man, who wrote a book in a single night, tossing each sheet as it was finished over his left shoulder, pursuing his work with a pen that hissed with the heat of the terrible friction, and fainting away into the arms of anxious friends when the task was finished. Preposterous as the fiction was, it hardly exaggerated an idea prevalent in many minds that literary production is a sort of miraculous birth, that is as strenuous and inevitable as the travail which brings a new being into life. Indeed, there are some, perhaps many, writers who practically entertain the same notion. They depend upon moods, and if the moods do not come, nothing comes. They go to their work without a will, and impotently wait for some angel to stir the pool; and if the angel fails to appear, that settles the question for them. Such men, of course, accomplish but little. Few of them ever do more than show what possibilities of achievement are within them. They disappoint themselves, disappoint their friends, and disappoint a waiting public that soon ceases to wait, and soon transfers its expectations to others. Literary life has very few satisfactions for them, and often ends in a resort to stimulating drinks or drugs in order to produce artificially the mood which will not come of itself.

There is a good deal of curiosity among literary men in regard to the habits of each other. Men who find their work hard, their health poor, and their production slow, are always curious concerning the habits of those who accomplish a great deal with apparent ease. Some men do all their writing in the morning. Some of them even rise before their households, and do half their day's work before breakfast. Others do not feel like going to work until after breakfast and after exercise in the open air. Some fancy that they can only work in the evening, and some of these must wait for their best hours until all but themselves are asleep. Some cannot use their brains at all immediately after exercise. Some smoke while writing, some write on the stimulus of coffee, and some on that of alcohol. Irregularity and strange whims are supposed to be characteristic of genius. Indeed, it rather tells against the reputation of a man to be methodical in his habits of literary labor. Men of this stripe are supposed to be mechanical plodders, without wings, and without the necessity of an atmosphere in which to spread them.

We know of no better guide in the establishment of habits of literary labor than common sense. After a good night's sleep and a refreshing breakfast, a man ought to be in his best condition for work, and he is. All literary men who accomplish much and maintain their health do their work in the morning, and do it every morning. It is the daily task, performed morning after morning, throughout the year—carefully, conscientiously, persistently—that tells in great results. But in order to perform this task in this way, there must be regular habits of sleep, with which nothing shall be permitted to interfere. The man who eats late suppers, attends parties and clubs, or dines out every night, cannot work in the morning. Such a man has, in fact, no time to work in the whole round of the hours. Late and irregular habits at night are fatal to literary production as a rule. The exceptional cases are those which have fatal results upon life in a few years.

One thing is certain: no great thing can be done in literary production without habit of some sort; and we believe that all writers who maintain their health work in the morning. The night-work on our daily papers is killing work, and ought to be followed only a few years by any man. A man whose work is that of literary production ought always to go to his labor with a willing mind, and he can only do this by being accustomed to take it up at regular hours. We called upon a preacher the other day—one of the most eloquent and able men in the American pulpit. He was in his study, which was out of his house; and his wife simply had to say that there was no way by which she could get at him, even if she should wish to see him herself. He was wise. He had his regular hours of labor, which no person was permitted to interrupt. In the afternoon he could be seen; in the morning, never. A rule like this is absolutely necessary to every man who wishes to accomplish much. It is astonishing how much a man may accomplish with the habit of doing his utmost during three or four hours in the morning. He can do this every day, have his afternoons and evenings to himself, maintain the highest health, and live a life of generous length.

The reason why some men never feel like work in the morning is, either that they have formed other habits, or that they have spent the evening improperly. They have only to go to their work every morning, and do the best they can for a dozen mornings in succession, to find that the disposition and power to work will come. It will cost a severe effort of the will, but it will pay. Then the satisfaction of the task performed will sweeten all the other hours. There is no darker or deadlier shadow than that cast upon a man by a deferred and waiting task. It haunts him, chases him, harries him, sprinkles bitterness in his every cup, plants thorns in his pillow, and renders him every hour more unfit for its performance. The difference between driving literary work and being driven by it is the difference between heaven and hell. It is the difference between working with a will and working against it. It is the difference between being a master and being a slave.

Good habit is a relief, too, from all temptation to the use of stimulants. By it a man's brain may become just as reliable a producer as his hand, and the cheerfulness and healthfulness which it will bring to the mind will show themselves in all the issues of the mind. The writings of those contemporaneous geniuses, Scott and Byron, illustrate this point sufficiently. One is all robust health, the result of sound habit; the other all fever and irregularity. What could Poe not have done with Mr. Longfellow's habit? No; there is but one best way in which to do literary work, and that is the way in which any other work is done—after the period devoted to rest, and with the regularity of the sun.

Literary Style.

We have Dr. Johnson's authority for the statement that "Whoever wishes to attain an English style, familiar but not coarse, and elegant but not ostentatious, must give his days and nights to the volumes of Addison." There is, undoubtedly, much to be gained by the writer through familiarity with pure models of style. The recognized classics of all languages, ancient and modern, assist in the direction and discipline of taste, for they yield instruction in certain common qualities, without which no style can be good, however strongly flavored by attractive individuality. Simplicity, directness, perspicacity and perspicuity form the basis of all good style, but a man may exhibit all these qualities in his literary performances without having any style at all. One can hardly be said to have a style who apprehends all things uncolored by imagination, and aims to record and interpret them with literal exactness. Dr. Johnson himself did what it would have been impossible for Noah Webster to do—he carried style into his dictionary. The man who could say: "I am not so lost in lexicography as to forget that words are the daughters of earth, and that things are the sons of heaven," was undoubtedly injured as a lexicographer by an imagination which made him the author of a style still recognized as "Johnsonian."

We do not hold an unquestioning faith in Dr. Johnson's prescription. A style may be corrected, chastened and modified in various ways by a familiarity with models, especially with models with which the writer finds himself in sympathy; but we do not believe that a good style was ever "attained" by conscious or unconscious imitation. Fish is good, but fishy is always bad. Nothing is more offensive than the coloring that a weak writer always receives from the last strong man he has read. Every possessor of a positive style, provided he be a valued writer, produces a school of imitators, who try to do their little things in the way in which he does his large ones, and make themselves ridiculous, of course. A worthy style must be the fitting expression of worthy thought. Chesterfield calls style "the dress of thoughts," but to have dressed Chesterfield's thoughts in Johnson's or Addison's style would have been the most absurd masquerading. The same may be said of almost any other man. Washington Irving might have received great good, in his early life, by giving "his days and nights to the volumes of Addison," because his was a cognate genius; but Carlyle could no more have clothed his thoughts in the style of Addison than he could have fenced or boxed in a strait-jacket. Style that is not the outgrowth of a man's individuality, is, of course, without significance or value in the expression of his thoughts. It is never thoroughly formed until character is formed, and until the expression of thought has become habitual.

No man of power can do himself a greater wrong than to make an attempt to acquire the style of another man, under the impression that that style will fit his thought. He might as well have his clothes made to his neighbor's measure. There is not one chance in a thousand of a fit, unless it be a fit of disappointment or disgust. The sensitiveness of language to the impulses and characteristics of the spirit that sits behind and utters it, is one of the marvels of the world. Its flexibility in shaping itself to every variety of thought and every form of imagination, its power to transmit an atmosphere or an aroma which no analysis of word or expression betrays, and the ease with which it is made either puerile or majestic, in accordance with the spirit of its maker, show that style, unborn of the individual, is an utterly valueless attainment. We can imagine no good to come from "attaining" a style by studying other men, except, perhaps, to cover up the literary coxcombry of such writers as Willis, the rhythmical follies of such men as Poe, or the affected barbarisms of—Mr. Emerson knows who, because he once did the world great mischief by praising him.

All direct aims at the acquisition of a style, for the style's sake, are always, in some sense or another, failures. We beg the lady's pardon for mentioning it, but Gail Hamilton's incisive, brusque and forceful style,—sometimes saucy, always clear, though often redundant, and strong beyond the average feminine quality,—has done, without any premeditated guilt, a great deal of harm to the lower grade of literary women in America. The weaker woman, undertaking to speak through such a style, is simply and insipidly pert. She lacks the strong common sense and the height and breadth of imagination of her model, and so appears as ridiculous as if she were to "assist" at a New York party in an old dress of Queen Elizabeth or the soldier-clothes of Jean d'Arc.

Some years ago Mr. Congdon was a writer on "The New York Tribune." He reduced sarcasm, irony,—we had almost said blackguardism,—to a fine art. He could abuse a political opponent, or a social or literary pretender, by ingenuities of badinage so brilliant as to attract and delight every reader, and, at the same time, leave the object of his attacks hopelessly floundering in the public contempt. The efforts that have been made in the newspaper world from that day to this, by editorial writers and sensational correspondents, to repeat his performances, have been pitiful. No one has equaled him, and the attempt to fight with another man's weapons has drawn upon the clumsy thief of the old lance the punishment of public contempt which he sought to inflict. Mr. Headly, in the hey-dey of his literary career, had some sins to answer for, even if he were not a sufferer for the sins of others; for it is almost impossible to believe that the writer of the exquisite "Letters from Italy" was also the author of the florid and forced periods of "Napoleon and His Marshals."

As a fair illustration of the absolute impossibility of one man writing in the style of another, take the two great poets of England now living, and let Browning and Tennyson undertake to acquire each the style of the other. It would absolutely ruin both. All writers who are good for anything have a style of their own. It can no more be transmitted or "attained" than the powers and qualities in which it had its birth; and a man who is so strongly impressed, or magnetized, by the style of another, that he finds himself trying to work in his way, has his own weakness and lack of individuality demonstrated to him. It follows that most of the criticisms of style are equally without common sense and common justice—so far, at least, as they are made with the idea that there is such a thing as a standard of style. There is abundant wealth of literary style in the world which has no characteristic similarity to Addison's; and the young writers who fancy that they must shape their style upon some approved or popular model, would do well to abandon the effort at once. A good style is always the natural offspring of a good literary mind. It is polished and chastened by self-criticism, and is a growth from the centre. A style thus formed is the only legitimate representative of a literary man. No lack of heart, or brains, or culture, or marked and large individuality, can be hidden by adopting another man's literary dress and presentment. If a man has no style of his own, he has no literary calling whatsoever.

Nature and Literature.

If we were to look for a demonstration of the existence of a spiritual world, of which the things apprehended by our senses are the typical expression, we should find it in literature, and on that beautiful field of illustration where we so readily apprehend spiritual truth through the forms and relations of material objects. A preacher rises in his desk and tells us that there is no awkward or rough element which can be introduced into home life that may not become the occasion of new beauty and loveliness to that life; and we wonder how it can be. Then he paints for us a pure rill gurgling from a rock, and picking its dainty way down the ravine into the grassy valley. Half way there thunders from the hill a huge bowlder, that plants itself squarely in its path, tearing its banks, and throwing the mud in every direction. Quietly the rill makes a little detour, goes around the rock, nourishes vines that weave the uncouth intruder all over with verdure, and builds for itself a temple of beauty just there—a wayside shrine, at which all pilgrims pause for worship. At once we see the spiritual truth, and recognize its perfect analogies. The rill verifies the proposition, and we no more think of questioning its word than if it were spoken to us from heaven. It is this utter truthfulness of nature to the realm of thought that demonstrates its origin in thought, and proves itself to be an expression of thought in various forms and motions of matter.

It follows that no one can be fully learned as a literary man who has not learned of nature. The strong men of the press, the pulpit, the platform, are those who are the most bountifully furnished with the natural analogies of their thoughts. The man who can illustrate best is the best teacher, as he is always the most attractive. The man who can make us see his thought—who can point out or paint to us its exact analogy in nature—is the successful man, in whatever department of intellectual or spiritual instruction. The more closely a man lives in sympathy with nature—the more deeply he looks into it—the more fully he realizes the fact that it is only the language of the spiritual, placed before him to read, and put in his hands to use. He builds its rocks into his thoughts, he weaves its beauty into his imaginations, he clothes his fancies with its atmosphere. The rhythmic day and night become poetry, the setting sun a god with flaming wings, the birds, chanting choirs of cherubim. He sees straight through all into a world of which these things are fading shadows, or startling intimations, or perfect demonstrations. In short, he sees, hears, smells, tastes, feels thought, as it appears in a material form, among material conditions; and with his thought thus apprehended, he has the power to represent it to those whom he is called upon to instruct.

We are led into this strain of remark by the consideration that there are great numbers of young men, scattered up and down the country, in schools and colleges, who lament that they have not the advantages of a city life. They feel that in the city there are great opportunities of education, wonderful stimulus to labor, inspiring competitions, large libraries, social advantages, contact with high literary culture, eloquence to be had for the seeking, centralized knowledge and brotherly sympathy. Their country lives seem poor and barren in comparison.

Well, what they think of the city is, in most respects, true; but what they think of their country conditions is not true at all. No man is fit for the literary or the productively intellectual life of the city who has not had either a country training, or, for a considerable period of his life, direct and sympathetic association with nature. Blessed is the literary man, the public man, the man of the pulpit, who was bred among the fields, and woods, and brooks; who has known the ocean in all its moods, and with whom the sky with its country blue and its silver stars and all its machinery and phenomena of summer and winter storms, has been an open and favorite book.

Suppose that Mr. Beecher had been confined to the city during all his young life. The result would have been that we should not have had Mr. Beecher at all. We should have had a strong, dramatic man, notable in many respects—but he would have been so shorn of his wonderful power of illustration, that his pulpit would have been but a common one. It is quite safe for us to say that he has learned more of that which has been of use to him, as a public teacher, from nature, than from his theological schools and books. He has recognized the word which God speaks to us in nature as truly divine—just as divine as that which he speaks in revelation. His quick apprehension of the analogies that exist between nature and the spiritual world has been the key by which he has opened the door into his wonderful success. A theologian who has mastered his science only, is as poorly armed for effective work as a child; and all these young men, pining for the advantages of city life, ought to realize that they are living where alone they can fit themselves for the highest success. They cannot know too much of nature, learned directly from her own wide-open book. It is all illuminated with analogies which are not only corrective of their crudely formed ideas, but full of all fruitful suggestions touching their work. There is not a glimpse of a brook, a whisper of a leaf, a habit of an animal, a sweep of a storm's wing, a blush of a flower, an uprising of a morning, a sparkle of a sea, or a sob of a wave, that is not eloquent, or may not be made eloquent, in the exposition of intellectual and spiritual truth; and he whose soul is fullest of these will have the most and best to say to the humanity that comes to him for instruction and inspiration.

The Rewards of Literary Labor.

Mr. Thackeray, in his notable letter to the editor of the "London Evening Chronicle," written in 1850, concerning the dignity of literature, says that every European state but his own, the English, rewards its men of letters; and he even cites America as more considerate in this regard than Great Britain. "If Pitt Crawley," he says, "is disappointed at not getting a ribbon on retiring from his diplomatic post at Pumpernickel, if General O'Dowd is pleased to be called Sir Hector O'Dowd, K. C. B., and his wife at being denominated My Lady O'Dowd, are literary men to be the only persons exempt from vanity, and is it to be sin in them to court honor?"

Probably no Englishman who has lived in the last century cared less for titles, and the sort of honor that belongs to them, than Thackeray. His plea was a general one for the literary craft. He simply intended to protest that if any literary man wanted the kind of reward or recognition of his work which a ribbon or a title would bestow, he had as good a right to it as anybody—a better right to it, indeed, than the average or usual recipient of it. And he was right, though he chose something better, as literary men usually do.

In looking over the recent volume compiled and partly furnished by Mr. Stoddard, in the "Bric-à-Brac Series," we find much of suggestion on this great subject of rewards for literary labor. Thackeray and Dickens, or Dickens and Thackeray,—as men may choose to order their coupling of the two great names,—were what may be called well-rewarded men. They had many personal friends in all ranks of society. They were held in great honor and admiration by multitudes of men and women whom they did not know. They had princely pay for their labor, and were enabled by their power to earn money to give good homes to their wives and children. Yet neither of them, by the usages of English society, was socially among the highest class. They were petted and patronized personally, but they have left no higher social position for their children than they themselves originally held. Wider the circle may be, but its plane is not raised. These literary men, whose labor was one of the highest glories of the realm, who carried untold pleasures, and exquisite culture, and pure sentiment, and fructifying thought into every hamlet and house in the kingdom, were not the social equals of an earl, though that earl may have been,—as many an earl undoubtedly has been,—an ass. That they both saw the injustice of this, and despised the constitution of society that made such injustice possible, is not to be doubted—thorough Englishmen as both of them were; and so thoroughly must they have seen the baselessness of the social distinctions which placed them where they stood in the social scale, that they could not but despise the titles and ribbons of which Mr. Thackeray spoke in his letter. The thought that the Queen of England can delight in having the works of her great novelists in her private apartments, and is shut away by social barriers from their genial, sparkling and fruitful society, and that those next below her must remain with those among whom they were born, may be a trial to them,—

it ought to be,—but it ought not to disturb the men whose society is so foolishly sacrificed.

After all, the matter is well enough as it is. In this country it is particularly so. In a free country like ours, where the social lines are not closely drawn, we do not see how a man can claim a right to any larger domain than he fairly conquers. The literary man who complains of lack of popular consideration and social reward for his labor, is, by rule, the man who has not comprehended the wants of his time, and has simply sought to serve himself. To complain of lack of public reward for the service of one's self is certainly childish; yet, the great mass of literary men in America who find fault with their winnings is made up of these. Those who are not up to their time, though they mean well, fail of necessity. Those who are above or beyond their time fail, perhaps, in a certain way, but, after all, the world knows enough to know who they are, and accredits them often with more than belongs to them. Emerson has a world of honor from men who do not pretend to understand him.

So we come back to the proposition that a man has no right to any more consideration for his literary labor than, in a fair, open field he can conquer.

Every literary man, by virtue of his constitution, owes a duty to his generation and his time; and if, comprehending that duty, he performs it well, he has no stint of honor. There is no man around whom gathers so much interest, admiration, affection and respect as around him who charms, teaches, and inspires by his literary work. The young man who boasted that he once saw a rail-road train passing, in one car of which sat Charles Dickens, and who felt exalted by the thought that though he had never looked upon his face, he had seen the car that held him, illustrates the enthusiastic affection in which eminent literary men are held. They are kings by right. Their kingdom may not be strictly of this world of titles, and dignities, and palaces, and lands, but it is a veritable kingdom, which holds only loyal subjects. The literary man who would not rather be Walter Scott than the Napoleon whom he described, or Thackeray than the Emperor William, or Charles Dickens than the Prince of Wales, or Mrs. Browning than the Queen of England, or Washington Irving than Gen. Jackson, or William Cullen Bryant than General Grant, is a disgrace to his craft, undeserving of any literary reward, and incapable of winning one.

This admitted, it is idle to talk of the inadequacy of literary rewards, so far as the social and personal honors of the world are concerned. They are abundant, and above all titular honors, all wealth, all official position. Mr. Everett is remembered to-day, not as our minister to England, but as an orator. Mr. Bancroft retires honorably from his Prussian mission; but Mr. Bancroft, the historian, has conferred more honor upon his office than the office has conferred upon him. The principle distinction that has ever come to the Liverpool consulate has come through Mr. Hawthorne's occupation of it. Names like those of Franklin, Adams, and Motley are those almost alone which have saved the bureaus of our diplomatic foreign service from absolute contempt. A hundred ordinary politicians come, go, and are forgotten; but glory lingers around the chairs once occupied by men whom office could not honor.

The great lack of reward to literary labor is in the matter of money. Not one author in twenty can live on his authorial earnings. We speak of this country of cheap books. We have altogether too many men who are still drudging for the bread that feeds themselves and their families, though thay have done good, marketable literary work all their lives. Copyright is contemptibly small. We do not mean that publishers make too much, but that the books are sold so cheap that neither publishers nor authors can get a fair living. The consumers of books must remember that out of every dollar they pay for a copyrighted book, the writer gets but ten cents, and the publishers would be quite willing, as a rule, to share the losses and gains of publication with the authors. If copyright were double what it is, authors could not get a living exclusively by authorship. That this is all wrong, is undoubted. That it ever will be right until we have an international copyright law, which will do away with the competition of American authors with stolen books, we do not believe. When this wrong is righted, authors will have nothing left to complain of.

Professional and Literary Incomes.

The clergyman, the lawyer, the physician, the editor, the teacher, and the writer of books, in order to excellence in their respective professions, are all obliged to go through the same amount of preliminary study. It costs as much of time, money and labor to thoroughly fit one for his work as the other; and we may add that it requires just as much talent and genius to be a teacher as to be an author, to be an editor as to be a clergyman or a lawyer. The special adaptation of natural gifts and dispositions is just as important and valuable to the community in one profession as in another. Each requires a whole man, who shall be a man outside of his special work—a man of culture, large acquaintance with men and things, a well-furnished and cleanly working intellect, a high character, and superlative devotion to the work from which he wins his living. In the nature of things, in the character of the work done, and in the amount and kind of preparation required, there is no reason why one should be better paid than the other; yet there is no field of human effort which presents a wider variety or contrariety of pecuniary rewards than that presented by professional and literary labor.

There are two forms of income attached to this variety of work; viz.: that which arises from salaries, and that which arises from fees. The former is fixed by the community for which the work is done, and the latter by those who do the work. The salaried man enters the market and sells his services at the highest rate which they will command in competition with others. The man of fees combines with his brethren to fix a compensation for his services, which compels the community to take them at his valuation or to do without them. To say that the lawyer and the physician have the advantage of all the other professions, is simply to repeat a notorious fact. The lawyer and the physician who are thoroughly prepared for and fitted to their work can, and do, get rich. The clergyman, the teacher, the editor, and the author cannot, and do not, get rich by their work. The brightest author in America, though he produce books of universal acceptation, can never get rich; and hardly one author in one hundred can realize enough from his labor at the present rates of copyright to rear a family in comfort. The teacher gets just enough to live on, and no more, while the clergyman and the hired editor, save in rare instances, are men who are obliged to practice the most rigid economy in order to live within their income.

We are not among those who believe that the salaried man gets enough for his work. We should be glad to see him better paid, in all departments of his labor. It so happens that he works at the very foundations of society, and has his office of ministry all through its superstructure. He has to do with the morality, the education, the information, the opinion, and the culture of the social mass. Take away his work, and society would degenerate into barbarism. The importance of his work cannot be calculated. He is the inspirer, instructor, and conservator of our civilization; and he is as powerless to-day to win a competence for his old age, while all around him are getting rich, and receiving the results of his labor, as if he were a child. The superannuated clergyman ekes out his life in the humblest way; the exhausted teacher peddles books or drifts into some petty clerkship; the editor breaks down or becomes a hack; and the author writes himself out, or runs into drivel that wins the scantiest pay and destroys whatever reputation he may have won when his powers were at their best productive activity. There may be exceptions to this rule; but that this is the rule is beyond dispute.

The men of fees are the physician and the lawyer. One has to do with the physical diseases of men, and the other with their legal quarrels and their crimes. We do not, in the slightest degree, disparage the usefulness of these two classes of professional men: we simply say that the better the other classes perform their work, the less these have to do. They live upon the moral and physical evils of the country; and there is no reason in the nature of their calling for their advantage in pecuniary rewards over the other classes. There is no reason why a general practitioner of medicine, or a specialist in medicine or surgery, should sit in his office, and take in a single fee, for a service that costs him fifteen minutes of time, a sum equal to that which a teacher or a clergyman works all day to win. There is no reason why a physician, called into a house in consultation, should charge for his service a sum that it takes an editor two days of hard work to earn. There is no good reason for the setting of a price upon a surgical operation, performed in half an hour, that the most successful author's copyright cannot pay in a month. It is simple, inexcusable and outrageous extortion. If we go from the physician to the lawyer, we find still higher fees. The simplest work, such as searching titles, work that only demands accuracy, and is usually done by clerks, commands a price that few men can afford to pay, while larger work involves fees that are startling and stupendous. Some of the incomes of lawyers in this city are large enough to swallow up the salaries of a dozen, or twice that number, of salaried professional men. The way in which the people are bled in the process of securing justice is often most shameful. So shameful is it, that thousands submit to wrong rather than go into any litigation whatever. People dread getting into a lawyer's hands as they dread getting into the hands of a New York hackman. There are honorable and reasonable lawyers, without doubt,—men in whose honor we may implicitly trust; but there are so many extortioners among them that they have given a bad flavor to the profession. There are shysters and scamps enough in New York, attached to the profession, to sink it, were it not that there are noble men in it who are unpurchasable. But lawyer's fees are notoriously large as a rule, and altogether outweigh the salaries of the salaried professional men.

Perhaps the fees the community is obliged to pay is a fitting punishment for the wrong it inflicts upon its salaried professional servants. There ought to be some remedy for both evils. Where it is to be found, we do not know. The physician has some apology for getting high fees of those who can pay, because he is obliged to do so much for the poor who cannot pay; but the lawyer, as a rule, does not undertake a case which promises him no remuneration. He "goes in" for money; and there ought to be some law which will enable the poor man to get justice without financial ruin. There is at least no good reason why one set of professional men should half starve while another gorges itself upon fees that bring wealth and luxury. That fees are too large and salaries too small has become a popular conviction, which can only be removed by a reform in both directions, that shall bring literary and professional men equivalent rewards.

Literary Hinderances.

There was something very impressive and suggestive in what Mr. Stedman once printed on the embarassments of Hood's literary life. The brave, cheerful, mirth-provoking man, spreading innocent pleasure all over a realm from his bed of pain, coining his wasting blood into pence with which to buy bread for himself and his family, presents to the imagination an object at once pitiful and inspiring. Yet the literary world is full of spectacles only less touching. Three-quarters of the literary men and women of the present time are loaded down with cares that seem to forbid the free development of their genius, and deny to them the power to do their best possible work. The painter, with the greatest ambition and the noblest genius, is obliged to come down to what he calls his "pot-boilers;" and most literary men and women do the same. They do work in which they take no pleasure, simply because it is necessary to win them bread and clothing. Even this work they do under a pressure that is sometimes degrading, and some of them are obliged to do so much of it that, after a time, the spontaneous, creative impulse dies out of them, and they become disheartened and demoralized literary hacks.

But suppose the case were as we would like to have it. Suppose that when genius should be discovered in any man, or woman, a competent pension were provided at once for his or her maintenance, so that all common cares could be forever set aside, and the song be sung, and the story be told in perfect freedom, and at perfect leisure. Suppose every writer could have Byron's wealth, or Tennyson's competence, or Dickens's literary income, would it be better for the world thus, or even better for literature? It is an open question, which it would be well for all repiners to examine. Would Byron have been a better or a worse writer with poverty? Would not Tennyson have had more for the great world of struggling and sorrowing life with smaller possibilities of self-seclusion? Were not Dickens's wide-mouthed wants, natural and artificial, among the productive motives which have given to the world the most remarkable series of novels that the English language holds among its treasures?

If the truth must be confessed, the literary men and women of the world can hardly be trusted with wealth, when we remember that literature has no uses save as it ministers to the comfort, the pure pleasure, the strength, the elevation and the spiritual culture of the race. To be placed beyond the common needs and the common struggles of men, is to be placed beyond their sympathies,—is to be placed outside of a realm of knowledge which all must possess whose function is that of artistic ministry.

That the operation of this law brings individual hardship may not be questioned, but we cannot afford to lose it because of this. Tennyson could never have sung "The Song of the Shirt," or "The Bridge of Sighs." It took a man to do those things who had lived close to London life, and who, in his own person and fortunes, had shared in the trials and tragedies of its struggling multitudes. Cowper is dearest to those whose lives have been clouded, and sings to them by a divine commission. We should have lost our Burns if he had been born in a palace, and reared in luxury. Mrs. Browning, like the lark, would have sung all her songs in the sky, beyond the hearing of the common ear, if she had not been bound to the earth by the chain of pain. Even Shakespeare, in his most wonderful plays, "meant business." How true, and sweet, and pure remains the spirit that still shines under the Quaker brown, and waits for translation within the consecrated cottage of Amesbury! God made Whittier poor, that every son of want, and every victim of wrong should have a sympathizing and ministering brother. Uncounted and inestimable literary successes have been founded upon a knowledge of, and sympathy with, the world, only won and only attainable by sharing that world's homely needs and homely work.

Sometimes, however, the conviction comes to the literary worker that he is having something too much of drudgery. There are undoubtedly cases of this kind, but, after all, we cannot afford to lose the test which work for bread furnishes in deciding upon the genuineness of a literary man's mission. He who becomes soured by toil shows that he is not fit for prosperity, and cannot be trusted with it. He who makes the best of his conditions, and bends them all to the service of his art; who keeps a good conscience in all his work, and makes men better and happier in winning the bread for himself and his dependents; who learns to love his kind while sharing their toils, and to serve his God in serving them, is the man whose name is safe in the keeping of his country. The man, on the contrary, who takes his lot with discontent; who ceases to do good work because he must work or starve, and becomes willing at last to do any work that offers, writing on any required side of any prescribed question, shows himself made of poor material—unworthy, under any circumstances, to hold a high place in the regard of his countrymen. If the ideal, literary life of freedom and leisure were best for the mass of literary workers, they would, doubtless, have it. If the pet notion of the modern *dilettanti*, that beauty is its own excuse for being, and that the artist has no mission which does not end in his art, were sound, we should find literary conditions adjusted to it. But the artist is a minister—a servant; and, that he may learn his duty to his race, he must mingle with it, work with it, weep with it. Only thus can he know how to charm it with story, and inspire it with song.

The Reading of Periodicals.

It is lamented by many that the reading of periodicals has become not only universal, but that it absorbs all the time of those who read them. It is supposed that, in consequence of these two facts, the quiet and thorough study of well-written books—books which deal with their subjects systematically and exhaustively—has been forsaken. As a consequence of this fact, it is farther supposed that readers only get a superficial and desultory knowledge of the things they study, and that, although their knowledge covers many fields, they become nothing better than smatterers in any.

We think these conclusions are hardly sustained by the large array of facts relating to them. We doubt whether the market for good books was ever any better than it is now. We have no statistics on the subject, but our impression is, that through the universal diffusion of periodical literature, and the knowledge of books conveyed and advertised by it, the book trade has been rather helped than harmed. It has multiplied readers and excited curiosity and interest touching all literature. There are hundreds of good books which would never reach the world but for the introduction and commendation of the periodical; and books are purchased now more intelligently than they ever were before. The librarians will tell us, too, that they find no falling off in their labors; and we doubt whether our scholars would be willing to confess that they are less studious than formerly. Science was never more active in its investigations than now; discovery was never pushed more efficiently and enthusiastically, and thought and speculation were never more busy concerning all the great subjects that affect the race.

No, the facts do not sustain the conclusions of those who decry the periodical; and when we consider how legitimately and necessarily it has grown out of the changes which progress has introduced, we shall conclude that they cannot do so. The daily newspaper, in its present splendid estate, is a child of the telegraph and the rail-car. As soon as it became possible for a man to sit at his breakfast-table and read of all the important events which took place in the whole world the day before, a want was born which only the daily paper could supply. If a man, absorbed in business and practical affairs, has time only to read the intelligence thus furnished, and the comments upon it and the discussions growing out of it, of course his reading stops there; but what an incalculable advantage in his business affairs has this hasty survey given him! If he has more time than this, and has a love of science, the periodical brings to him every week or month the latest investigations and their results, and enables him to keep pace with his time. If the work of the various active scientists of the day were only embodied in elaborate books, he would never see and could never read one of them. In the periodical all the scientific men of the world meet. They learn there just what each man is doing, and are constant inspirers and correctors of each other, while all the interested world studies them and keeps even-headed with them. A ten-days' run from Liverpool brings to this country an installment of the scientific labor of all Europe, and there is no possible form in which this can be gathered up and scattered except that of the periodical. In truth, we do not know of any class of men who would be more disastrously affected by a suspension of periodical literature than those who have particularly decried it—the scholars and the scientists.

Within the last twenty years, not only have the means of communication been incalculably increased, but the domain of knowledge has been very greatly enlarged; and the fact is patent that periodical literature has been developed in the same proportion. It has grown out of the new necessities, and must ultimately arrange itself by certain laws. At present, it is in a degree of confusion; but at last the daily paper will announce facts, the scientific journal will describe discoveries and processes, the weekly paper will be the medium of popular discussion, the magazine and review will furnish the theatre of the thinker and the literary artist, and the book, sifting all—facts, processes, thoughts and artistic fabrics, and crystallizations of thought—will record all that is worthy of preservation, to enter permanently into the life and literature of the world. This is the tendency at the present time, although the aim may not be intelligent and definite, or the end clearly seen. Each class of periodicals has its office in evolving from the crude facts of the everyday history of politics, religion, morals, society and science those philosophic conclusions and artistic creations that make up the solid literature of the country; and this office will be better defined as the years go by.

We do not see that it is anything against the magazine that it has become the medium by which books of an ephemeral nature find their way to the public. The novel, almost universally, makes its first appearance as a serial. Macdonald, Collins, Reade, George Eliot, Mrs. Stowe, Mrs. Whitney, Trollope—in fact, all the principal novelists—send their productions to the public through the magazines; and it is certainly better to distribute the interest of these through the year than to devour them *en masse.* They come to the public in this way in their cheapest form, and find ten readers where in the book form they would find one. They are read, too, as serials, mingled with a wider and more valuable range of literature, as they always should be read. Anything is good which prevents literary condiments from being adopted as literary food.

If the fact still remains that there are multitudes who will read absolutely nothing but periodical literature, where is the harm? This is a busy world, and the great multitude cannot purchase large libraries. Ten or fifteen dollars' worth of periodicals places every working family in direct relations with the great sources of current intelligence and thought, and illuminates their home life as no other such expenditure can do. The masses have neither the money to buy books nor the leisure to read them. The periodical becomes, then, the democratic form of literature. It is the intellectual food of the people. It stands in the very front rank of the agents of civilization, and in its way, directly and indirectly, is training up a generation of book-readers. It is the pioneer: the book will come later. In the meantime, it becomes all those who provide periodicals for the people to take note of the fact, that their work has been proved to be a good one by the growing demand for a higher style of excellence in the materials they furnish. The day of trash and padding is past, or rapidly passing. The popular magazine of to-day is such a magazine as the world never saw before; and the popular magazine of America is demonstrably better than any popular magazine in the world. We are naturally more familiar with this class of periodical literature than any other, and we make the statement without qualification or reservation. That it is truly educating its readers is proved by the constant demand for its own improvement.

The Morals of Journalism.

In the discussions of journalism which have been started by editorial conventions and the establishment of chairs of journalism in one or two academic institutions, it is well not to forget the matter of morals. A great deal of indignation has been meted out to those presses which publish quack advertisements, calculated to encourage vice and crime. In this thing, a gnat is strained at that a camel may be swallowed; for, almost without exception, the papers which denounce and refuse to publish these advertisements, take endless pains to spread before their readers the details of the crimes which the advertisements are supposed to engender or encourage. Murders, suicides, seductions, adulteries, burglaries, thefts, scandals —all disagreeable and disgraceful things—detailed histories of events which appeal to prurient tastes and a morbid desire for coarse and brutal excitements—are not these the leading material of a great number of our daily papers? We may be mistaken, but we believe that there is no department of the world's news given with such exhaustive particularity as that which relates to vice and crime. If this be doubted, let the first paper at hand be taken up, and the fact will, we think, be determined as we apprehend it. We know that in many papers the remedial agencies of society—the churches, schools, social conventions—private and organized charities—beg for space that is freely accorded to the record of a petty theft or a husband's or wife's infidelity. That which will make a spicy paragraph is chosen before that which will make a healthy one.

Nor is this all. The crimes which are thus spread before

the public for its daily food are often treated like anything but crimes. Some of our papers have a way of doing up their columns of local crime as if it were all a joke. The writer makes an ingenious jest of everything he is called upon to notice. The poor women who are lost to virtue and society, with hell within them and before them, furnish grateful themes for the reporter's careless pleasantries. Their arraignment, their trial, their sentence, their appearance, their words, are chronicled in unfeeling slang, with the intent to excite laughter. That which to a good man or woman is infinitely pathetic is made to appear a matter to be laughed at, or to be passed over as of no account. A case of infidelity in the marriage relation, involving the destruction of the peace of families, the disgrace of children, and the irremediable shame of the parties primarily concerned, comes to us labeled: "rich developments." The higher the life involved and the purer the reputation, the "richer" the "developments," always. Nothing pleases our jesting reporter like large game. A clergyman is the best, next a lay member, and then any man or woman who may be in a high social position. "Crime in high life" is a particularly grateful dish for those to serve up who cater for the prurient public. It is impossible not to conclude that the men who write these items and articles delight in them, and that the men who publish them regard them only with relation to their mercantile value. We know of nothing more heartless than the way in which criminals and crime are treated by a portion of the daily press, and nothing more demoralizing to the public and to those who are guilty of trifling with them under the license of the reporter's pen. It is a bad, bad business. It is an evil which every paper claiming to be respectable ought to cut up, root and branch. So long as crime is treated lightly it is encouraged. So long, too, as the edifying, informing, remedial and purifying agencies of the world are subordinated in the public notice to the records of vice and crime, simply because they are less startling or spicy, it is nonsense to talk about quack advertisements, and a parade of mock virtue which deserves both to be pitied and laughed at.

The daily paper has now become a visitor in every family of ordinary intelligence. It has become the daily food of children and youth all over our country, and it ought never to hold a record which would naturally leave an unwholesome effect upon their minds. If crime is recorded, it should be recorded as crime, and with a conscientious exclusion of all details that the editor would exclude were he called upon to tell the story to his boy upon his knee, or to his grown-up daughter sitting at his side. The way in which nastiness and beastliness are advertised in criminal reports is abominable. It is not necessary: it is not on any account desirable. A thousand things of greater moment and of sweeter import pass unnoticed by the press every day. The apology that the press must be exact, impartial, faithful, literal, etc., is a shabby one. A press is never impartial, when, by the predominance it gives to crime in its reports, it conveys the impression that crime is the most important thing to be reported, when, in truth, it is the least important. Its records do not hinder crime, do not nourish virtue, do not advance intelligence, do not purify youth, do not build up the best interests of society; and the absorption of the columns of the public press by them is a stupendous moral nuisance that ought to be abated.

We do not expect the press to be very much in advance of the people, either in morality or intelligence. It is quite as much the outgrowth as the leader of our civilization, but it ought to be an emanation from the best American spirit and culture and not the worst. We shall have, probably, so long as crime exists, professional scavengers who follow in its way to glean and gorge its uncleanness. We have such now, and a beastly brood who glean after them even; but why a press claiming to be respectable should deem it its duty to assist in their dirty work surpasses our comprehension. We repeat—it is not necessary: it is not on any account desirable.

Lord Lytton.

One of the most striking and memorable statements made by George MacDonald, in his lecture on Robert Burns, was, that the first grand requisite of a poet is a heart. No matter how brilliant a man's intellect may be, no matter how high and fine his culture, no matter how cunning and careful his art, if he have not a heart that brings him not only into sympathy with his kind, but with all life of plant and animal, and all life of God as it breathes through, and is manifested in, inanimate nature, the essential qualification of the poet is wanting. This proposition may stand as a canon of criticism by right of its own self-evident truthfulness, no less than by the testimony of all literary history. A thousand brilliant men have risen and passed away, attracting wide attention while they lived, but warming and fructifying no mind by their light, and expiring at last like a burnt-out star, leaving no trace in the sky. So near the earth were they, that their light failed at once when the fountain failed, while many a lesser star, by burning nearer heaven, has been able to send down its rays for centuries after its fires were extinguished.

Lord Lytton had what may be called a very successful literary life, and, politically and socially, was a power in his day and generation. He had wealth, he had position, he had a marvelous culture, he had fame, he had great industry, he held the curious eye and the attentive ear of the world, he had an imperious ambition, he had something more than talent,—gifts which only needed the talismanic touch of love to make them genius,—he had everything but the one thing needful to make him a poet. That one needful thing was a heart. No man ever accused or suspected him of possessing anything that could bear so precious a name. His neighbors tell us that he was a bad man; his wife affirms the same fact; and all that he has left to us of his enormous literary work sustains their personal testimony. Marvelous jewelry of thought and fancy has he bequeathed to us—beautiful stones in beautiful settings—but there is no blood in his rubies: there is no heaven in his sapphires; and all his diamonds are "off color." He has a place in history; his works stand in long rows upon many a library shelf in his own and other lands; but Lord Lytton is dead, and his works are nearly so. They enter no more into the life of the world. They never did enter into the life of the world as a beneficent power. Were it not for two or three plays which still hold to the boards, he, with all his works, would be as dead to-day as Julius Cæsar.

Simple Bobby Burns, with morals hardly less offensive than his of whom we write, goes singing down the centuries, and making music through the silence that shrouds the memory of our titled *littérateur*. It is not because he was good, or pure, or true even to himself, but because he was in sympathy with life, and did not sit and sing, poised in the superb selfishness from which Lord Lytton addressed the world. He loved nature, he loved mankind, he entered sympathetically into human trial and trouble; he hated oppression, he despised cant, he respected and defended manhood; and with all his weaknesses, over which he mourned and with which he struggled, he revered Christian goodness. The high and the humble recognize him as a brother. In brief, he had a heart, and without that heart all his wonderful gifts would have availed him nothing. Without that heart, and its manifestation in song, his name would long since have been forgotten, and the poetry he left would have been swept away among the vulgar trash of earlier and coarser times.

The same thing may be said, only less emphatically, of Dickens. The personal character of Dickens can hardly be regarded as admirable, even by those who loved him most; yet he had a heart which brought him into sympathy with all those phases of humanity which were intellectually interesting to him. He loved the rascals whom he painted, and enjoyed the society of the weakest men and women of his pages; and it is this sympathy which gives immortality to his novels. Pickwick and David Copperfield are as fresh to-day as when they were written, and are sure to be read by many generations yet to come; yet the learning, culture, and position of the man—his gifts and acquirements and art—were all inferior to those of Lord Lytton. His superiority was in his heart and his sympathy, and on these he stands far above his titled contemporary in the popular regard. Bulwer is a name whose home is in catalogues and biographical dictionaries. Dickens is a man whom the people love. One is a memory; the other a living and abiding presence.

No poet or novelist can greatly benefit the world who does not become the object of popular affection; and this popular affection cannot be secured without the manifestation of sympathy. There was no lack of power in Bulwer, but there was a lack of that quality which was necessary to bring him inside the better sympathies of human nature. No art emanating from supreme selfishness can ever command a permanent place in the world. Heartless art is loveless art, useless art, dead art. Fine art without fine feeling is a rose without fragrance,

Poetry without sympathy bears the same relation to true poetry that the music of the orchestrion, turned by a water-wheel, bears to that of the violin, singing or moaning in the passionate hands of a master.

Lord Lytton passes away, and no man stops his neighbor in the street to speak of it. He lived the splendid, selfish life he chose to live; he was the admired, the petted, the courted, the titled, the rich man of literature; but his fame was as heartless and loveless as himself. No worthy man covets his name and fame. No young man finds in him virtues to emulate, or excellences to inspire. No man finds in his work the stimulus to purity, to nobleness, to goodness. He lived to his autumn, but his fruit, brought to premature beauty by the worms it bred, rots where it fell, and his leaves, brilliant with many dyes, fall at the touch of the frost, to be trodden under foot or swept away by the wind.

The Difficulty with Dickens.

"Was Charles Dickens a believer in our Saviour's life and teachings?" is the question which a few men have attempted to answer. Now we beg the privilege of suggesting that it is not of the slightest consequence to the world or to Christianity whether Mr. Dickens believed in our Saviour's life and teachings or not. He could do that without having the belief of the least advantage to himself or his fellow-men. The devils believe—and—tremble. Have we any certificate that Mr. Dickens trembled? It should have gone as far as that, at least.

No; if Mr. Dickens was a Christian—and this, after all, is the real question that the world cares for—there must be better evidences of the fact than appear in the defenses under consideration. If he was a Christian, he was fond during his life of Christian people. With as hearty a hatred of sectarianism and bigotry and cant as Mr. Dickens himself ever entertained, we declare in all candor that there are men and women in the world who are informed and moved by the spirit of the Master. They love mankind for His sake. They devote their lives and labors, and yield their hearts' best love to Him. They are pure, and sweet, and good. They live lives of prayer and benevolence. If Mr. Dickens was a Christian, he loved the society of these people, and was supremely interested in their aims and ends of life. When between these and those who so often invited him to the convivial table he was called upon to choose, he made a Christian choice. So his defenders should not have been content to tell what Mr. Dickens believed, but they should have shown by his sympathies with Christian people that he possessed the Christian spirit. They should have shown how he always labored heart and hand with the Christian Church in every good work; how for that religion which is the hope of the world he spent money and sacrificed time and talents, that its benign influence might be spread among the nations of the earth and the ignorant multitudes of his own nation. His ardent sympathy with Christian missions should have been brought forward, and his love and respect for Christian ministers, as displayed in his novels. If all this had been done, the question would have been more nearly settled than it is.

It may be suggested again that Mr. Dickens's friendliness to Christian reforms would do much, when properly presented, to establish his Christian character before the world.

In the long period of his literary life, during which he had the ear and the heart of the English-reading world, a million men and women—more or less—in Great Britain sank into the miserable grave of the drunkard. The liquor-fiend desolated the kingdom. He burned up the health and the prosperity of the nation. He instigated murder, robbery, and all forms of cruel violence. He beat women and maimed little children, even before they were born. He assumed all seductive forms, and tempted the young to their ruin. Everywhere his work was degradation, desecration, and destruction. No pen can record—nay, no imagination can picture—the evils—the loathsome horrors—inflicted upon the British nation during those thirty years, by the demon of strong drink. To show how valiantly, how persistently, and how powerfully Mr. Dickens worked to stem the tide of intemperance in his own and other lands, to repeat his words of cheer to all who labored for the suppression of the great curse, to present his immaculate example of abstinence for the sake of one of the least of those who possibly might be helped by it, to picture the noble characters he has left upon his printed pages to represent his ideal temperance reformers—this would certainly be better than to tell what he believed, and would go to show something of the practical power of his belief.

Still again: Mr. Dickens lived during a period when the sanctities of Christian marriage were assailed by pretended revelations and infidel philosophies and bold beastliness. He belonged to a guild whose members had been conspicuously unhappy in their marriage relations. Hundreds of literary men and literary women had separated from their companions, and brought disgrace upon themselves, their class, and the sacred institution whose bonds they so lightly snapped asunder. To such lengths had one of them gone, that, after absorbing the lovely youth of his wife—nay, after having lived with her for twenty years, and seen pillowed in her maternal arms his large family of beautiful children, he decided that her nature was incompatible with his own, and that they must separate—a decision which seems so sadly cruel that we can find no words to give it fitting characterization. To be able to say that in such a time as this Mr. Dickens, though sorely tempted by his own temperament and by the circumstances in which he found himself, stood with Christian resignation and Christian honor by his vows, would be grand indeed, and would do much to relieve his eulogists of future questions relating to the Christian character of their subject. We marvel that means of vindication so close at hand as these should have been entirely overlooked.

For thirty years we have been an interested reader and a devoted admirer of Charles Dickens. We believe we have appreciated his rare genius and all his good and noble impulses. Kind things have been said of him and his memory in this magazine, and it is only when his self-appointed champions insist on holding him up before the American people as a Christian saint that we feel compelled to protest. If Christianity is something to be bottled up in a last will and testament, or only used for the purposes of art and literature, it is very cheap stuff and is not, really, worth making much ado about. If it is something which softens, purifies, and elevates character, and reforms and regulates life, it is not at all necessary to inquire what a man believes. If Mr. Dickens yielded his life to the supreme control of Christian motives he was a Christian man; and, for the life of us, we do not see how he could have been otherwise. Nor do we see how we can do better in the attempt to determine this—and we are not responsible for this attempt—than to examine with the eye of common sense the manifestations and outcome of his life.

CRITICISM.

A Heresy of Art.

More than fifty years ago Wordsworth said, in one of his most carefully prepared utterances, that "poetry is most just to its divine origin when it administers the comforts and breathes the spirit of religion." It was no new proposition, either to him or to the world. The connections in which he placed it showed that he regarded it as soundly established and universally accepted. Of course, poetry can only "administer the comforts" of religion by direct design; and, by necessity, the design to fulfill this function is not only legitimate, but laudable in the exercise of poetic art. A recent writer, discoursing of poetry, speaks of an exceptionally successful poem, whose title and authorship he does not give us, as originating in a moral rather than a poetic inspiration. If he had been more explicit, and said all that he intended to convey, he would have said that no true poem can spring from a purely moral inspiration. If he had gone still further, and revealed to us the fully rounded heresy of his school, he would have said that there can be no true poem and no true work of art that by original and carefully executed design is framed and armed to produce a moral result upon the souls of men. If this school is to be believed, the poetic muse is never to be either teacher or preacher; and a poem with a moral is a work of art with that one fatal blot, or taint, or weakness, or unseemly superfluity which destroys its genuineness.

During our recent civil war, a gifted woman of New England gave utterance to the overflowing religious and patriotic sentiments of her section by writing a hymn which was sung by the Union armies wherever they bore their banners, or whitened the hills with their camps. It was one of the grandest and most stirring of all the tuneful utterances of the time. Suppose some man, speaking of this, were to say that the most successful army hymn or song that had been given to the world within the last ten years was the offspring of a patriotic rather than a poetic inspiration! Suppose he should sneer at Burns's *Highland Mary* because those immortally sweet verses were born of a boy's pure love, that only sought expression in them! What should we think of such a man? What ought to be thought of such a man? Simply, that he is so utterly misled by a false theory of art as to be incapable of saying any worthy and valuable thing about it.

But the critic does not say this, and he will not say it. It is not that a poem may not be inspired by the love of a woman, or by the love of country, or by the love of fame, or by the love of beauty; it is that it cannot be inspired by the love of God—Himself the Great Inspirer! So long as the poet deals with the flowers of the field, that rise to his eye and beat with soft wings at the bars of all his senses for admission to his soul, he writes poetry; but when he touches those sentiments of the religious spirit which open themselves to The Divine, and rise with aspiration, adoration, love, and praise, he strikes prose, and writes stuff! We declare this to be a heresy so degrading to art, so belittling to the minds entertaining it, so subversive and perversive of all sound criticism, that until it shall be overthrown there can be no such thing as progress in literary art among those who entertain it. Even our beloved Whittier, singing away his beautiful life, and soaring while he sings, is impatiently accused of "preaching" because his songs are less and less of the earth from which he retires and more and more of the heaven into which he rises!

If art may convey one lesson, it may another. If it is legitimate for art to bear one burden, it may bear a hundred; and the heresy of which we speak, in condemning all art that springs from a moral inspiration, condemns the best, nay, the only worthy things that have been created in every department of art. If George MacDonald is not a true artist, there is no true artist writing the English language; yet he literally writes nothing that is not the offspring of a moral or a religious inspiration. The lady who writes over the *nom de plume* of George Eliot is the greatest living Englishwoman,—a woman who, since Mrs. Browning died, has had no peer as a literary artist among her sex; but she carefully elaborates in her best work a high moral purpose, and, lest some fool may possibly miss or mistake it, she works it all into the last page of *Romola*. "It is only a poor sort of happiness that could ever come by caring very much about our own narrow pleasures. . . . . There are so many things wrong and difficult in the world that no man can be great—he can hardly keep himself from wickedness—unless he gives up thinking about pleasures and rewards, and gets strength to endure what is hard and painful." What is *Aurora Leigh*, by the greatest poetess of our century, if not of all time, but one long and carefully elaborated lesson of life? Every book that comes from the pens of Mrs. Stowe and Mrs. Whitney, our best living female writers in America, is thoroughly charged with moral purpose; and Hawthorne, than whom no writer of English stands higher as an artist, was not content in his best book—*The Scarlet Letter*—to permit his lesson to be inferred, but he put it into words: "Be true, be true, be true!" With the heretics under discussion, it is entirely legitimate for a heathen to embody his religion in his poetry, and to use his religion as material of poetry; but when a Christian undertakes to do the same thing he is warned off, and informed that no poetry can come of a purely moral or religious inspiration.

There is a noteworthy coincidence in the fact that the theories of the nature and province of art upon which we have animadverted exist only or mainly in association with infidel opinions. It is not to be denied that there is in America a large circle of literary men and women from whom all sincere faith in Christianity and in the interest of God in the affairs of men has gone out. They are just as fond of preaching in and through art as they are of preaching in the pulpit. They regard with pitying contempt those whose faith still stands by the revelations of The Great Book, and read with impatience all those utterances of literary art which are inspired by it. That their lack of faith in the grand, central truths of their own nature, relations, and history should lead them into absurd and inconsistent theories of art, is not strange; but it is strange that Christian men and women have not more openly protested against those theories, and strange that many have not only been puzzled by them, but have been half inclined to accept them. It is well that Heaven takes care of its own, and impels each man whom it moves to artistic utterance to speak forth that which is in him in his own best way, and, regardless of theories, to go on doing so while he lives. More than this: it is well that the world has a sense of its own needs, and gratefully recognizes the heavenly credentials of that art which comes to it with gifts and deeds of ministry.

Criticism as a Fine Art.

A brief article, entitled "Criticism as a Fine Art," which appeared not long since in a foreign magazine, from the pen of Mr. Arthur Mattheson, was a notable production that did not receive the attention in America which its merits deserved. Nothing more remarkable for acuteness of insight, justness of judgment, and appositeness of illustration has appeared, within our knowledge, upon this subject. The conclusion arrived at by the writer is, that there is no such thing as a science of criticism—that there are no such universally recognized canons of critical art as will enable any two writers of differing mental organization and differing education and opinions to arrive at identical decisions regarding a literary work, worthy of being criticised at all. This being proved or admitted, it follows that criticism is nothing more nor less than the method by which the critic reveals, not the characteristics of the author criticised, but those of himself. Thus all the science there is in the matter applies to the critic, and not to the work he criticises. Given a certain book, and a critic of certain social, political, and religious opinions, with a certain grade of culture, and the critique he will write can be predetermined. The abstract or absolute merits of the book, if it have any, have nothing whatever to do with the critic's decision. What he does is simply to describe himself and define his standpoint; and the book is used simply as a means for the end aimed at in entire unconsciousness.

The truthfulness of Mr. Mattheson's theory is proved by the history of criticism; for nothing is better known than that the great books of the world have made their way and their place in total disregard of its decisions. Though a thousand critics determine that a book ought not to live, if it is a real book it lives, without the slightest reference to their opinions and protests. What the critics prove by their work is, simply, their lack of power to comprehend and appreciate it. They prove nothing against the book whatever. There has not lived a great British author within the last century whose works have not been subjected to the most scorching criticisms and the most slashing and sweeping condemnations. Yet those criticisms and condemnations have passed for nothing. The criticisms, often profoundly ingenious, and full of learning and power, die, and the books live. They are often exceedingly creditable productions—so creditable, indeed, that they form the basis of great personal reputations—but they accomplish absolutely nothing except the revelation of the men who produce them. Criticism thus becomes a form of personal expression, and is just as thoroughly individualized as if it were poetry, or picture, or sculpture. The critic takes a book in one hand, and uses the other to paint himself with. When his work is done, we may fail to find the book in it, but we are sure to find him.

The growth in the popular regard of the music of Wagner might have furnished a forcible illustration to Mr. Mattheson of the soundness of his position, had he needed more than he used. No great musician of the century has been so persistently sneered at by the critics as Wagner. His music has been called, in derision, "The music of the future," until the phrase is everywhere identified with his productions. The young King of Bavaria has been supposed to be half daft, because, in addition to his other eccentricities, he has believed in Wagner, and devoted himself to him. During this storm of detraction which has rattled over the whole world, Wagner has been quietly and most fruitfully at work; and, as a single home-comment on his music, it is pleasant to recall the Wagner-evening given at Thomas's Garden among the closing summer concerts by the finest of our orchestras. The last work of the season was expended upon Wagner's music, and it drew together a great crowd of the first musicians of the city and of the country about us. "The music of the future" has become the music of the present. The critics, in deriding or denouncing it, simply proclaimed their inability to comprehend it, and their mocking phrase stares them in the face as a grand prophecy fulfilled.

Viewed from Mr. Mattheson's position, criticism becomes one of the most amusing branches of our literature. The opinion of a journal upon a literary work is, after all, only the self-revelation of a man. When we look through the pretentious and authoritative types, into the manuscript written by some unfledged *littérateur*, or some disappointed and soured hireling, or some pretender charged with the affectation of learning, or some specialist possessed by his one idea, or some zealot or partisan, or some greedy seeker for sensation and notoriety, we lose our respect for much that passes for criticism, and learn the reason of its powerlessness in determining the public opinion. A poor fellow who pumps his brain and levies contributions on his commonplace books, and crams himself with the lumber of libraries, to show how much more he knows than the authors upon whom he presumes to sit in judgment, is a funny spectacle to everybody but his unconscious self.

The general worthlessness of criticism is shown best, perhaps, in the fact that the view which any given periodical will take of any given book can always be predicted by any man thoroughly conversant with the views, prejudices, and spirit of its conductors. Two periodicals, edited with equal talent and learning, can always be selected which will present opinions diametrically opposed to each other on any book of positive qualities. As a general thing, criticism has no drift. It is a confused mass of individual opinions whose tendency is to destroy each other. It may assist the public in getting a view of the different sides of a literary work, but it does not determine anything, and is not relied upon to determine anything. Indeed, it is so contradictory that it cannot possibly determine anything but its own worthlessness. In view of these facts, the *ex-cathedra* judgments of some of our journals are laughable enough, especially when we remember how sincerely their authors believe in their own judicial wisdom, and how disgusted they are with the fact that the world will not endorse it. Mr. Mattheson has at least helped us to apprehend one office of criticism, not commonly known hitherto. It quite reverses the point of observation and study, but it makes it more interesting, and ought to make it more useful.

THE INDECENCIES OF CRITICISM.

The uses of competent and candid criticism are various. The first is to assist the public in arriving at a just judgment of the various productions of literature and art, and the enlightenment and correction of their producers. Nothing that passes for, or pretends to be, criticism, is worthy of the name, that does not accomplish these objects; and these results, in various forms, may be grouped under the head of information. The next object is one of education. The processes of criticism are educational, both to the critic and to the public. The study of the various forms of art—literary, architectural, pictorial, plastic; the discussions of relations, proportions, details; the exposition of the rules of construction as they relate to the body of a work, and of vitalizing principle, purpose and taste, as they relate to its spirit—all these are educational. They fit not only the public, but the critic himself, to judge of other works. They assist in building up a public judgment, and in training the public mind for the trial of that which comes before it for sentence. The office of criticism is one of the most important, dignified, and difficult, that a writer is ever called upon to assume. It requires not only a sound head but a good heart. It calls not only for wide knowledge, fine intellectual gifts, and a closely discriminating judicial mind, but for a catholicity of sympathy and a broad good-will that will enable a man to handle his materials without prejudice, and lead him to his work with the wish to find, and the purpose to exhibit, all of worthiness it possesses. A critic must be able to find the inside of an author's design, and to get his outlook from the inside. In brief, he must be a very rare man. He need not be able to produce the works upon which he sits in judgment, but he should, at least be able sympathetically to apprehend the nature and purpose of the producer, and large and many-sided enough to grasp and entertain the great variety of human genius and power and their multifarious products.

How many competent critics have we in America? Not many. The critical judgment furnishes the most notable jargon of the literary world. There is not a work of art worth noticing at all that does not use up, in its critical characterization, all the adjectives of praise and dispraise. To one, a book may be a farrago of nonsense; to another, the finest flight of human genius. So ludicrous do these contrarieties of opinion appear, and so little do publishers and the public care for them, that they are published side by side in the advertisements of booksellers as "the unbiased opinions of the press." So ludicrous are they, indeed, that the public have ceased to be guided by them. It is often the case that books which win the widest praise find no market whatever, while those which are greeted with critical derision reach no end of editions. The shameful fact is, or seems to be, that the public have no faith in the criticism of the day. They read criticism for amusement as they would read a novel, and straightway buy the book, the record of whose condemnation is fresh in their minds, tolerably sure of finding the worth of their purchase-money. Who are these men of warring counsels and conclusions?

A. runs a country paper. He writes no criticisms himself, but there is a young man at his elbow, fresh from college, who is literary, or nothing. He has read little, and thought less; but criticism gives him practice in writing; so he writes. He has no well-formed opinion on anything, but he must express an opinion. The solid work of some old man of letters comes into his hands, and then the young progressive gets his chance. Woe to the old fogy who presumes to write a book! Incapable of writing his mother tongue well, with nothing in his head but the contents of his college text-books, with no experience of life, with no culture, with no practical knowledge of the great questions that engage the thinkers of the age, the young man sits down and demolishes the work of one by the side of whom he is but an infant of days. He parades what little knowledge he possesses, through legitimate study or illegitimate cram, and when his critique appears, he prances around it and parades it before his friends. This sort of job is supposed to assist the public in forming an intelligent opinion!

B. writes his own criticisms. He edits a country paper by downright hard work. He is fond of receiving the favors of publishers, and anxious to please them. All the week long the books accumulate upon his table until, on Friday or Saturday, they must be attended to, or they will overwhelm him. So he starts at the top of the pile and works down through. Up to the moment of his beginning, he has not looked inside of a cover. He copies the titles, looks at the preface, glances at an expression here and there, and then records his judgment. In three hours he has finished; and the batch of "book notices" goes in, with the knowledge on the part of the writer that there is not a competent criticism in the number, though there may be twenty *ex-cathedra* opinions. Not a book has been read, and nothing beyond a first impression has been recorded; and, again, the public is supposed to have been very much enlightened!

C. is the editor of a feeble sheet to which he wishes to attract attention. He knows that his candid judgment is not accounted for much, so he tries an uncandid one. He will win notice by the amount of fur which he can strip off and set flying; by the streams of blood he can set flowing; by the hurts he can inflict; by the outrages he can commit. To him, an author or an artist is fair game. His paper must live. His paper shall live. He sails under a black flag, and, because people think a pirate interesting, they flock around to look upon his ugly craft and examine his ensanguined shirt-sleeves. He is a man who stands no nonsense, and acknowledges no loyalty to the amenities of life. He caricatures women in his pages, or tells them that they are old and ugly. He perpetrates personal affronts, for which he ought to be knocked down like a dog; and when taken to task for them, he talks about the sacrifices that all men suffer who undertake thorough criticism! So here is another manufacturer of public opinion.

D. is a dyspeptic, who simply voids his spleen on paper. He is obliged to write for a living, and his breakfast invariably rises sour in his gorge. His physician can prescribe for him as well by reading his criticism as a quack can by examining his glandular secretions in a vial, and can see just where an antacid, or a mercurial, or a tonic, would tone down a judgment, or modify an expression, or elevate him to appreciation. He uses a sharp pen, and tempers his ink with vinegar. He is cross and crotchety. It is as hard for an author or an artist to get along with him as it is for his wife and children. He must have vent for his humor, and the innocent books that come to him must suffer. The boy who pounds his thumb with a hammer, throws his hammer through the nearest mirror, purely as an expression of his mingled pain and anger. The mirror is not in the least to blame, but something must be smashed to avoid swearing. The dyspeptic critic operates in the same way, and his criticisms are the natural outcome of the horrors and irritations of his indigestion.

E. is a partisan, and the member of a clique. All that is done inside the circle in which, by choice or circumstances, he finds himself placed, is rightly done. The pets of that clique can do no wrong. To exhibit their excellences, to paint their superiorities, to cackle vicariously over their eggs, is one-half of the business of his life. The other half is to cheapen, pick in pieces, ridicule, condemn, and, so far as he can, destroy the work of all outside of the charmed line which circumscribes the area of his sympathies. Within his field, all growths are divine: sun-flowers are suns, daisies are dahlias, crab-apples are pomegranates, and an onion is the fountain of tearful emotion. Outside of his field, the land is desert, and the people are barbarians, who not only do nothing well, but who are guilty of great presumption in attempting to do anything at all. It is the land of the thorn and the thistle. There dwells the wild ass. There hammers, among senseless echoes, the lonely bittern. There poisonous waters break on barren shores, and there dwell the graceless infidels who do not worship toward the holy hill, humbly at whose foot he has reared his tabernacle.

F. is a man whose theory of criticism compels him to simple fault-finding. He may have brains, culture, acumen, or none or little of all these, but it has never entered into his head that criticism calls for the discrimination of excellences. His business is to pick flaws, and he does it without reference to any man's standard of taste, or point of purpose, but his own. He takes no account of an author's peculiar power, or the kind of audience he addresses and seeks to move. He belongs to no clique; vaunts his independence; and demonstrates that independence by finding all the fault possible with everything that comes to him. He assumes to be a sort of inspector-general of literary and artistic wares, and sorts them, as they come along, by their defects. A rose may be beautiful and fragrant, but if he finds a petal over-colored or under-colored, or decayed, or imperfectly formed, it is tossed aside among the worthless. If it have a rose-bug in it, or a worm, it is thrown among those infested with insects or vermin. The more faults he can find, the more pride he takes to his eyes for their discovery. It is not his business to nurse art, or to encourage merit. It is not his business, perhaps, to depress either, but he has an office like the English sparrow, which is to kill vermin. If he also drives away all the singing birds, it is not his affair. The blue-bird may flee his society, the robin may build his nest otherwhere, the songs of the summer morning may cease; it matters not, so long as he can swab his greedy throat with a caterpillar, and save the tree on which he holds his perch, and in which he builds his nest.

G. is a man of learning, whose simple effort in criticism is to prove to an author and the public how much more than the author he knows of the subject which he discusses. His criticisms are disquisitions, expositions, treatises. The book in hand is the occasion of his performance, not in any way the subject of it. It is simply a peg on which he hangs his clothes for an airing, or a graceful apology for calling attention to himself. In short, he uses the book in hand for the purpose of putting himself forward, not as a critic, but as an author! Of the dreariness and essential indecency of this kind of criticism, we have left ourselves no room to speak. Its egotism and arrogance would be ludicrous, if they were not disgusting.

H. regards criticism as an instrument of rewards and punishments. He pays his friends with it, and revenges himself upon those whom he chooses to consider his enemies. He approaches either task without the slightest conscience. Every book, and every work of art, is handled without any regard to its merits, and only with relation to his own selfish interests and feelings. He "takes down" a man by assailing his productions, and lifts him up by praising them. In the whole range of what, by courtesy, is called "criticism," there is nothing more indecent than this. The only thing that makes it tolerable is, that its motive is too apparent to permit it to have any marked effect on public opinion.

There are other classes of indecent critics and indecent criticism that we should be glad to notice, but the list is already long, and when we have fairly exhausted it—when we have assigned to these classes all the critics and all the criticism that justly belong to them—what have we left? It is a painful question to ask, and a hard one to answer. We certainly have not much left, but we have something. Let us be grateful, at least, to those men and women, scattered here and there over the country, who, with well-cultured brains and catholic hearts, make of criticism, a careful, conscientious, discriminating task—who, with sympathy for all who are honestly trying to build up their country's literature and add to its treasures of native art, approach their work with kindness and candor, and so perform it as to educe the best that every worker can do. Such men and women are public benefactors, the dignity and importance of whose office it would be hard to exaggerate. We need more of them—need them sadly. In the meantime, it is probable that incompetency, flippancy, arrogance, partisanship, ill-nature, and the pertinacious desire to attract attention, will go on with their indecent work, until criticism, which has now sunk to public contempt, will fall to dirtier depths beneath it.

Conscience and Courtesy in Criticism.

The lack of sound value in current literary criticism, both in this country and Europe, is notorious. It is so much the work of cliques and schools, or so much the office of men who have a chronic habit of finding fault, or so coarse in its personalities, or so incompetent in its judgments through haste and insufficient examination, that it is rarely instructive, either to the authors reviewed or to the public. The average column of book-notices in a daily paper is quite valueless, by necessity. The reviewer seems to forget that all the influence of the journal for which he works stands behind his hastily-written words, and that sensitive men and women are to be warmed or withered by them. Just a little more conscience, or a more candid consultation of such as he may have, would teach him that he has no moral right to give publicly an opinion of a book of which he knows nothing. In so small a matter as noticing a book before a competent examination of it, the chances are that he will mislead the public and do injustice to those who nearly always have some claim to the good opinion of the reading world. Publishers expect impossibilities of the daily press, and are largely responsible for what is known as the "book-notice;" but the daily press ought to declare its independence, and absolutely refuse to notice any book which has not been thoroughly read. The best and richest of the city press has already done this; but the country press keeps up its column of book-notices every week, written by editors who never have time to look beyond the preface.

In England, criticism is probably more the work of partisanship than it is here. The interests of parties in church and state, and of cliques and schools of literary art, seem to determine everything. It appears to be perfectly understood that everything written by the members of a certain clique will be condemned, and if possible killed, by the combined efforts of another clique, and *vicè versa.* Criticism is simply a mode of fighting. Mr. Blank, belonging to a certain literary clique, writes a volume of verses and prints it. He sends advance copies to his friends, who write their laudations of it, and communicate them to sympathetic journals and magazines. So when it is published, the critiques appear almost simultaneously, and the public is captured by the stratagem. The condemnations come too late to kill the book, and the clever intriguers have their laugh over the result. It is not harsh to say that all criticism born of this spirit is not only intrinsically valueless, but without conscience. The supreme wish to do right and to mete out simple justice to authorship is wanting. The praise is as valueless as the blame.

The old and fierce personalities of English criticism, which so aroused the ire of Byron, and crushed the spirit of some of his less pugnacious contemporaries, have, in a measure, passed away; but really nothing better in the grand result has taken their place. Men stand together for mutual protection, fully aware that they have nothing to expect of justice and fair dealing by any other means. We do not know why it is that the ordinary courtesies of life are denied to authors more than to painters or sculptors or architects, except, perhaps, that painters and sculptors and architects are not judged by their own co-laborers in art. We presume that these, and that singers and actors would fare badly, if all the criticisms upon them were written by their professional brethren; and this fact suggests the animus of those who criticise current literature. It seems impossible to get a candid and conscientious judgment of a literary man until after he is dead, and out of the way of all envyings and jealousies and competitions. It seems impossible, also, until this event occurs, to separate a man from his works, and to judge them as they stand. There is no good reason, however, for the personal flings dealt out to authors, whose only sin has been a conscientious wish to deserve well of the public, except what is to be found in the meanest qualities of human nature. The lack of personal, gentlemanly courtesy in current criticism is a disgrace to the critical columns of our newspapers and magazines.

The majority of those who write are sensitive to a high degree, and could not possibly be notable writers were they otherwise. They do the best they can, and that which they do is the record of the highest civilization and culture of their country and period. They publish, trembling to think that what they publish is to be pounced upon and picked to pieces like prey. Their best thoughts and best work are not only treated without respect, but they find themselves maligned, cheapened, maliciously characterized, or summarily condemned. All this they are obliged to bear in silence, or suffer the reputation of being thin-skinned and quarrelsome. There is no redress and no defense. They have published a book, in which they have incorporated the results of a life of labor and thought and suffering, with the hope of doing good, and of adding something to the literary wealth of their country; and they have in so doing committed a sin which places them at the mercy of every man who holds a periodical press at his command. It is said that the greatest literary woman living fled her country at the conclusion of that which is perhaps her greatest work, in order to be beyond the reading of the criticisms which the book would call forth. The woman was wise. It was not criticism that she feared: it was the malevolence and injustice of its spirit, to which she would not subject her sensibilities.

There is but one atmosphere in which literature can truly thrive, viz.: that of kindness and encouragement. A criticism from which an author may learn anything to make him better, must be courteous and conscientious. All criticism of a different quality angers or discourages and disgusts him. Our literary men and women are our treasures and our glory. They are the fountain of our purest intellectual delights, and deserve to be treated as such. All that is good in them should have abundant recognition, and all that is bad should be pointed out in a spirit of such friendliness and courtesy that they should be glad to read it and grateful for it. If many of them become morbid, sour, resentful, impatient or unpleasantly self-asserting, it ought to be remembered on their behalf that they have been stung by injustice, and badgered by malice, and made contemptuous by discourteous treatment. It is not unjust to say that all criticism which does not bear the front of personal courtesy and kindness and the warrant of a careful conscience is a curse to literature, and to the noble guild upon which we depend for its production.

THE POPULAR LECTURE.

Star-Lecturing.

Mr. Proctor does not need to look upward to find the star-depths. The phrase may fitly characterize American society, which consists of stars and blank spaces. We run our politics on the starring system. A man becomes a star, and we make him president. The "red light of Mars" is the favorite color. Not statesmanship, not personal character, not intellectual culture, not eminent knowledge, not anything and not any combination of things that constitute superlative fitness, fixes the American choice for the chief magistracy. The star which, for the moment, can attract the greatest number of eyes, becomes the lord of the heavens and the earth. Votes must be had at any sacrifice; and votes can only be counted on for stars. Availability is the political watch-word, and such statesmanship as we get is that with which we manage to surround the star that so quickly cools and flickers in its new and alien atmosphere. Political rewards do not go where they belong; public trust is not reposed in the best men; and so politics degenerate, and second and third rate men are everywhere uppermost. The starring system in politics is a failure. It is bad for the country, it is bad for politics; it is a discouragement to personal and political worth; it is a nuisance.

The starring system in theatricals is even more obviously

destructive to all that is worthy in the popular drama. We go to a theatre, not to witness a play, but to see Booth, or Joe Jefferson, or some other star. The opera is nothing without Kellogg, or Patti, or Nilsson, or some miraculous tenor who to-day is, and to-morrow is not. The orchestras,—trained, laborious, patient, admirable,—pass for nothing. The choruses are not thought so much of as an orchestrion would be. The great mass of singers and players who sustain the minor parts, have no more consideration than puppets. What is the consequence? The money is mainly absorbed by the stars, who shine the brighter in a sky of mediocrity or absolute inferiority. So long as the starring system prevails, mediocrity will be the rule. Stars must have space, to be seen; and we have had for years, in the theatrical world, nothing but stars and spaces—the latter, wide. A first-class drama, well presented in every part, is not often witnessed in New York; and for this fact the starring system is alone responsible. An actor nowadays can get no consideration except as a star, and, to succeed, he is often obliged to confine himself to a single play.

How has the starring system worked upon the platform? It has been tried pretty thoroughly for the last five years, and the results ought to be, and are, apparent. Ten and fifteen years ago, a course of lectures consisted of eight or ten discourses on topics of popular interest, or social and political questions of public moment. They were prosperous, well attended, and profitable in many ways. Then came the star-fever. Men were summoned to the platform simply because they would draw, and not because the people expected instruction or inspiration from them. A notoriety had only to rise, to be summoned at once to the platform. If he could lift a great many kegs of nails; if he was successful as a showman; if he was a literary buffoon, and sufficiently expert in cheap orthography; in short, if he had been anything, or had done anything, to make himself an object of curiosity to the crowd, he was regarded as a star, and called at once into the lecture field, for the single purpose of swelling the receipts at the door. Of course the stars called for high prices, and under high prices the number of lectures given in a course was cut down. The people who came to bask in the blaze, finding too often only a twinkle, and sometimes only a fizzle, that left an unpleasant odor, became disgusted, and the best of them,—the very men and women upon whom the whole lecture system relied for steady prosperity,—left the lecture-room altogether. Still the starring system went on, with a new agency to push it, established by the lecture bureaus. Men were invited to come from England, and promised great results. Some of these have been genuine accessions to the corps of good lecturers, while many have proved to be sorry failures. Many a famous name, "far-fetched and dear-bought," has shone upon the list for a season, never to be recalled and always to be remembered with disappointment. The bureaus have pushed and puffed their pets,—both imported and domestic,—until lecture committees have ceased to believe in them altogether.

And now, what is the condition of the platform? In the large towns, where they have been able to get "the stars," it is difficult to get a first-rate audience together on any night, and still more difficult to maintain a steady, prosperous course of lectures. In the smaller towns, where want of funds has compelled them to dispense with the stars, the system was never more prosperous than it is to-day. In New England and New York, generally, the towns with 20,000 inhabitants and upwards, have difficulty in sustaining a course of lectures, while there are many towns of less than five thousand people that maintain a good course every winter, and make money by it.

If there is anything in the lecture system worth saving, let us save it. Those who know what it used to be, will be glad to see it restored to its old position, and if they have studied its history, they will conclude, with us, that the starring system must be stopped. The lecture-room must cease to be the show-room of fresh notorieties, at high prices. Men must be called to lecture for the simple reason that they have something to say. The courses must be lengthened, and made in themselves valuable. The pushing by interested bureaus of untried men must be ignored or resisted. Men must be called to teach because they can teach, and not because they can do something else. The lecture must cease to be regarded simply as an entertainment. Wherever it has been so regarded and so managed, the system has gone down, and wherever the stock lecturer has been sacrificed to the star, the audiences have gradually dwindled until it has become almost impossible to sustain a course of lectures at all. Stars have been so much in fashion that we have establishments now for the manufacture of fictitious reputations, and these establishments must go under. They always were an impertinence, and they have become a nuisance. The lecture is a necessity. Let us restore the institution to its old footing of direct friendly relations between the lecturers and the lyceum, and give no man access to the platform who does not come there in a legitimate way, and who is not held there because he has something valuable to say. No system can stand when its best and most reliable workers are pinched in their prices, that those may be overpaid, who not only bring no strength to it, but weaken it in its finances and in its hold upon the respect and affection of the people.

Triflers on the Platform.

There was a time in the history of our popular "lecture system" when a lecture was a lecture. The men who appeared before the lyceums were men who had something to say. Grave discussions of important topics; social, political, and literary essays; instructive addresses and spirited appeals—these made up a winter's course of popular lectures. Now, a lecture may be any string of nonsense that any literary mountebank can find an opportunity to utter. Artemus Ward "lectured;" and he was right royally paid for acting the literary buffoon. He has had many imitators; and the damage that he and they have inflicted upon the institution of the lyceum is incalculable. The better class that once attended the lecture courses have been driven away in disgust, and among the remainder such a greed for inferior entertainments has been excited that lecture managers have become afraid to offer a first-class, old-fashioned course of lectures to the public patronage. Accordingly, one will find upon nearly every list, offered by the various committees and managers, the names of triflers and buffoons who are a constant disgrace to the lecturing guild, and a constantly degrading influence upon the public taste. Their popularity is usually exhausted by a single performance, but they rove from platform to platform, retailing their stale jokes, and doing their best and worst to destroy the institution to which they cling for a hearing and a living.

This thing was done in better taste formerly. "Drollerists" and buffoons and "Yankee comedians" were in the habit of advertising themselves. They entered a town with no indorsement but their own, and no character but that which they assumed. They attracted a low crowd of men and boys as coarse and frivolous as themselves, and the better part of society never came in contact with them. A woman rarely entered their exhibitions, and a lady never; yet they were clever men, with quite as much wit and common decency as some of the literary wags that are now commended to lecture committees by the bureaus, and presented by the committees to a confiding public.

There are, and have been for years, men put forward as lecturers whose sole distinction was achieved by spelling the weakest wit in the worst way—men who never aimed at any result but a laugh, and who, if they could not secure this result by an effort in the line of decency, did not hesitate at any means, however low, to win the coveted response. If there is any difference between performers of this sort and negro minstrels, strolling "drollerists," who do not even claim to be respectable, we fail to detect it; and it is high time that the managers of our lecture courses had left them from their lists, and ceased to insult the public by the presumption that it can be interested in their silly utterances.

It would be claimed, we suppose, by any one who should undertake to defend the employment of these men, that they draw large houses. Granted: they do this once, and perhaps do something to replenish the managerial exchequer; but they invariably send away their audiences disappointed and disgusted. No thoughtful or sensible man can devote a whole evening to the poorest kind of nonsense without losing a little of his self-respect, and feeling that he has spent his money for that which does not satisfy. The reaction is always against the system, and in the long run the managers find themselves obliged to rely upon a lower and poorer set of patrons, who are not long in learning that even they can be better suited by the coarse comedy of the theatre, and the dances and songs of the negro minstrel. Nothing has been permanently gained in any instance to the lyceum and lecture system by degrading the character of the performances offered to the public. A temporary financial success consequent upon this policy is always followed by dissatisfaction and loss, and it ought to be. Professional jesters and triflers are professional nuisances, who ought not to be tolerated by any man of common sense interested in the elevation and purification of the public taste.

But shall not lyceums and the audiences they gather have the privilege of laughing? Certainly. Mr. Gough's audiences have no lack of opportunity to laugh, and there are others who have his faculty of exciting the mirthfulness of those who throng to hear them; but Mr. Gough is a gentleman who is never low, and who is never without a good object. He is an earnest, Christian man, whose whole life is a lesson of toil and self-sacrifice. Mr. Gough is not a trifler; and the simple reason that he continues to draw full houses from year to year is, that he is not a trifler. Wit, humor, these are never out of order in a lecture, provided they season good thinking and assist manly purpose. Wit and humor are always good as condiments, but never as food. The stupidest book in the world is a book of jokes, and the stupidest man in the world is one who surrenders himself to the single purpose of making men laugh. It is a purpose that wholly demoralizes and degrades him, and makes him unfit to be a teacher of anything. The honor that has been shown to literary triflers upon the platform has had the worst effect upon the young. It has disseminated slang, and vitiated the taste of the impressible, and excited unworthy ambition and emulation. When our lyceums, on which we have been wont to rely for good influences in literary matters, at last become agents of buffoonery and low literary entertainments, they dishonor their early record and the idea which gave them birth. Let them banish triflers from the platform, and go back to the plan which gave them their original prosperity and influence, and they will find no reason to complain of a lack of patronage, or the loss of interest on the part of the public in their entertainments.

PERSONAL DANGERS.

Moths in the Candle.

Every moth learns for itself that the candle burns. Every night, while the candle lasts, the slaughter goes on, and leaves its wingless and dead around it. The light is beautiful, and warm, and attractive; and, unscared by the dead, the foolish creatures rush into the flames, and drop, hopelessly singed, their little lives despoiled.

It has been supposed that men have reason, and a moral sense. It has been supposed that they observe, draw conclusions, and learn by experience. Indeed, they have been in the habit of looking down upon the animal world as a group of inferior beings, and as subjects of commiseration on account of their defenselessness; yet there is a large class of men, reproduced by every passing generation, that do exactly what the moths do, and die exactly as the moths die. They learn nothing by observation or experience. They draw no conclusions, save those which are fatal to themselves. Around a certain class of brilliant temptations they gather, night after night, and with singed wings or lifeless bodies, they strew the ground around them. No instructions, no expostulations, no observation of ruin, no sense of duty, no remonstrances of conscience, have any effect upon them. If they were moths in fact, they could not be sillier or more obtuse. They are, indeed, so far under the domination of their animal natures that they act like animals, and sacrifice themselves in flames that the world's experience has shown to be fatal.

A single passion, which need not be named,—further than to say that, when hallowed by love and a legitimate gift of life to life, it is as pure as any passion of the soul,—is one of the candles around which the human moths lie in myriads of disgusting deaths. If anything has been proved by the observation and experience of the world it is that licentiousness, and all illicit gratification of the passion involved in it, are killing sins against a man's own nature,—that by it the wings are singed not only, but body and soul are degraded and spoiled. Out of all illicit indulgence come weakness, a perverted moral sense, degradation of character, gross beastliness, benumbed sensibilities, a disgusting life, and a disgraceful death. Before its baleful fire the sanctity of womanhood fades away, the romance of life dies, and the beautiful world loses all its charm. The lives wrecked upon the rock of sensuality are strewn in every direction. Again and again, with endless repetition, young men yield to the song of the siren that beguiles them to their death. They learn nothing, they see nothing, they know nothing but their wild desire, and on they go to destruction and the devil.

Every young man who reads this article has two lives before him. He may choose either. He may throw himself away on a few illegitimate delights which cover his brow with shame in the presence of his mother, and become an old man before his time, with all the wine drained out of his life; or he may grow up into a pure, strong manhood, held in healthy relation to all the joys that pertain to that high estate. He may be a beast in his heart, or he may have a wife whom he worships, children whom he delights in, self-respect which enables him to meet unabashed the noblest woman, and an undisputed place in good society. He may have a dirty imagination, or one that hates and spurns all impurity as both disgusting and poisonous. In brief, he may be a man, with a man's powers and immunities, or a sham of a man,—a whited sepulchre,—conscious that he carries with him his own dead bones, and all uncleanness. It is a matter entirely of choice. He knows what one life is, and where it ends. He knows the essential quality and certain destiny of the other. The man who says he cannot control himself not only lies, but places his Maker in blame. He can control himself, and, if he does not, he is both a fool and a beast. The sense of security and purity and self-respect that come of continence, entertained for a single day, is worth more than the illicit pleasures of a world for all time. The pure in heart see God in everything, and see him everywhere, and they are supremely blest.

Wine and strong drink form another candle in which millions of men have singed themselves, and destroyed both body and soul. Here the signs of danger are more apparent than in the other form of sensuality, because there is less secrecy. The candle burns in open space, where all men can see it. Law sits behind, and sanctions its burning. It pays a princely revenue to the government. Women flaunt their gauzes in it. Clergymen sweep their robes through it. Respectability uses it to light its banquets. In many regions of this country it is a highly respectable candle. Yet, every year, sixty thousand persons in this country die of intemperance; and when we think of the blasted lives that live in want and misery—of wives in despair, of loves bruised and blotted out, of children disgraced, of alms-houses filled, of crimes committed through its influence, of industry extinguished, and of disease engendered—and remember that this has been going on for thousands of years, wherever wine has been known, what are we to think of the men who still press into the fire? Have they any more sense than the moths? It is almost enough to shake a man's faith in immortality to learn that he belongs to a race that manifests so little sense, and such hopeless recklessness.

There is just one way of safety, and only one; and a young man who stands at the beginning of his career can choose whether he will walk in it, or in the way of danger. There is a notion abroad among men that wine is good,—that when properly used it has help in it,—that in a certain way it is food, or a help in the digestion of food. We believe that no greater or more fatal hallucination ever possessed the world, and that none so great ever possessed it for so long a time.

Wine is a medicine, and men would take no more of it than of any other medicine if it were not pleasant in its taste, and agreeable in its first effects. The men who drink it, drink it because they like it. The theories as to its healthfulness come afterwards. The world cheats itself, and tries to cheats itself in this thing; and the priests who prate of "using this world as not abusing it," and the chemists who claim a sort of nutritious property in alcohol which never adds to tissue (!) and the men who make a jest of water-drinking, all know perfectly well that wine and strong drink always have done more harm than good in the world, and always will until that millenium comes, whose feet are constantly tripped from under it by the drunkards that lie prone in its path. The millenium with a grog-shop at every corner is just as impossible as security with a burglar at every window, or in every room of the house. All men know that drink is a curse, yet young men sport around it as if there were something very desirable in it, and sport until they are hopelessly singed, and then join the great, sad army which, with undiminished numbers, presses on to its certain death.

We do not like to become an exhorter in these columns, but, if it were necessary, we would plead with young men upon weary knees to touch not the accursed thing. Total abstinence, now and forever, is the only guaranty in existence against a drunkard's life and death, and there is no good that can possibly come to a man by drinking. Keep out of the candle. It will always singe your wings, or destroy you.

THE YOUNG IN GREAT CITIES.

The world learns its lessons slowly. Much of the world does not learn its lessons at all. The young are everywhere growing up amid the ruins of other lives, apparently without inquiring or caring for the reasons of the disasters to life, fortune and reputation that are happening, or have happened, everywhere around them. One man, with great trusts of money in his hands, betrays the confidence of the public, becomes a hopeless defaulter, and blows his brains out. Another, led on by love of power and place, is degraded at last to a poor demagogue, without character or influence. Another, through a surrender of himself to sensuality, becomes a disgusting beast, with heart and brain more foul than the nests of unclean birds. Another, by tasting and tasting and tasting of the wine-cup, becomes a drunkard at last, and dies in horrible delirium, or lives to be a curse to wife, children, and friends. There is an army of these poor wretches in every large city in the land dying daily, and daily re-enforced. A young girl, loving "not wisely, but too well," yields herself to a seducer who ruins and then forsakes her to a life of shame and a death of despair. Not one girl, but thousands of girls yearly, so that, though a great company of those whose robes are soiled beyond cleansing hide themselves in the grave during every twelve-month, another great company of the pure drop to their places, and keep filled to repletion the ranks of prostitution. Again and again, in instances beyond counting, are these tragedies repeated in the full presence of the rising generation, and yet it seems to grow no wiser. Nothing has been more fully demonstrated than that the first steps of folly and sin are fraught with peril. Nothing has been better proved than that temperate drinking is always dangerous, and that excessive drinking is always ruinous. Nothing is better known than that a man cannot consort with lewd women for an hour without receiving a taint that a whole life of repentance cannot wholly eradicate. Since time began have women been led astray by the same promises, the same pledges, the same empty rewards. If young men and young women could possibly learn wisdom, it would seem as if they might win it in a single day, by simply using their eyes and thinking upon what they see. Yet in this great city of New York, and in all the great cities of the country, young men and young women are all the time repeating the mistakes of those around them who are wrecked in character and fortune. The young man keeps his wine bottle, and seeks resorts where deceived and ruined women lie in wait for prey, knowing perfectly well, if he knows anything, or has ever used fairly the reason with which Heaven has endowed him, that he is in the broad road to perdition,—that there is before him a life of disgust and a death of horror.

When the results of certain courses of conduct and certain indulgences are so well known as these to which we allude, it seems strange that any can enter upon them. Every young man knows that if he never tastes a glass of alcoholic drink he will never become, or stand in danger of becoming, a drunkard. Every young man knows that if he preserves a chaste youth, and shuns the society of the lewd, he can carry to the woman whom he loves a self-respect which is invaluable, a past freely open to her questioning gaze, and the pure physical vitality which shall be the wealth of another generation. He knows that the rewards of chastity are ten thousand times greater than those of criminal indulgence. He knows that nothing is lost and everything is gained by a life of manly sobriety and self-denial. He knows all this, if he has had his eyes open, and has exercised his reason in even a small degree; and yet he joins the infatuated multitude and goes straight to the devil. We know that we do not exaggerate when we say that New York has thousands of young men, with good mothers and pure sisters, who, if their lives should be uncovered, could never look those mothers and sisters in the face again. They are full of fears of exposure, and conscious of irreparable loss. Their lives are masked in a thousand ways. They live a daily lie. They are the victims and slaves of vices which are just as certain to cripple or kill them, unless at once and forever forsaken, as they live. There are thousands of others who, now pure and good, will follow evil example unwarned by what they see, and within a year will be walking in the road that leads evermore downward.

One tires of talking to fools, and falls back in sorrow that hell and destruction are never full—in sorrow that men cannot or will not learn that there is but one path to an honorable, peaceful, prosperous, and successful life, and that all others lead more or less directly to ruin.

The Good Fellow.

We wonder if "The Good Fellow" ever mistrusts his goodness, or realizes how selfish, how weak, how unprincipled, and how bad a fellow he truly is. He never regards the consequences of his acts as they relate to others, and especially those of his family friends. Little fits of generosity towards them are supposed to atone for all his misdeeds, while he inflicts upon them the disgraces, inconveniences, and burdens which attend a selfishly dissolute life. The invitation of a friend, the taunts of good-natured boon companions, the temptations of jolly fellowship, these are enough to overcome all his scruples, if he has any scruples, and to lead him to ignore all the possible results to those who love him best, and who must care for him in sickness and all the unhappy phases of his selfish life.

The Good Fellow is notoriously careless of his family. Any outside friend can lead him whithersoever he will—into debauchery, idleness, vagabondage. He can ask a favor, and it is done. He can invite him into disgrace, and he goes. He can direct him into a job of dirty work, and he straightway undertakes it. He can tempt him into any indulgence which may suit his vicious whims, and, regardless of wife, mother, sister, who may be shortened in their resources so as legitimately to claim his protecting hand,—regardless of honorable father and brother,—he will spend his money, waste his time, and make himself a subject of constant and painful anxiety, or an unmitigated nuisance to those alone who care a straw for him. What pay does he receive for this shameful sacrifice? The honor of being considered a "Good Fellow," with a set of men who would not spend a cent for him if they should see him starving, and who would laugh over his calamities. When he dies in the ditch, as he is most likely to die, they breathe a sigh over the swill they drink, and say, "after all, he was a Good Fellow."

The feature of the Good Fellow's case which makes it well nigh hopeless, is, that he thinks he is a Good Fellow. He thinks that his pliable disposition, his readiness to do other good fellows a service, and his jolly ways, atone for all his faults. His love of praise is fed by his companions, and thus his self-complacency is nursed. Quite unaware that his good fellowship is the result of his weakness; quite unaware that his sacrifice of honor, and the honor and peace of his family, for the sake of outside praise is the offspring of the most heartless selfishness; quite unaware that his disregard of the interests and feelings of those who are bound to him by the closest ties of blood, is the demonstration of his utterly unprincipled character; he carries an unruffled, or a jovial front, while hearts bleed or break around him. Of all the scamps society knows, the traditional good fellow is the most despicable. A man who for the sake of his own selfish delights, or the sake of the praise of careless or unprincipled friends, makes his home a scene of anxiety and torture, and degrades and disgraces all who are associated with him in his home life, is, whether he knows it or not, a brute. If a man cannot be loyal to his home, and to those who love him, then he cannot be loyal to anything that is good. There is something mean beyond description, in any man who cares more for anything in this world than the honor, the confidence, and love of his family. There is something radically wrong in such a man, and the quicker and the more thoroughly he realizes it, in a humiliation which bends him to the earth in shame and confusion, the better for him. The traditional good fellow is a bad fellow from the crown of his head to the sole of his foot. He is as weak as a baby, vain as a peacock, selfish as a pig, and as unprincipled as a thief. He has not one redeeming trait upon which a reasonable self-respect can be built and braced.

Give us the bad fellow, who stands by his personal and family honor, who sticks to his own, who does not "treat" his friends while his home is in need of the money he wastes, and who gives himself no indulgence of good fellowship at the expense of duty! A man with whom the approving smile of a wife, or mother, or sister, does not weigh more than a thousand crazy bravos of boon companions, is just no man at all.

Easy Lessons from Hard Lives.

No man ever died a more natural death than James Fisk, Jr., excepting, perhaps, Judas Iscariot. When the devil entered into the swine, and they ran violently down a steep place into the sea, it was only the going down that was violent. The death that came was natural enough. When a man pushes his personality so far to the front of aggressive and impertinent schemes of iniquity as Fisk did, it is the most natural thing in the world for him to run against something that will hurt him, for dangers stand thick as malice and revenge can plant them in the path of godlessness and brutality. The captain of a piratical ship who undertakes, in addition to the duties of his office, to serve as the figure-head of his own vessel, will receive, naturally, the first blow when she drives upon the rocks. Yet we join in the general sorrow that Mr. Fisk is dead, for it is possible that the lesson of his life may fail to be impressed upon Young America as it ought to be, in consequence of the sympathy awakened by the manner of his taking off. It is not to be denied that a pretty universal execration of this man's memory has been saved to him through the bloody mercy of a murder. Yes, people talk of his fund of humor, his geniality, his generosity, etc., etc. If this kind of talk is a source of satisfaction to anybody, of course he will indulge in it; but Fisk certainly is none the better for having been killed. He was a bad man—bold and shameless and vulgar in his badness—with whom no gentleman could come in contact on terms of familiar intercourse without a sense of degradation. As for his geniality, that was as natural as his death. A cow that has spent the night in a neighbor's corn-field, and stands whisking her tail and ruminating in the morning sun, is one of the blandest and most genial creatures living. More than this, she does not care particularly who drinks the milk she has won; and so we suppose that the cow too, is generous as well as genial!

Ah! we forgot about Mr. Tweed. It was Mr. Tweed who was a great man a little while ago, was it not? Mr. Tweed had power in his hands and patronage at his disposal, and had thousands to come at his beck and go at his bidding. His name was a tower of strength on a great many Boards of Directors. The legislature elected by the State managed the State, and he managed the legislature. He had confederates in iniquity; but he was "The Boss," and his will was imperative and imperial. Intrenched behind laws that were the product of corruption, ballots that could be increased or diminished at will, and wealth that came to him in dark and mysterious ways, he dictated the administration of the government of the first city of the new world, and shaped the policy of the proudest State of the Union. His path was strewn with luxuries for himself and largess for his friends. He lived a right royal life, and the power-worshiping multitude and the vulgar seekers for place hung around him with abject and obsequious fawning. Where and what is Mr. Tweed now? Where and what are his *confrères?* All, from the Boss down to the meanest menial of the Ring, are writhing and shriveling under the heat of a great popular indignation. Their deeds of darkness are uncovered, their shameless betrayals of trust are exposed, their power is passed hopelessly from their hands, and a great city, which once felt helpless in their grasp, has risen in its might and crowded them all to their utter overthrow. Every man who was a participator in the power and plunder of the Ring, shakes in his shoes wherever he walks, or stands, or skulks, and shows what it is to have a fearful looking for of judgment. Good men everywhere breathe freer for this revolution, and the republic and the world have won new hope.

The overthrow of these men—sudden, awful, complete—brings home to young men a much-needed lesson. A short time ago there were thousands of young men regarding with an eager, curious gaze the careers which have terminated and are terminating so tragically. It was a question in many minds, alas! whether honesty was the best policy—whether virtue paid—whether, after all that the preachers and the teachers might say, the rascality which received such magnificent rewards at the hands of the people was not the best investment for a young man cherishing a desire for wealth and power. Who can begin to measure the effects of these poisonous examples on American blood? Let every man who wields a pen or has audience with the public do what he can to counteract them, by calling popular attention to the fact that these men have simply met the natural and inevitable fate of eminent rascality. Honesty *is* the best policy. Virtue *does* pay. Purity *is* profitable. Truthfulness and trustworthiness *are* infinitely better than basely won gold. A good conscience *is* a choicer possession than power. When a man sacrifices personal probity and honor, he loses everything that makes any earthly possession sweet. When these men were dazzling the multitude with their shows and splendors, they knew that the world they lived in was unsubstantial; and we have no question that they expected and constantly dreaded the day of discovery and retribution. We do not believe that rascality ever paid them for a day, even when it seemed to be most triumphantly successful.

The storm which has wrecked these men has cleared the sky.

The air is purer, and has tone and inspiration in it. Honesty is at a premium again, and honest men may stand before rogues unabashed. The lesson of the day is one which teaches young men that lying and stealing and committing adultery are unprofitable sins, against which Nature as well as Revelation protests. It has not come too soon. We hope that it may not be learned too late.

Prizes for Suicide.

We have all heard of the testimony of the Boston physicians against the system of forcing pursued by the public schools of that city,—of its tendency to produce nervous diseases, and even, in some instances, insanity itself. The testimony is so strong and positive, and so unanimous, that it must be accepted as true. Some weeks ago, at the commencement anniversary of a college, not in Boston or New England, a long row of young men was called up to receive the prizes awarded to various forms of acquisition and scholarship. It was pleasant to see their shining faces, and to witness their triumph; but the pleasure was spoiled by the patent fact that their victories had been won at the expense of physical vitality. Physically, there was not a well-developed man among them; and many of them were as thin as if they had just arisen from a bed of sickness. After they had left the stage, a whole class was called on, to receive their diplomas. The improvement in the average physique was so great that there was a universal recognition of the fact by the audience; and whispered comments upon it went around the assembly. The poorer scholars were undeniably the larger and healthier men. The victors had won a medal, and lost that which is of more value than the aggregate of all the gold medals ever struck.

There is one lesson which teachers, of all men living, are

the slowest to learn, viz.: that scholarship is not power, and that the ability to acquire is not the ability to do. The rewards of excellence in schools and colleges are, as a rule, meted out to those who have demonstrated their capacity for acquiring and cramming. The practical world has ceased to expect much of its valedictorians and its prize-medal bearers. Those whose growth of power is slow, and whose vitality has been unimpaired by excessive study during the years of physical development, are the men who do, and who always have done, the work of the world. Thousands of educated men go through life with feeble health, and power impaired, and limited usefulness, in direct consequence of their early triumphs, or, rather, of the sacrifices by which those triumphs were won.

We cannot but believe that prizes do more harm than good, and that it would be a blessing to the nation if they could be abolished in every school and college in the country. They are won invariably by those who need rather to be restrained than stimulated, and are rarely contended for by those whose sluggish natures alone require an extraordinary motive to exertion and industry. Their award is based upon the narrowest grounds. Their tendency is to convey a false idea of manly excellence, and to discourage the development of the stronger and healthier forms of physical and mental life. The young man who goes to the work of his life with a firm and healthy frame, a pure heart, and the ability to use such knowledge as he possesses, is worth to himself, his friends, and the world, a thousand times more than the emaciated scholar whose stomach is the abode of dyspepsia and whose brain is a lumber-house of unused learning. If we have any prizes to give, let us give them to those young men of delicate organizations and the power of easy acquisition who restrain their ambition to excel in scholarship, and build up for themselves a body fit to give their minds a comfortable dwelling-place and forcible and facile service. These would be prizes worth securing, and they would point to the highest form of manhood as their aim and end.

The tendency in all these educational matters is to extremes. It is quite as much so in England as here. We have no sympathy with the aim which is fostered in some institutions of making athletes of the students. Base-ball matches, and rowing matches, and acrobatic feats are well enough for those who have no brains to cultivate, or who are not engaged in educating and storing them; but they are not the things for studious young men. The awful strain that they inflict upon the body draws all the nervous energy to the support of the muscular system, and kills the ability to study. More than all, they wound the vitality of every man who engages in them. We once heard an English clergyman say that every noted athlete of his (the clergyman's) class in the university was either dead or worse. Moderate play every day in the open air, limited hours of study in the day-time, pleasant social intercourse, unlimited sleep, good food, the education of power by its use in writing, speaking, and debating—these are what make men of symmetry, health, and usefulness. The forcing process, in whatever way applied, and to whatever set of powers, is a dangerous process. We make a great stir over the flogging of a refractory boy by a teacher. Whole communities are sometimes convulsed by what is regarded as a case of physical cruelty in a school, but the truth is that the ferule and the raw-hide are the mildest instruments of cruelty in the hands of more teachers than can be counted. The boy who is crowded to do more than he ought to do in study, and so crowded that he is enfeebled, or takes on disease of the brain and nervous system at the first onset of sickness, is the victim of the subtlest cruelty that can be practiced upon him.

We write strongly of these things because we feel strongly. We believe that there is a wrong practiced upon the children and young men of the country that ought to be righted. We believe, too, that not only teachers but parents are blameworthy in this matter. It all comes of a false idea of education. To acquire what is written in books—in the quickest way and in the greatest quantity—this is education in the popular opinion. The enormous mistakes and fatal policies of which we complain all grow out of this error. Half of the schooling which we give those children who go to school would be better than the whole; while the poor third, who do not go to school at all, would give employment to the unused energies of those teachers whose time would be released to them by such a reduction of school hours. Six hours of daily imprisonment for a child is cruelty, without any reference to the tasks to which he is held during that period.

Keeping at It.

Every man has his own definition of happiness; but when men have risen above the mere sensualities of life,—above eating and drinking, and sleeping, and hearing and seeing,—they can come to something like an agreement upon a definition which, when formulated, would read something like this: "Happiness consists in the harmonious, healthy, successful action of a man's powers." The higher these powers may be, and the higher the sphere in which they move, the higher the happiness. The genuine "fool's paradise" is ease. There are millions of men, hard at work, who are looking for their reward to immunity from work. They would be quite content to purchase twenty-five years of leisure with twenty-five years of the most slavish drudgery. Toward these years of leisure they constantly look with hope and expectation. Not unfrequently the leisure is won and entered upon; but it is always a disappointment. It never brings the happiness which was expected, and it often brings such a change of habits as to prove fatal, either to health or to life.

A man who inherits wealth may begin and worry through three-score years and ten without any very definite object. In driving, in foreign travel, in hunting and fishing, in club-houses and society, he may manage to pass away his time; but he will hardly be happy. It seems to be necessary to health that the powers of a man be trained upon some object, and steadily held there day after day, year after year, while vitality lasts. There may come a time in old age when the fund of vitality will have sunk so low that he can follow no consecutive labor without such a draft upon his forces that sleep cannot restore them. Then, and not before, he should stop work. But, so long as a man has vitality to spare upon work, it must be used, or it will become a source of grievous, harassing discontent. The man will not know what to do with himself, and when he has reached such a point as that, he is unconsciously digging a grave for himself, and fashioning his own coffin. Life needs a steady channel to run in—regular habits of work and of sleep. It needs a steady, stimulating aim—a trend toward something. An aimless life can never be happy, or, for a long period, healthy. Said a rich widow to a gentleman, still laboring beyond his needs: "Don't stop; keep at it." The words that were in her heart were: "If my husband had not stopped, he would be alive to-day." And what she thought was doubtless true. A greater shock can hardly befall a man who has been active than that which he experiences when, having relinquished his pursuits, he finds unused time and unused vitality hanging upon his idle hands and mind. The current of his life is thus thrown into eddies, or settled into a sluggish pool, and he begins to die.

We have, and have had, in our own city some notable examples of business continued through a long life with unbroken health and capacities to the last. Mr. Astor, who has just passed away, undoubtedly prolonged his life by his steady adherence to business. There is no doubt that he lived longer and was happier for his continued work. If he had settled back upon the consciousness of assured wealth, and taken the ease that was so thoroughly warranted by his large possessions, he would undoubtedly have died years ago. Commodore Vanderbilt, now more than eighty years old, is a notable instance of healthy powers, continued by use. How long does any one suppose he would live if his work were taken from his hands, and his care from his mind? His life goes on in a steady drift, and he is as able now to manage vast business enterprises as when he was younger. There was never a time apparently when his power was greater than it is to-day. Our Nestor among American editors and poets, though an octogenarian, not only mingles freely in society, makes public speeches, and looks after his newspaper, but writes verses, and is carrying on grand literary enterprises. Many people wonder why such men continue to work when they might retire upon their money and their laurels; but they are working, not only for happiness, but for life.

The great difficulty with us all is that we do not play enough. The play toward which men in business look for their reward should never be taken in a lump, but should be scattered all along their career. It should be enjoyed every day, every week. The man who looks forward to it wants it now. Play, like wit in literature, should never be a grand dish, but a spice; and a man who does not take his play with his work never has it. Play ceases to be play to a man when it ceases to be relaxation from daily work. As the grand business of life, play is the hardest work a man can do.

Besides the motives of continued life and happiness to which we have called attention in this article, there is another of peculiar force in America, which binds us to labor while we live. If we look across the water, we shall find that nearly all the notable men die in the harness. The old men are the great men in Parliament and Cabinet. Yet it is true that a man does not so wholly take himself out of life in Europe as in America when he relinquishes business. A rich man in Europe can quit active affairs, and still have the consideration due to his talents, his wealth, and his social position. Here, a man has only to "count himself out" of active pursuits, to count himself out of the world. A man out of work is a dead man, even if he is the possessor of millions. The world walks straight over him and his memory. One reason why a rich and idle man is happier in Europe than at home is that he has the countenance of a class of respectable men and women living upon their incomes. A man may be respectable in Europe without work. After a certain fashion, he can be so here; but, after all, the fact that he has ceased to be active in affairs of business and politics makes him of no account. He loses his influence, and goes for nothing, except a relic with a hat on, to be bowed to. So there is no way for us but to "keep at it;" get all the play we need as we go on; drive at something, so long as the hand is strong and steady, and not to think of rest this side of the narrow bed, where the sleep will be too deep for dreams, and the waking will open into infinite leisure.

PERSONAL DEVELOPMENT.

The American Gentleman of Leisure.

Did the reader ever see a lost dog in a great city? Not a dog recently lost, full of wild anxiety and restless pain and bewilderment, but one who had given up the search for a master in despair, and had become consciously a vagabond? If so, he has seen an animal that has lost his self-respect, traveling in the gutters, slinking along by fences, making acquaintance with dirty boys, becoming a thorough coward, and losing every admirable characteristic of a dog. A cat is a cat even in vagabondage; but a dog that does not belong to somebody is as hopeless a specimen of demoralization as can be found in the superior race among which he has sought in vain for his master. We know him at first sight, and he knows that we know him. The loss of his place in the world, and the loss of his objects of loyalty, personal and official, have taken the significance out of his life and the spirit out of him. He has become a dog of leisure.

We do not know how it may be in trans-Atlantic countries. It is quite possible that in Constantinople, where dogs are plenty and masters comparatively scarce, the canine vagabonds keep each other in countenance. There is a sort of self-respect among human thieves, if only enough of them get together. Where beggars are plenty, there are sometimes generated a sort of professional ambition and a semblance, at least, of professional pride and honor. Liquor-dealers form a society, publish a newspaper, call themselves "Wine Merchants," and make themselves believe that they are respectable. Stock-gamblers in Wall street, by sheer force of numbers in combination, make a business semi-respectable which never added a dollar of wealth to the country and never will, and which constantly places the business interests of the country in jeopardy. So it is possible that in Constantinople lost dogs maintain their self-respect, by community of feeling and a consciousness that they are neither exceptional nor eccentric. A dog's sense of vagabondage would seem, therefore, to depend much upon his atmosphere and circumstances. In New York he loses himself with his home; in Constantinople he joins a community.

The American man of leisure is a sort of lost dog. The people are so busy, they have so long associated personal importance with action and usefulness, that it is all a man's life is worth to drop out of active employment. If a Vanderbilt should quietly release his hold of the vast railroad interests now in his hands, and should never more show his face in Wall Street, he would practically shrink to a nonentity and cease to be of interest to anybody. It is undeniably true that there is nobody in America who has so hard a time as the man of leisure. The man who has nothing to do, and nobody to help him do nothing, may properly be counted among the unfortunate classes, without regard to the amount of wealth he possesses. This is, doubtless, the reason why so many who retire from a life of profitable labor come back, after a few months or years, to their old haunts and old pursuits. They see that the moment they count themselves out of active life, they are counted by their old acquaintances out of the world. They become mere loafers and hangers-on; and a certain sense of vagabondage depresses them. The climate is stimulating, time hangs heavy on their hands, business is exciting, business associations are congenial and attractive; and so they go back to their industries, never to leave them again till sickness or death or old age removes them from the theatre of their efforts.

In Europe we know that the case is widely different. The number of men who live upon their estates,—estates either won by trade or inherited from rich ancestors,—is very large, while those who have small, fixed incomes, which they never undertake to increase, is larger still. The Englishman of leisure who cannot live at home on his income goes to the Continent, and seeks a place where his limited number of pounds *per annum* will give him genteel lodgings, with a life of idle leisure. In such a place he finds others in plenty who are as idle as he, and who have come there for the same reason that brings him. He finds it quite respectable to do nothing, and knows that his command of the means that give him leisure is the subject of envy on the part of the inhabitants. He eats, sleeps, reads, visits, writes letters, and kills time without any loss of self-respect, and without feeling the slightest attraction for busier life. Indeed, the tradesmen who are active around him are looked down upon as social inferiors, on account of the fact that they are under the necessity of work. Work is not a genteel thing to do, unless it be done in an office or profession. Shop-keeping and labor of the hands are accounted vulgar.

It seems impossible to conclude that the man of leisure can ever hold a desirable position where labor holds its legitimate position. We wish the American could have more leisure than he has. It would, in many respects, be well for society that men who have property enough, and ten times more than enough, should retire from active life to make place for others rather than go on accumulating gigantic fortunes which become curses to their owners and the community. After all, if idleness can only be made respectable and desirable by making labor vulgar, we trust that the American gentleman of leisure will be as rare in the future as he has been in the past.

We are glad, on the whole, that every American deems it essential to belong to somebody, to belong to something, to sustain some active relation to some industry, or enterprise, or charity, to be counted in at some point among the useful forces of society. He is the better and the happier for it, and he helps to sustain the honor and self-respect of all those with whom labor is a constant necessity.

The Improved American.

Those Americans who have traveled over Europe during the past three or four years, expecting to be shocked by the vulgar display of their countrymen and countrywomen, and shamed by their gaucheries, have been pleasantly surprised to find their expectations unrealized. The American in Europe is now a quiet person, who minds his own business, takes quickly to the best habits of the country in which he finds himself, pays his bills, and commands an ordinary degree of respect. The vulgar displays on the continent are now made mainly by men who were born there, and who, having made money in America, have returned to their early homes to show themselves and their wealth. These people do more to bring America into disrepute in Germany than all the native Americans have ever done; and many of them, we regret to say, have been sent there by the American government as consuls and other governmental agents whose end in securing such appointments was simply that of commanding respect and position in communities in which neither they nor their friends had ever had the slightest consideration. In railway carriages and diligences and steamers the American is always a courteous and well-behaved person, who bears with good-nature his full share of inconveniences, is heartily polite to ladies of all nationalities, is kind to children, and helpful to all. He and his wife and daughters are invariably more tastefully and appropriately dressed than their English fellow-travelers, and at the *table d' hôte* their manners are irreproachable, while very little that is pleasant can be said of the "table manners" of the subjects of the Kaiser William. In brief, the traveling American is greatly improved, and it is time that he were relieved of the lampoons of ill-natured correspondents and penny-a-liners, and placed where he belongs—among the best bred of all those who are afloat upon the tide of travel.

Again, those who have visited the various American watering-places during the past season, have not failed to remark that a great change has occurred among the summer pleasure-seekers. At Newport and Saratoga the efforts at vulgar display, which were frequent during the last years of the war and the first of peace, have been entirely wanting. The vulgar love of the dance and the display which it involves, in all the popular places of resort, have almost entirely disappeared. With the most inspiring bands of music there is but little dancing except at the small family hotels in out-of-the-way places. Bathing, driving, walking, rowing, sailing, bowling, and croquet and pic-nic give a healthful tone to the seaside and inland places of recreation, and dress and dancing are at a discount. People speak of this change as if it were a fashion of the year, but in truth it is the evidence of an improvement in the national character and life. We are less children and more men and women than we were—finer and higher in our thoughts and tastes

There are other signs of improvement in the American, and these relate mainly to the female side of the nation. The American woman has long been regarded by Europeans as the most beautiful woman in the world. This she is and has been for twenty-five years, without a doubt; and as the circumstances of her life become easier, her labor less severe, and her education better, she will be more beautiful still. America never possessed a more beautiful generation of women than she possesses to-day, and there is no doubt that the style of beauty is changing to a nobler type. The characteristic American woman of the present generation is larger than the characteristic American woman of the previous generation. It comes of better food, better clothing, better sleep, more fresh air, and less of hard work to mothers during those periods when their vitality is all demanded for their motherly functions. We venture to say that the remark has been made by observers thousands of times during recent summers, at the various places of resort, that they had never seen so many large women together before. Indisputably they never had.

The same fact of physical improvement is not so apparent among the men, and the cause is not too far off to be found. It need not be alluded to, however, until something has been said about the reasons of the superior beauty of American women over those of other Christian nationalities. The typical American woman is not, and never has been, a beer-drinking or a wine-drinking woman; and to this fact mainly we attribute her wealth of personal loveliness. In America it has always been considered vulgar for a woman to be fond of stimulating liquors in any form, and horribly disgraceful for her to drink them habitually. As a rule, all over the country, the American woman drinks nothing stronger than the decoctions of the tea-table, and those she is learning to shun. She is a being raised to maturity without a stimulant, and as this is the singular, distinguishing fact in her history, when we compare her with the woman of other nations, it is no more than fair to claim that it has much to do with her pre-eminence of physical beauty.

This will appear still more forcibly to be the case when we find that physical improvement in the American man is not so evident as it appears to be in his wife and sister. The American man is better housed, better clothed, and better fed than formerly, but his habits are not better. Our students are done with bran-bread and scant sleep, and are winning muscle and health in the gymnasium; but they smoke too much. The young men in business everywhere understand the laws of health and development better than the generation that preceded them, but they drink too much. This whole business of drinking is dwarfing the American man. It stupefies the brain and swells the bulk of the Englishman and the German, but it frets and rasps and whittles down the already over-stimulated American. The facts recently published concerning the enormous consumption of liquor in America are enough to account for the disparity between the degrees of physical improvement that have been achieved respectively by the two sexes. The young American who drinks habitually, or who, by drinking occasionally, puts himself in danger of drinking habitually, sins against his own body beyond the power of nature to forgive. He stunts his own growth to manly stature, and spoils himself for becoming the father of manly men and womanly women. The improved American will not drink, and he will not be improved until he stops drinking.

Room at the Top.

To the young men annually making their entrance upon active life, with great ambitions, conscious capacities and high hopes, the prospect is, in ninety-nine cases in a hundred, most perplexing. They see every avenue to prosperity thronged with their superiors in experience, in social advantages, and in the possession of all the elements and conditions of success. Every post is occupied, every office filled, every path crowded. Where shall they find room? It is related of Mr. Webster that when a young lawyer suggested to him that the profession to which he had devoted himself was overcrowded, the great man replied: "Young man, there is always room enough at the top." Never was a wiser or more suggestive word said. There undoubtedly is always room enough where excellence lives. Mr. Webster was not troubled for lack of room. Mr. Clay and Mr. Calhoun were never crowded. Mr. Evarts, Mr. Cushing, and Mr. O'Conor have plenty of space around them. Mr. Beecher, Dr. Storrs, Dr. Hall, Mr. Phillips Brooks would never know, in their personal experience, that it was hard to obtain a desirable ministerial charge. The profession is not crowded where they are. Dr. Brown-Sequard, Dr. Willard Parker, Dr. Hammond, are not troubled for space for their elbows. When Nélaton died in Paris, he died like Moses on a mountain. When Von Graefe died in Berlin, he had no neighbor at his altitude.

It is well, first, that all young men remember that nothing will do them so much injury as quick and easy success, and that nothing will do them so much good as a struggle which teaches them exactly what there is in them, educates them gradually to its use, instructs them in personal economy, drills them into a patient and persistent habit of work, and keeps them at the foot of the ladder until they become strong enough to hold every step they are enabled to gain. The first years of every man's business or professional life are years of education. They are intended to be, in the order of nature and

Providence. Doors do not open to a man until he is prepared to enter them. The man without a wedding garment may get in surreptitiously, but he immediately goes out with a flea in his ear. We think it is the experience of most successful men who have watched the course of their lives in retrospect, that whenever they have arrived at a point where they were thoroughly prepared to go up higher, the door to a higher place has swung back of itself, and they have heard the call to enter. The old die, or voluntarily retire for rest. The best men who stand ready to take their places will succeed to their position and its honors and emoluments.

The young men will say that only a few can reach the top. That is true, but it is also true that the further from the bottom one goes, the more scattering the neighborhood. One can fancy, for illustration, that every profession and every calling is pyramidal in its living constituency, and that while only one man is at the top, there are several tiers of men below him who have plenty of elbow-room, and that it is only at the base that men are so thick that they pick the meat out of one another's teeth to keep themselves from starving. If a man has no power to get out of the rabble at the bottom, then he is self-convicted of having chosen a calling or profession to whose duties he has no adaptation.

The grand mistake that young men make, during the first ten years of their business and professional life, is in idly waiting for their chance. They seem to forget, or they do not know, that during those ten years they enjoy the only leisure they will ever have. After ten years, in the natural course of things, they will be absorbingly busy. There will then be no time for reading, culture, and study. If they do not become thoroughly grounded in the principles and practical details of their profession during those years; if they do not store their minds with useful knowledge; if they do not pursue habits of reading and observation, and social intercourse, which result in culture, the question whether they will ever rise to occupy a place where there is room enough for them will be decided in the negative. The young physicians and young lawyers who sit idly in their offices, and smoke and lounge away the time "waiting for something to turn up," are by that course fastening themselves for life to the lower stratum, where their struggle for a bare livelihood is to be perpetual. The first ten years are golden years, that should be filled with systematic reading and observation. Everything that tends to professional and personal excellence, should be an object of daily pursuit. To such men the doors of success open of themselves at last. Work seeks the best hands, as naturally as water runs down hill; and it never seeks the hands of a trifler, or of one whose only recommendation for work is that he needs it. Young men do not know very much any way, and the time always comes to those who become worthy, when they look back with wonder upon their early good opinion of their acquirements and themselves.

There is another point that ought not to be overlooked in the treatment of this subject. Young men look about them and see a great measure of worldly success awarded to men without principle. They see the trickster crowned with public honors, they see the swindler rolling in wealth, they see the sharp man, the overreaching man, the unprincipled man, the liar, the demagogue, the time-server, the trimmer, the scoundrel who cunningly manages, though constantly disobeying moral law and trampling upon social courtesy, to keep himself out of the clutches of the legal police, carrying off the prizes of wealth and place. All this is a demoralizing puzzle and a fearful temptation; and multitudes of young men are not strong enough to stand before it. They ought to understand that in this wicked world there is a great deal of room where there is integrity. Great trusts may be sought by scoundrels, but great trusts never seek them; and perfect integrity is at a premium even among scoundrels. There are some trusts that they will never confer on each other. There are occasions when they need the services of true men, and they do not find them in shoals and in the mud, but alone and in pure water.

In the realm of eminent acquirements and eminent integrity there is always room enough. Let no young man of industry and perfect honesty despair because his profession or calling is crowded. Let him always remember that there is room enough at the top, and that the question whether he is ever to reach the top, or rise above the crowd at the base of the pyramid, will be decided by the way in which he improves the first ten years of his active life in securing to himself a thorough knowledge of his profession, and a sound moral and intellectual culture.

THE NEXT DUTY.

This is an epoch of elevators. We do not climb to our rooms in the hotel; we ride. We do not reach the upper stories of Stewart's by slow and patient steps; we are lifted there. The Simplon is crossed by a railroad, and steam has usurped the place of the Alpen-stock on the Rhigi. The climb which used to give us health on Mount Holyoke, and a beautiful prospect, with the reward of rest, is now purchased for twenty-five cents of a stationary engine.

If our efforts to get our bodies into the air by machinery were not imitated in our efforts to get our lives up in the same way, we might not find much fault with them; but, in truth, the tendency everywhere is to get up in the world without climbing. Yearnings after the Infinite are in the fashion. Aspirations for eminence—even ambitions for usefulness—are altogether in advance of the willingness for the necessary preliminary discipline and work. The amount of vaporing among young men and young women, who desire to do something which somebody else is doing—something far in advance of their present powers—is fearful and most lamentable. They are not willing to climb the stairway; they must go up in an elevator. They are not willing to scale the rocks in a walk of weary hours, under a broiling sun; they would go up in a car with an umbrella over their heads. They are unable, or unwilling, to recognize the fact that, in order to do that very beautiful thing which some other man is doing, they must go slowly though the discipline, through the maturing processes of time, through the patient work, which have made him what he is, and fitted him for his sphere of life and labor. In short, they are not willing to do their next duty, and take what comes of it.

No man now standing on an eminence of influence and power, and doing great work, has arrived at his position by going up in an elevator. He took the stairway, step by step. He climbed the rocks, often with bleeding hands. He prepared himself by the work of climbing for the work he is doing. He never accomplished an inch of his elevation by standing at the foot of the stairs with his mouth open, and longing. There is no "royal road" to anything good—not even to wealth. Money that has not been paid for in life is not wealth. It goes as it comes. There is no element of permanence in it. The man who reaches his money in an elevator does not know how to enjoy it; so it is not wealth to him. To get a high position without climbing to it, to win wealth without earning it, to do fine work without the discipline necessary to its performance, to be famous, or useful, or ornamental without preliminary cost, seems to be the universal desire of the young. The children would begin where the fathers leave off.

What, exactly, is the secret of true success in life? It is to do, without flinching, and with utter faithfulness, the duty that stands next to one. When a man has mastered the duties around him, he is ready for those of a higher grade, and he takes naturally one step upward. When he has mastered the duties at the new grade, he goes on climbing. There are no surprises to the man who arrives at eminence legitimately. It is entirely natural that he should be there, and he is as much at home there, and as little elated, as when he was working patiently at the foot of the stairs. There are heights above him, and he remains humble and simple.

Preachments are of little avail, perhaps; but when one comes into contact with so many men and women who put aspiration in the place of perspiration, and yearning for earning, and longing for labor, he is tempted to say to them: "Stop looking up, and look around you! Do the work that first comes to your hands, and do it well. Take no upward step until you come to it naturally, and have won the power to hold it. The top, in this little world, is not so very high, and patient climbing will bring you to it ere you are aware."

PREACHERS AND PREACHING.

The Power of the Affirmative.

The power of positive ideas and the power of the positive affirmation and promulgation of them move the world. Breath is wasted in nothing more lavishly than in negations and denials. It is not necessary for truth to worry itself, even if a lie can run a league while it is putting on its boots. Let it run, and get out of breath, and get out of the way. A man who spends his days in arresting and knocking down lies and liars will have no time left for speaking the truth. There is nothing more damaging to a man's reputation than his admission that it needs defending when attacked. Great sensitiveness to assault, on the part of any cause, is an unmistakable sign of weakness. A strong man and a strong cause need only to live an affirmative life, devoting no attention whatever to enemies, to win their way, and to trample beneath their feet all the obstacles that malice, or jealousy, or selfishness throws before them. The man who can say strongly and earnestly "I believe," has not only a vital and valuable possession, but he has a permanent source of inspiration within himself, and a permanent influence over others. The man who responds: "I do not believe what you believe," or "I deny what you believe," has no possession, and no influence except a personal one.

In nothing is this principle better exemplified and illustrated than in the strifes of political parties. The party that adopts a group of positive ideas, and shapes a positive policy upon them, and boldly and consistently affirms and promulgates both ideas and policy, has an immense advantage over one which undertakes to operate upon a capital of negations. The history of American politics is full of confirmations of this truth. No party has ever had more than a temporary success that based its action simply on a denial of a set of positive ideas held by its opponent. The popular mind demands something positive—something that really possesses breath and being—to which it may yield its allegiance. There is no vitalizing and organic power in simple opposition and negation. Earnest, straightforward affirmation has a power in itself, independent of what it affirms, greater than negation when associated with all the influences it can engage.

The Author of Christianity understood this matter. His system of religion was to be preached, proclaimed, promulgated. Its friends were not to win their triumphs by denying the denials of infidelity, but by persistently affirming, explaining and applying the truth. With this system of truth in his hands—so pure, so beneficent, so far-reaching in its results upon human character, happiness, and destiny—the Christian teacher commands the position. Infidelity and denial can make no permanent headway against faith, unless faith stop to bandy words with them. That is precisely what they would like, and what would give them an importance and an influence which they can win in no other way. Why should an impregnable fortress exchange shots with a passing schooner? Silence would be a better defense than a salvo, and deprive the schooner of the privilege of being reported in the newspapers. The world whirls toward the sun, and never stops to parley with the east wind. The great river, checked by a dam, quietly piles up its waters, buries the dam, and, rolling over it, grasps the occasion for a new exhibition of its positive power and beauty. The rip-rap shuts an ocean door, but the ocean has a million doors through which it may pour its tides. Stopping to deny denials is as profitless as stopping to deny truths. It is consenting to leave an affirmative for a negative position, which is a removal to the weak side.

So a man who has really anything positive in him has nothing to do but persistently to work and live it out. If he is a politician or a statesman, or a reformer or a literary man, he can make himself felt most as a power in the world, and be securest of ultimate recognition, by living a boldly affirmative life, and doing thoroughly that which it is in him to do, regardless of assault, detraction and misconstruction. The enemies of any man who suffers himself to be annoyed by them will be certain to keep him busy. The world has never discovered anything nutritious in a negation, and the men of faith and conviction will always find a multitude eager for the food they bear. Men will continue to drink from the brooks and refuse to eat the stones that obstruct them. Even error itself in an affirmative form is a thousand times more powerful than when it appears as a denial of a truth.

Modern Preaching.

We cannot more forcibly illustrate the difference between ancient and modern preaching than by imagining the translation of a preacher of fifty years ago to a modern pulpit. The dry and formal essays, the long homilies, the dogmatism and controversy that then formed the staple of public religious teaching, would be to-day altogether unsatisfactory in the hearing, and unfruitful in the result. Experience has proved that

Christians are more rarely made by arguments addressed to the reason than by motives addressed to the heart. The reliable and satisfactory evidences of Christianity are found less in the sacred records than in its transformations of character and its inspirations of life. Though a thousand Strausses and Renans were at work endeavoring to undermine the historical basis of the Christian scheme, their efforts would prove nugatory when met by the practical results of that scheme in reforming character, in substituting benevolence for selfishness as the dominant motive in human commerce, in sustaining the heart in trial, in comforting it in sickness, and supporting it in dissolution. With the results of Christianity before him and in him, the Christian may confidently say to all his enemies: "If a lie can do all this, then a lie is better than all your truth, for your truth does not pretend to do it; and if our lie is better in every possible legitimate result than your truth, then your truth is proved to be a lie, and our lie is the truth." The argument is not only fair but it is unanswerable, and saves a world of trouble. Of all "short methods" with infidelity, this is the shortest. It is like the argument of design in proving the existence of an intelligent first cause. The man who ignores or denies it, is either incapable of reason or viciously perverse.

So the modern preacher preaches more and argues less. He declares, promulgates, explains, advises, exhorts, appeals. He does more than this. Instead of regarding Christianity solely as a scheme of belief and faith, and thus becoming the narrow expounder of a creed, he broadens into a critic and cultivator of human motive and character. We do not assert that modern preaching is entirely released from its old narrowness. There are still too many who heat over the old broth, and ladle it out in the old way which they learned in the seminary. This "preaching of Jesus Christ" is still to multitudes the preaching of a scheme of religion, the explanation of a plan, the promulgation of dogmata. But these men, except in the most ignorant and unprogressive communities, preach to empty walls, or contemptuous audiences. The man who preaches Christ the most effectively and acceptably, in these days, is he who tries all motive and character and life by the divine standard, who applies the divine life to the every-day life of the world, and whose grand endeavor is not so much to save men as to make them worth saving. He denounces wrong in public and private life; he exposes and reproves the sins of society; he applies and urges the motives to purity, sobriety, honesty, charity, and good neighborhood; he shows men to themselves, and then shows them the mode by which they may correct themselves. In all this he meets with wonderful acceptance, and, most frequently, in direct proportion to his faithfulness. This, after all, is the kind of talk men are willing to hear, even if it condemns them. All truth relating to the faults of character and life, if presented in a Christian spirit, by a man who assumes nothing for himself, and who never loses sight of his own weakness and his brotherhood with the erring masses whom he addresses, is received gladly.

The world has come to the comprehension of the fact that, after all that may be said of dogmatic Christianity, character is the final result at which its author aimed. The aim and end of Christianity is to make men better, and in making them better to secure their safety and happiness in this world and the world to come. The Christianity which narrows the sympathies of a man, and binds him to his sect, which makes the Christian name of smaller significance to him than the name of his party, which thinks more of soundness of belief than soundness of character, is the meanest kind of Christianity, and belongs to the old and outgrown time. It savors of schools and books and tradition. The human element in it predominates over the divine. The typical modern preacher mingles with men. He goes into the world of business—into its cares, its trials, its great temptations, its overreachings, its dangers and disasters—and learns the character and needs of the men he meets there. He sits in the humble dwelling of the laborer, and reads the wants of the humanity he finds there. In workshops, in social assemblies, in schools, among men, women and children, wherever they live, or meet for labor or for pleasure, his presence is familiar. Human life is the book he reads preparatory to his pulpit labors, and without the faithful reading of this book he has no fitting preparation for his task. No matter how much a preacher knows of the divine life, if he has not an equal knowledge of the human, his message will be a barren one.

The great mistake of the modern preacher is in not keeping up with the secular thought of his time. It is quite as essential to the preacher to know what men are thinking about as what they are doing. Comparatively few preachers are at home in the current progress of science, and too many of them look coldly upon it, as upon something necessarily inimical to the system of religion to which they have committed their lives. They apparently forget that their indifference or opposition wins only contempt for themselves and their scheme. There are few laymen so devoid of common sense as to be unable to see that any scheme which is afraid of scientific truth—nay, any scheme which does not gladly welcome every new realm won to the grand domain of human knowledge—is unworthy of confidence. An unreasoning loyalty to old interpretations of revealed truth is a weakness of the pulpit that becomes practically a reproach to Christianity itself. If the God of nature undeniably disputes the God of revelation, as the preacher interprets him, let him give up his interpretation gladly, and receive the correction as from the mouth of God himself. It is only in this way that he can maintain his hold upon his age, and win honor to the religion he tries to serve. All truth is divine, and the mode of utterance makes it neither more so nor less. A man who denies a truth spoken to him by the God of nature is as truly and culpably an infidel as if he were to deny a plainly spoken truth of the Bible.

Fewer Sermons and More Service.

There is, without any question, a good deal of "foolishness of preaching," and a good deal of preaching which is "foolishness" by its quantity alone. Preachers are aware of it, pretty generally, and the people are slowly learning it. Indeed, a reform is begun, and is making headway—a reform which all the intelligent friends of Christian progress will help by ready word and hand. There is no man living, engaged in literary work, who does not know that a minister who writes, or in any way thoroughly prepares, two sermons a week, can have no time for any other work whatsoever. Pastoral duty is out of the question with any man who performs this task month after month. A man who faithfully executes this amount of literary labor, and then, on Sunday, preaches his two sermons and performs the other services which are connected with public worship, does all that the strongest constitution can endure. When it is undertaken to add to this work universal pastoral visitation, attendance at funerals, weddings, and all sorts of meetings during the week, and the care of personal and family affairs, a case of cruelty is established a great many times worse than any that engages the sympathies and demands the interference of the humane Mr. Bergh. To do all this work without a fatal break-down before middle age, requires an amount of vitality and a strength of constitution which few men in any calling possess, and which a youth devoted to study is pretty certain to damage or destroy.

The country is full of ministerial wrecks, three-fourths of which were stranded early upon the sands of exhaustion. There are many towns in America in which there are now living more preachers out of business—and hopelessly out—than the number engaged in active life and employment. We think that a census of New York city would give us some startling facts connected with this matter, though it is into country towns, where the cost of living is small, that the exhausted preachers drift at last. We know a little New England town in which there are now residing more than twenty ex-clergymen,—a number four times as large as that of the active pulpits and churches in the town. The early studies of these men, and the excessive service demanded of them, have reduced the majority of them to the comparatively useless persons they are.

In speaking of the exhausting nature of the task of writing two sermons a week, we have made no distinctions. The average preacher needs as much time for, and expends as much hard work on, the preparation of a single sermon as Mr. Beecher does on two. To demand two sermons of this man—the average man—that shall be even tolerably well prepared, is to demand what is not in him to give. He works in constant distress—conscious all the time that under the pressure that is upon him he can never do his best, and fearful always that his power over his flock is passing with the weekly drivel of commonplace which he is obliged to breathe or bellow into their drowsy ears. Yet the average preacher manages in some way to preach two sermons a week, to attend any number of meetings, to visit every family of his charge twice a year, to officiate at weddings and funerals, to rear his children, and to do this until he breaks down or is dismissed, and with his old stock of sermons on hand, as capital, begins a new life in another parish, from which in due time he will pass to another.

Now if such work as this were necessary, or even extraordinarily useful, there would be some apology for it, and some justification of it; but it is neither. If it is impossible for the average minister to prepare competently two sermons a week, it is just as impossible for the average parishioner to receive and remember and appropriate two sermons in a day. No man of ordinary observation and experience—no man who has carefully observed his own mental processes in the reception and appropriation of truth—has failed to notice that the digestive powers of the mind are limited. The man who hears and appropriates a good sermon in the morning has no room in him for another sermon in the afternoon or evening. To hear three sermons in a day is always to confuse and often to destroy the impression left by each. Every discourse that a man hears after his first strong impression and his first hungry reception is a disturbing, distracting, and depressing force. The second sermon on a single Sabbath makes every man poorer who heard and was interested in the first, and not richer; while both sermons were damaged in their quality by the simple fact that the time devoted to both should have been bestowed on one alone. We know of no walk of life in which there is such a profligacy of resources as in this—none in which such unreasonable demands are made upon public servants with such a damaging reaction upon those who make them. The preachers are killed outright, or permanently damaged in their power, by a process that results in the impoverishment of the very men who demand its following.

The truth is, that half of this fondness for preaching that we see in many parishes arises from hunger for some sort of intellectual entertainment, and even for some sort of amusement. The hearers go away from their Sunday sermons and talk about them as coolly as if they had only been to a show. They gorge themselves—many of them preferring three sermons to two. Then they go into their weekly work, and do not look into a book from Monday morning until Saturday night. The Sunday sermons are all the amusement and intellectual food and stimulus they get. They fancy they are very religious, and that their delight in endless preaching is an evidence of their piety, when in truth it is an evidence mainly of social and intellectual starvation, and of a most inconsiderate or cruel demand upon the vitality of the poor man who does their preaching.

Well, the world has been preached to pretty thoroughly for the last hundred years. The advocates of many sermons have had it all their own way, and we should like to ask them whether the results of preaching—pure and simple—satisfy them? What preacher is there who has not been a thousand times discouraged by the result of his labors in the pulpit? How small are the encroachments made upon the world by it! With all our preaching in America—and we have had more of it, and better, than has been enjoyed in any other country—we should, but for the prevalence and power of Sunday-schools, have drifted half-way back to barbarism by this time. Preaching to a great population of lazy adults, who do nothing for themselves or the children, and nothing for the Church but grumblingly to pay their pew-rent, and nothing for the world around them, is about as thriftless a business as any man can engage in. Let us saw wood and eat pork and beans, for to-morrow we die.

And now let us state our conclusions, for this article, which we intended should be brief, is opening into a long discourse.

1st. There is no way to improve the character and quality of our preaching except by reducing the quantity. The advancing intellectual activity and capacity of the people demand a better sermon than the fathers were in the habit of preaching—such a sermon as our preachers cannot possibly produce with the present demand for two sermons on a Sunday.

2d. For all practical purposes and results, one sermon on a Sunday is better than two. It is all that the average preacher can produce, doing his best, and all that the average hearer can receive and "inwardly digest."

3d. One sermon each Sunday gives the whole church half a day in which to engage in Sunday-school and missionary work, and a Sunday evening at home—an evening of rest and family communion.

Of course we shall be met by the stereotyped questions: "Will not our people go somewhere else to hear preaching if they cannot get the two sermons at our church?" "Will not young people go to worse places on Sunday night if the churches should be shut?" The answer to the first question is, that no one will leave "our church" who is worth anything in and to it; and to the second, that whether the young will go to worse places will depend something upon the attractiveness of Christian homes, which are now rather lonely and cheerless places on a Sunday, we confess. Still, if places of worship must be open for them, it is easy to have union services, dividing the work among the pastors. There are a thousand ways to meet special exigencies like this, for which we shall find our means amply sufficient when the broad reform moves through the land, for the reform must come, and the sooner the better.

The Dragon of the Pews.

A little direction to the popular imagination is only necessary to point out to it a dragon that, every Sunday, enters every church. It is handed like Briareus, headed like Hydra, and footed like the centiped. It is beautiful to look at, with its silken scales of many colors flashing in the sun, but its stomach, like that of all respectable dragons, is the seat of an insatiable greed. Its huge bulk fills the church, and the moment it is at rest it opens its mouth. It gorges prayers, hymns, exhortations and sermons, as the pale man in the desk tosses them out, and opens its mouth for more and better. But for this pale man, who is under a contract to feed it, and is at his wits' and strength's end to accomplish his work, it could not live. When, in the morning, he has done all he can for it, it crawls out, to come back in the afternoon, with its maw just as empty, its feverish eyes just as expectant, its mouth just as wide open as it was in the morning. It swallows more prayers, more hymns, another sermon, other exhortations. It crawls out again to go somewhere in the evening, to glut, or try to glut, its horrible greed. Like those young women of veterinary parentage it cries, "give! give!" But the sermon is the special object of its awful appetite. Prayer is but a prelude to the solid dish of the feast. Singing is only the Yorkshire-pudding that goes with the beef, and the plum-pudding that comes after it. Sermons, sermons, sermons!—it swallows them whole. They are taken at a gulp, without mastication or digestion, and wide open spring the mouths again, in marvelous multiplication.

To drop the dragon, for he is a clumsy fellow, and a somewhat bulky figure to drag on through a whole article, let us have a plain word about the greed for sermons, so prevalent in these latter days. We doubt whether there ever was a time in the history of the Christian Church when its ministers were placed in so awkward, difficult, and unjust a position as they are to-day. Great, expensive edifices of worship are built, for which the builders run heavily in debt. That debt can only be handled, the interest on it paid, and the principal reduced, by filling it with a large and interested congregation. That congregation cannot be collected and held without brilliant preaching. Brilliant preaching is scarce, because, and only because, brilliant men are scarce, and scarcer still the brilliant men who have the gift of eloquence. So soon, therefore, as a man shows that he cannot attract the crowd, "down goes his house." He may be a scholar, a saint, a man whose example is the sweetest sermon that a human life ever uttered, a lovely friend, a faithful pastor, a wise spiritual adviser, and even a sermonizer of rare attainments and skill, but if he cannot draw a crowd by the attractive gifts of popular eloquence, he must be sacrificed to the exigencies of finance. The church must be filled, the interest on the debt must be paid, and nothing can do this but a man who will "draw." The whole thing is managed like a theatre. If an actor cannot draw full houses, the rent cannot be paid. So the actor is dismissed and a new one is called to take his place.

There is an old-fashioned idea that a church is built for the purposes of public worship. It is not a bad idea; and that exhibition of Christianity which presents a thousand lazy people sitting bolt upright in their best clothes, gorging sugar-plums, is not a particularly brilliant one. It was once supposed that a Christian had something to do, even as a layman, and that a pastor was a leader and director in Christian work. There certainly was a time when the burden of a church was not laid crushingly upon the shoulders of its minister, and when Christian men and women stood by the man who was true to his office and true to them. We seem to have outlived it; and a thousand American churches, particularly among the great centres of population, are groaning over discomfiture in the sad results. Instead of paying their own debts like men, they lay them on the backs of their floundering ministers, and if they cannot lift them, they go hunting for spinal columns that will, or tongues that hold a charm for their dissipation. It is a wrong and a shame which ought to be abolished, just as soon as sensible men have read this article.

Who was primarily in the blame for this condition of things, we do not know; but we suspect the ministers themselves ought to bear a portion of it. Beginning in New England years ago, the sermon in America has always been made too much of. The great preachers, by going into their pulpits Sunday after Sunday with their supreme intellectual efforts, have created the demand for such efforts. Metaphysics, didactics, apologetics, arrayed in robes of rhetoric, have held high converse with them. The great theological wrestlers have made the pulpit their arena of conflict. Homilies have grown into sermons and sermons into orations. Preachers have set aside the teacher's simple task for that of the orator. Even to-day, they cannot see, or they will not admit, that they have been in the wrong. With a knowledge of the human mind which cannot but make them aware that no more than a single good sermon can be digested by a congregation in a day, and that every added word goes to the glut of intellect and feeling, and the confusion of impressions, they still go on preaching twice and thrice, and seem more averse than any others to a change of policy. It is all intellectual gormandizing, and no activity, and no rest and reflection. It is all cram and no conflict, and they seem just as averse to stop cramming as they did before they apprehended and bemoaned the poverty of its results.

But we are consuming too much of their time. The great dragon, with its multitudinous heads, and arms, and feet, is to meet them next Sunday with its mouths all open. It has done nothing all the week but sleep, and it is getting hungry. Woe to him who has not his two big sermons ready! Insatiate monster, will not one suffice?

"No," says the dragon; "No," says his keeper and feeder. Brains, paper, ink, lungs—he wants all you can give, and you must give him all you can. The house must be filled, the debt must be paid, and you *must* be a popular preacher, or get out of the way. Meantime, the dragon sleeps, and meantime the city is badly ruled; drunkenness debauches the people under the shield of law, harlotry jostles our youth upon the sidewalks, obscene literature stares our daughters out of countenance from the news-stands, and little children, with no playground but the gutter, and no home but a garret, are growing up in ignorance and vice. If this lazy, overfed, loosely articulated dragon could only be split up into active men and women, who would shut their mouths and open their eyes and hands, we could have something different. But the sermon is the great thing; the people think so, and the preachers agree with them. We should like to know what the Master thinks about it.

Shepherds and Their Flocks.

A mischief-breeding mistake is made when pastors and people fail to establish and maintain between each other a business relation just as independent of the spiritual as it is possible to make it. The physician may be, and in multitudes of instances is, the dearest family friend; but he lives by his profession, and his services have a recognized money value which he expects to receive without a question. He would prefer, perhaps, to render his services without reward, especially to those whom he loves; but he has mouths to feed and provision to make for rainy days, and for the days of helplessness that come at last to all. So, though love and sympathy, and self-denial for love and sympathy's sake may have actuated him in all his daily round of duty, he goes home at night, takes down his blotter, and enters his charges as formally as if he had been selling farm-produce or tin-ware.

There is a feeling in many parishes that it is a gift by whatsoever any pastor may be profited by his people,—that a pastor earns nothing, and that in all things he is the beneficiary of the parish. To make this matter a thousand times worse, there are pastors not a few who take the position to which the parishes assign them, and assist in perpetuating the mistake. They are men whose hands are always open to receive whatever comes; who delight in donation parties, and who grasp right and left, with insatiable greed, at gifts. They become so mean-spirited that they do not like to pay for anything, and do not really think it right that they should be called upon to pay for anything. They are sponges upon their people and the community. Wherever they happen to be, they "lie down" on the brethren. There is nothing of value that they are not glad to receive, and there is nobody that they are not glad to be indebted to for favors. Sometimes they are extravagant, and have a graceless way of getting into debt, out of which they are helped yearly, and out of which they expect to be helped yearly. The abject meanness into which a pastor can sink, and the corresponding and consequent powerlessness into which he can descend, find too frequent illustration among the American ministry. It is shocking and sickening that there are some men who seem forced by their parishes to live in this way, and it is still more disgusting to find men who seem tolerably comfortable and contented while living in this way. If a man is fit to preach, he is worth wages. If he is worth wages, they should be paid with all the business regularity that is demanded and enforced in business life. There is no man in the community who works harder for the money he receives than the faithful minister. There is nò man—in whose work the community is interested—to whom regular wages, that shall not cost him a thought, are so important. Of what possible use in a pulpit can any man be whose weeks are frittered away in mean cares and dirty economies? Every month, or every quarter-day, every pastor should be sure that there will be placed in his hands, as his just wages, money enough to pay all his expenses. Then, without a sense of special obligation to anybody, he can preach the truth with freedom, and prepare for his public ministrations without distraction. Nothing more cruel to a pastor, or more disastrous to his work, can be done than to force upon him a feeling of dependence upon the charities of his flock. The office of such a man does not rise in dignity above that of a court-fool. He is the creature of the popular whim, and a preacher without influence to those who do not respect him or his office sufficiently to pay him the wages due to a man who devotes his life to them. Manliness cannot live in such a man, except it be in torture—a torture endured simply because there are others who depend upon the charities doled out to him.

Good, manly pastors and preachers do not want gifts: they want wages. It is not a kindness to eke out insufficient salaries by donation parties and by benefactions from the richer members of a flock. It is not a merit, as they seem to regard it, for parishes or individuals to do this. It is an acknowledgment of indebtedness which they are too mean to pay in a business way. The pastor needs it and they owe it, but they take to themselves the credit of benefactors, and place him in an awkward and a false position. The influence of this state of things upon the world that lies outside of the sphere of Christian belief and activity is bad beyond calculation. We have had enough of the patronage of Christianity by a half-scoffing, half-tolerating world. If Christians do not sufficiently recognize the legitimacy of the pastor's calling to render him fully his just wages, and to assist him to maintain his manly independence before the world, they must not blame the world for looking upon him with a contempt that forbids approach and precludes influence. The world will be quite ready to take the pastor at the valuation of his friends, and the religion he teaches at the price its professors are willing to pay, in a business way, for its ministry.

The Relations of Clergymen to Women.

Recent events have given rise to a fresh discussion of the relations of clergymen to women, some of which have been wise and some widely otherwise. It is supposed by many that the pastor is a man peculiarly subjected to temptations to unchaste "conversation" with the female members of his flock. It is undoubtedly and delightfully true that a popular preacher is the object of genuine affection and admiration to the women who sit under his ministry. A true woman respects brains and a commanding masculine nature; but if there is any one thing which she naturally chooses to hide from her pastor it is her own temptations—if she has any—to illicit gratifications. She naturally desires to appear well to him upon his own ground of Christian purity. To expose herself to his contempt or condemnation would be forbidden by all her pretensions, professions, and natural instincts. A bad woman might undertake to atone for, or to cover up, her outside peccadillos by the most friendly and considerate treatment of her pastor, but she would not naturally take him for her victim. It is precisely with this man that she wishes to appear at her best. Any man with the slightest knowledge of human nature can see that her selfish as well as her Christian interests are against any exhibitions of immodest and unchaste desires in the presence of her spiritual teacher.

There are only two classes of women with whom a minister is liable to have what, in the language of the world, would be called "dangerous intimacies." The first consists of discontented wives—discontented through any cause connected with their husbands or themselves. A woman finds herself married to a brute. She suffers long in silence; her heart is broken or weary, and she wants counsel, and is dying for sympathy. She tells her story to the one man who is—to her—guide, teacher, inspirer, and friend. He gives her the best counsel of which he is capable, comforts her if he can, sympathizes with her, treats her with kindness and consideration. That a woman should, in many instances, look upon such a man as little less than a god, and come to regard him as almost her only solace amid the daily accumulating trials of her life, is as natural as it is for water to run down hill. That she should respect him more than she can respect a brutal husband—that half-an-hour of his society should be worth more to her heart and her self-respect than the miserable years of her bondage to a cruel master—is also entirely natural. He cannot help it, nor can he find temptation in it, unless he chooses to do so. Women, under these circumstances, do not go to their pastors either to tempt or to be tempted.

There is another class of women who are thrown, or who throw themselves, into what may be called an intimate association with the clergy. It is a class that have nothing else to do so pleasant as to be petting some nice man, to whose presence and society circumstances give them admission. They are a very harmless set—gushing maiden ladies, aged and discreet widows with nice houses, sentimental married women who, with no brains to lend, are fond of borrowing them for the ornamentation of all possible social occasions. A popular minister receives a great deal of worship from this class, at which, when it is not too irksome, we have no doubt he quietly laughs. The good old female parishioner who declared that her pastor's cup of tea would be "none too good if it were all molasses," was a fair type of these sentimental creatures, to whom every minister, possessing the grace of courtesy, is fair game. To suppose that a pastor, sufficiently putty-headed to be pleased with this sort of worship, or sufficiently manly to be bored by it, is in a field of temptation to unchastity, is simply absurd. One is too feminine for such temptation, and the other altogether too masculine.

When these two classes are set aside, what have we left? Virtuous and contented mothers of virtuous daughters—daughters whom he baptizes in their infancy, trains in his Sunday-school, marries when they are married, and buries with sympathetic tears when they die. In such families as these his presence is a benediction; and to suppose that he is tempted here, is to suppose him a brute and to deny the facts of human nature. We verily believe there is no class in the community so little tempted as the clergy, and there certainly is no class surrounded on every side with such dissuasives from unchaste conduct. To a clergyman, influence and a good name are inestimable treasures. To stand before confiding audiences, Sunday after Sunday, and preach that which he knows condemns himself in the eyes of a single member of his flock, must be a crucifixion from whose tortures the bravest man would shrink. There are bad men in the pulpit without doubt. There is now and then a woman who would not shrink from an intrigue with such, but women do not choose ministers for lovers, nor do ministers, as a class, find themselves subjected to great temptations by them. If ministers are tempted by the circumstances of their office, they may be sure that they are moved by their own lust and enticed, and that their office may very profitably spare their services.

As a class, the Christian ministers of the country are the purest men we have. We believe they average better than the Apostles did at the first. Jesus, in his little company of twelve, found one that was a devil. The world has improved until, we believe, there is not more than one devil in a hundred. In any scandal connected with the name of a clergyman and a female member of his flock, the probabilities are all in favor of his innocence. The man of the world who keeps his mistress, the sensualist who does not believe in the purity of any man, the great community of scamps and scalawags, are always ready to believe anything reflecting upon a clergyman's chastity. It only remains for clergymen themselves to be careful to avoid the appearance of evil. Nothing can be more sure and terrible than their punishment when guilty of prostituting their office, and nothing is so valuable to them as an unsullied name. To preserve this, no painstaking can be too fatiguing, no self-denial too expensive, no weeding out of all untoward associations too exacting.

A New Departure.

One of the great problems, apparently insoluble, that has vexed the pastors and churches of the great cities, more particularly during the last ten years, relates to the means by which they shall get hold of the great outlying world of the poor. So difficult has this question become, that pastors and churches alike have been in despair over it. The poor have not come into the churches of the rich, and few of them, comparatively, have had the Gospel preached to them. The results of mission-schools and missions have not been satisfactory. The efforts made have not built up self-supporting institutions; those who were benefited have been quite content to remain beneficiaries, and the most strenuous efforts have been constantly necessary to keep schools and congregations together. In the meantime, the working churches have been comparatively small, and attended only by the higher classes. All has gone wrong. The high and the humble, who, if anywhere in the world, should come together in the churches, have kept themselves separate, and the work of Christianization has been carried on slowly, and at a tremendous and most discouraging disadvantage.

One of the leading reasons for the unanimous feeling of friendly interest in the late efforts of Messrs. Moody and Sankey, on the part of the ministers of all denominations, rested in this difficulty. These men drew the poor to them in great numbers, and not only attracted, but helped them and held them. To learn how it was done, ministers from all quarters assembled in convention, and the professional teachers became eager learners at the feet of the two successful laymen. The first result of this convention will undoubtedly be a modification of pulpit work—a modification so marked that it will amount to a revolution. The old-fashioned, highly intellectual and largely theological sermon will go out, and the simple preaching of Jesus Christ as the Saviour of the world and the hortatory appeal, will come in. The ministers, however, have all been tending toward this for some years. The results of public discussion have been in this direction, so that the modification in preaching will not be a violent one, save in special instances. Still, the change may legitimately be noted as a new departure, and one on which the highest hopes may be built.

But the most important part of the problem is undoubtedly to be solved in another way. For some years it has been seen that the great non-church-going public has been quite ready to hear preaching, provided they could hear it in some other building than the church. Wherever the theatre, the opera-house, or the hall has been opened, it has been uniformly filled, and often to overflowing. In Boston, Philadelphia, Brooklyn, Chicago, and New York, the poor have pressed into the theatres and public halls whenever there was preaching to be heard that promised to be worth the hearing. We are not going to stop to discuss the reason of this. We simply allude to it as a most significant fact in connection with the policy of the future. The distance between the poor, uneducated man, and the rich and cultured church, is proved to be too great to be spanned by a single leap.

The non-professional teacher and the public hall are to furnish the stepping-stones by which the poor are to reach the Church. When a man from the poorer walks of life—from the ranks of the laborer—stands in a public hall where all can come together on common ground, and talks to the people in his simple, straightforward way, upon subjects connected with their highest interests, he furnishes all the means, and is surrounded by all the conditions necessary to success in his endeavors. He can do what no professional man can do in any building devoted to religious purposes. We make this statement, not as a matter of theory, but as a matter of well-established fact. The preachers know it; the people know it. It is a thing that has been marvelously demonstrated, and if the Christian world is not ready to accept this demonstration, with all its practical indications, it will show itself to be criminally blind.

Any new departure in the methods of Christian work will, therefore, be very incomplete—nugatory, in fact—which does not recognize lay preaching in public halls as an important part of its policy. We have seen just how the poor are to be reached and lifted into the churches, because we have seen just how they have been reached and lifted into the churches. During the efforts of Mr. Moody in London, Brooklyn, Philadelphia, and New York, thousands whom no pulpit could ever influence have found their way through his audience-rooms into the Church. He has officiated as a mediator between the world and the Church, and has been a thousand times wiser than he knew, or the Church suspected. He has solved the one grand problem that has puzzled the Church and its ministry for years, and they will be short-sighted indeed if they fail to make his work the basis of a permanent policy.

In every considerable city of the United States, all Christian sects should unite in the establishment of halls for the work of evangelists—of men who have a special gift for preaching the simple Gospel. The example of such a man as Mr. Moody cannot but be fruitful in calling out from the ranks of Christian laymen a little army of talented and devoted workers, who will enter into his methods and swell the results of his work. All evangelists whose work is worth the having should labor in this field. No man should be in it who cares more for building up one church than another; for one of the prime conditions of his success is, that he shall not be regarded as the mouthpiece of any Christian sect or party. The essential thing is, that he shall be a Christian, moved by the love of God and man, and desirous only of bringing men to God. If the Church does not see a new light upon its path, poured upon it by the events to which we have alluded, it must be strangely blind. But it does see the new light, and we believe that its leaders and teachers are ready to walk in it.

CHRISTIANITY AND SCIENCE.

Mr. Tyndall's Address.

Mr. Tyndall recently delivered a notable address before the British Association—notable for its brilliant panoramic presentation of the various philosophies and speculations concerning God and Nature, and for his own personal confession. Democritus, Epicurus, Lucretius, Plato, Aristotle, Copernicus, Giordano, Bruno, Père Gassendi, Bishop Butler, Darwin, Herbert Spencer, and John Stuart Mill are all passed in review, their respective discoveries, speculations and opinions presented and commented upon, and, at last, we get at Mr. Tyndall himself. It would be hard to find, in equal compass, so valuable a mass of information on the subject discussed, and for this the intelligent reading public will be grateful; but, after all, the great English scientist teaches us absolutely nothing about the origin of matter, motion and life. We rise from the perusal of his address with no new light on the great problems he presents. The existence of matter is a mystery, the origin and perpetuation of life are mysteries. God is a mystery. The sources of the force that builds, and holds, and wheels the worlds, endows every particle of matter with might which it never for a moment relinquishes in its myriad combinations,—vital and chemical,—adapts organisms to conditions and conditions to organisms, and weaves all into cosmical harmony, are brooded over by clouds which science can never pierce.

There are limits to thought, and none "by searching" can find out God. Because Mr. Tyndall cannot find God, is there, therefore, no God? He says: "Either let us open our doors freely to the conception of creative acts, or, abandoning them, let us radically change our notions of matter." In other words, he would say to us that there is a God who created all things, and endowed them with the principle of life, or matter has an innate power to evolve life in organic forms. The alternative is as inevitable as it is simple, and our scientific teacher does not hesitate to say that he finds in matter "the promise and potency of every form and quality of life." This declaration he endeavors to soften by intimations that matter itself may possibly have no existence, save in our consciousness, and that all we know of it is that our senses have been acted upon by powers and qualities which we attribute to it. The existence of matter therefore, is not an established fact, but an inference. The logic of his doctrine leads, of course, to what, in common language, is called "annihilation." If life is evolved by the potency of matter, it depends for its continual existence on the potency of matter. When any vital organism dissolves, that is the end of it. Its matter passes into new forms, and evolves new life. Thought is a product of matter. Love, joy, sorrow, heroism, worship are products of matter. All this Mr. Tyndall sees and accepts.

Well, who knows but God is a product of matter? Mr. Tyndall himself is a pretty brilliant and powerful product of matter: who knows but that, by the infinite evolutions of this eternal matter, a being has been produced so powerful that he has been able to take the reins of the Universe, and to have everything his own way? It has evolved man, and thus produced a form of life that lords it over seas and storms, that controls animal life, that builds enormous cities, that threads the world with telegraphs, railroads and cables, writes books, measures the heavens, mounts from power to power. Is it any more remarkable that it should evolve or create a God, who, going from might to might and glory to glory, through infinite ages, should have something to say about Mr. Tyndall and the rest of us? Matter was just as likely to possess the power to evolve a "moral and intelligent Governor of the Universe" as to evolve a man. So perhaps we have a God after all!

We sympathize with Mr. Tyndall—heartily—in his enmity to bigotry and ecclesiastical domination, but the intolerance with which science has been treated in various ages of the world deserves much of charitable consideration. Men in their ignorance have seen that certain doctrines which they thought they found in what they in all honesty believed to be the revealed word of God were controverted by scientific men. They have clung to their Bible because they supposed that, with their views of the Bible, their religion and their own personal salvation were identified. Let us be charitable to such. Not much can be expected of men who are evolved from matter! There must be a great choice in matter when the production of men is concerned, and really matter is doing better than it did! When Mr. Tyndall can say what he says, and do what he does, without hinderance and without any danger of dungeon or fagot, it seems as if matter had done a good deal to deserve his gratitude and ours. After all, intolerance and bigotry were in matter to begin with. They have simply been evolved! The promise of them and the potency to produce them were in them at the start!

In view of the materialism of Mr. Tyndall, what he says concerning the religious element in life is about as feeble nonsense as that in which Mr. Matthew Arnold indulges in his "Literature and Dogma." With Mr. Arnold religion is morality warmed and heightened by emotion. Mr. Tyndall speaks of the "immovable basis of the religious sentiment in the emotional nature of man." What does he mean? Does he mean that there is the possibility of religious sentiment in a man who does not believe in the existence of God as his creator, preserver, benefactor, father, governor—the source and sum of all moral perfections? If he does, then the less he talks about religion the better, for he can only do so to manifest his childish lack of comprehension of the subject. If man is evolved by the potency of matter—if there is no soul within him that bears a filial relation to the great soul of the universe, and will exist when its material dwelling goes back to dust; if there is no ordaining intelligence behind all moral law; if there is no object of worship, or faith, or trust, or love, or reverence to be apprehended by the heart—what a mockery is it to talk about the religious sentiment! We are assured by Mr. Tyndall that the region of emotion is the proper sphere of religion. The statement shows how shallow his apprehensions are of this great subject. A religion which touches neither motives, character nor conduct may well pass for little with any man; and we really do not see why Mr. Tyndall should pay any attention to it whatever. Even science can be ignorant of the simplest things, and it certainly does not become it to be supercilious or contemptuous in its treatment of those who question its dicta when it invades the region of their faith.

The question will naturally occur to many minds, whether Mr. Tyndall gives us anything worthy to take the place of that which he undertakes to read out of our beliefs. Does his materialistic view dignify human life and destiny, tend to enlarge and strengthen the motives which bind us to virtue, give us comfort in affliction, add new meaning to existence and experience? Not at all. He brings us out of matter; he gives us back to matter. He makes us indebted to matter for all our joys and for all our sorrows, and places us to walk on a level with brute life, only our heads being above it. That is all, and he must not be disappointed to see the Christian world turning away from his conclusions, with content in its faith and pity for him. He knows nothing on this subject beyond the rest of us. He offers us a material universe that made itself, stamped with laws that made themselves, and informed with the promise and the potency of all forms of life. This is his speculation, and it is worth just as much as the speculation of a peasant and no more. He offers it to those who believe that nothing was ever made without a maker; that nothing was ever designed without a designer; that no law was ever given without a lawgiver—in short, that power and intelligence necessarily precede all results of power that betray intelligence, through the analogies apprehended by the human mind. We do not see how his confession can do more than prove how utterly incompetent the pure scientist is to apprehend religion and its fundamental truths.

Science and Christianity.

In the current discussions of the relations of Christianity to science, there is one fact that seems to have dropped out of notice; yet it is full of meaning, and deserves, for Christianity's sake, to be raised and kept before the public. Who, or what, has raised science to its present commanding position? What influence is it that has trained the investigator, educated the people, and made it possible for the scientific man to exist, and the people to comprehend him? Who built Harvard College? What motives form the very foundation-stones of Yale? To whom, and to what, are the great institutions of learning, scattered all over this country, indebted for their existence? There is hardly one of these that did not have its birth in, and has not had its growth from, Christianity. The founders of all these institutions, more particularly those of greatest influence and largest facilities, were Christian men, who worked simply in the interest of their Master. The special scientific schools that have been grafted upon these institutions are children of the same parents, reared and endowed for the same work. Christianity is the undoubted and indisputable mother of the scientific culture of the country. But for her, our colleges would never have been built—our common schools would never have been instituted. Wherever a free Christianity has gone, it has carried with it education and culture.

The public, or a considerable portion of it, seems to forget this, or has come to regard Christianity as opposed to science in its nature and aims. It is almost regarded, by many minds, as the friend of darkness, as the opponent of free inquiry and the enslaver of thought. The very men who have been reared by her in some instances turn against her, disowning their mother and denying the sources of their attainments, and to-day she has herself almost forgotten that it is her hand that has reared all the temples of learning, framed the educational policy of the nation, and, with wide sacrifice of treasure, reared the very men who are now defaming her.

Now, if Christianity is the foe of science, has she not taken a singular method of demonstrating her enmity? To-day, as freely as ever, she is feeding the fountains of scientific knowledge. Her most devoted ministers, crowned with the finest culture of the time, preside over the schools which educate her enemies. Where is the sign of her illiberality, the evidence of her timidity, the show of a lack of confidence in ultimate results in all this? The easily demonstrable, nay, the patent truth is, that Christianity was the first, as she remains the fast and fostering, friend of science; and all attempts to place her in a false position will be sure to react upon those who engage in them. The devotion of the Christian Church of this country to education is one of the most notable facts in its history; and there is nothing to which it points with so much pride and satisfaction as to its educational institutions.

The radical difference in the stand-points of the two parties in this great controversy explains the controversy, and shows its motives at their sources. To the man of faith all science is a knowledge of God, through a knowledge of his works and his processes. That which increases the knowledge of the great Creator of all, through the study of His creations and His methods, is regarded as a purely Christian work. That which enlarges the mind of man, gives him power over nature, carries him farthest toward the Being in whose image he was made, comes within the office of Christian teaching. Science is thus the handmaid of Christianity, and will, in all coming ages, be cherished as such. To the man of science who rejects faith, science is simply the study of nature. He sees no God where the Christian apprehends him. He finds in matter all the potencies which produce its combinations, qualities, life. He dismisses a personal God from the universe, and makes of himself only an exalted brute, whose physical death ends him. The real controversy touches simply the question of the existence of a God. The question of revelation is practically nothing to the ultra scientist, because he does not believe in the personality revealed.

Now, if this is simply a question of opinion, we would like to ask—granting for the nonce that there has been no demonstration on either side—which opinion has been and is most fruitful of good results to the world? Can motives be found in that of the ultra scientist sufficient to elevate a race to knowledge and culture? Would our country be as learned, enlightened, scientific, and polite as it is to-day, if a community of ultra scientists had settled Plymouth colony and Massachusetts Bay? We presume that no man would be so simple as to suppose it would. Where, in that science which recognizes no personal God, is to be seen the motive of self-sacrifice which would have founded the institutions of learning that are the glory of our country? It is not there; and, if not, is a lie better than the truth? Has it more vitality, more munificence, a better estimate of human nature, more power for human good, more liberality, than the truth? These are questions that it would be well for scientific men to answer in a scientific way. Simply to show that the Christian idea of a personal God is one which leads to the abnegation of self in devotion to the common good; simply to show that there is something in the Christian scheme which furnishes motives for making mankind happier and better, and happier and better than any scientific affirmation or negation can make them, is scientifically to demonstrate that a personal God lives, and that Christianity is a scheme of truth. Would it be hard to show this? It certainly would be impossible to show the contrary.

The strife between science and Christianity is misunderstood on the part of Christianity. It goes deeper than Christianity. It is a strife between those who do not believe in a personal God and those who do, of all faiths, all over the world. That settled, the scientific opponents of Christianity would leave the field or occupy it. Until their proposition is proved or abandoned, we suggest that it will be a decent thing for them to treat with respect the mother who bore them, and cover with their charity the paps they have sucked.

By Their Fruits.

Was it Thackeray who said that the difference between genius and talent was the difference between the length of two maggots? It was worthy of him, at least, and like him. When a man gets large enough to know that he is almost infinitely small, he is tolerably ripe. When he becomes wise enough to realize that his wisdom is folly, his profoundest learning ignorance, and his opinions, drawn from partial views of truth and its relations, of little value, he has risen into a realm where he drops his robe of pride, and drapes himself in the garment of docility. The simplicity and the teachableness of great men have been the wonder of the vulgar through all time. At the beginning of our late civil war, a capitalist from the country came to New York for the purpose of acquiring a stock of financial information. What was to be the effect of this war upon the finances of the country? How should he manage to save his wealth? How should he manage to increase it? These were the questions he put to the wisest financier he knew. The old man pointed to an apple-woman across the street. "Go and ask her," he said; "she knows just as much about it as I do." Yet opinions were as plenty as blackberries, in Wall street, while the results of the war, as they accumulated, proved that they were beyond human sagacity to foresee, and that the man most competent to foresee them had no more financial prescience than the ignorant apple-woman.

There is a realm of inquiry—indeed, there are many realms of inquiry—where the opinions and speculations of one man are just as valuable as those of another man—no more so, no less—for those of both are valueless. The speculations of such a man as Mr. Tyndall on the origin of life attract a great deal of attention; yet Mr. Tyndall knows just as much about the origin of life as the apple-woman on the corner, and no more. The speculations about development and atoms, and molecules, form, perhaps, an elevated amusement. They are better than the Hippodrome and the Negro Minstrels, without being more instructive. It is better to speculate on the atomic theory than to play battledoor and shuttlecock. It is better to speculate a personal God out of the universe than to go on a spree—better to ignore his work than to mar it. But the whole thing rises no higher than elevated amusement. It does not give even the smallest basis for sound opinion. All these speculators, wrapped around with scientific reputations, battering vainly against the limits of thought and scientific knowledge, and coming back with their reports of having seen something more than their fellows, are pretenders—to be praised, perhaps, for their enterprise, but laughed at for their conclusions.

Mr. Tyndall finds in matter the promise and the potency of all forms and qualities of life. Who put the promise and the potency there? Ah! that is the question, and Mr. Tyndall has not solved it. He goes no farther, perhaps, than to say that he finds them there. Has he found them there? In what form have they presented themselves to his scientific investigation? Can he show what he has found? Alas! he has found nothing new—seen nothing that others have not seen. He has only come to a personal conclusion and indulged in a personal speculation, and that conclusion and that speculation are not only unscientific, but they are valueless.

Is there not some way—some scientific way—in which a just conclusion may be arrived at concerning this great subject? If we should stand at the beginning of the world, and know the want of bread, would it not be very unscientific for us to get together a bundle of seeds or germs, and speculate as to which would be the most likely to give us bread? Would it not be better to plant every seed, label its bed, watch its growth, and examine its fruits? Would not that be the scientific way of ascertaining the nature and characteristics of the great power that was to feed us? Certainly that seed which would yield the best results, and address itself most directly and beneficently to our wants, would be the one to which we should give our faith. To do anything else would be to rebel against the law of our nature. To do anything else would be irrational and unscientific.

Well, certain seeds have been planted in the world of mind. They have borne, in various times, and in many countries, their legitimate fruits. Can we not find, in the adaptation of those fruits to human want, a scientific conclusion concerning the tree or plant that bears them? Is it not strictly scientific to conclude that the better the fruit, and the better its results, the more thoroughly is the seed vitalized by everlasting and essential truth? If certain ideas of the nature and character of God, and of the immortality of the soul—if certain ideas of human responsibility—have dignified humanity more, elevated it more, civilized it more, purified its morals, sweetened its society, stimulated its hopes, assuaged its sorrows, developed its benevolence, and repressed its selfishness, more than any other ideas, are not those ideas scientifically ascertained to be nearer the truth than any others? If they are not, then we misunderstand the nature and the processes of science.

There has been abroad in the world, for many centuries, an idea, advanced and maintained by more religions than one, that there is at the head of the universe an Almighty God,—a Spirit who has created all material things, and informed them with law,—a Spirit that is in itself the source of all life. There has been the further idea that this God is a person, who, though His mode of being is beyond human ken, recognizes the persons He has created, loves them, regards them as His family, and holds them personally responsible to His moral law. There has been the further idea that mankind, in consequence of their common parentage, are a band of brothers and sisters, who owe to one another good-will and unselfish service. There has been a further idea that this personal God is a being to be worshiped as the sum and source of all perfection—to be thanked, praised, prayed to, in the full recognition of filial relationship, and a full faith in His providential and paternal care. Out of this group of ideas has come the world's best civilization. Out of it have come churches and schools, and colleges, and hospitals, and benign governments and missions, and a thousand institutions of brotherly benevolence. From it have sprung untold heroisms. It has recognized human rights. It has had no smaller aim than that of human perfection. It has armed millions of men and women with fortitude to bear the ills of life. It has made society safe wherever it has been dominant; it has transformed death into a gate that opens upon immortality. Associated with a thousand dogmas invented by mistaken men, it has still done all that has been done to redeem the world to peace and goodness; and if this group of ideas has not scientifically demonstrated itself to be nearer the truth than are all the negations and speculations of scientific dreamers, then there is no such thing as science.

Prayers and Pills.

A singular article, containing an unprecedented proposition, appeared recently in the *Contemporary Review*, entitled: "The Prayer for the Sick: Hints towards a serious attempt to estimate its value." Prof. Tyndall regarded it as of sufficient importance to claim from him a word of introduction. He thinks it quite desirable to have clearer notions than we now possess of the action of "Providence" in physical affairs. The proposition of the writer is to establish a scientific, experimental test of the power of prayer in the healing of the sick. He asks: "that one single ward, or hospital, under the care of first-rate physicians and surgeons" (including Sir Henry Thompson, we presume, the author of the proposition), "containing certain numbers of persons afflicted with those diseases which have been best studied, and of which the mortality rates are best known, whether the diseases are those which are treated by medical or by surgical remedies, should be, during a period of not less, say, than three or five years, made the object of special prayer by the whole body of the faithful, and that, at the end of that time, the mortality rates should be compared with the past rates, and also with that of other leading hospitals, similarly well managed, during the same period." Prof. Tyndall, in his introduction, says: "Two opposing parties here confront each other—the one affirming the habitual intrusion of supernatural power, in answer to the petitions of men; the other questioning, if not denying, any such intrusion."

It seems, therefore, that the whole question of Providence and prayer is to be decided by this experiment, and it will also be seen that Christianity itself will thus be placed on trial. This is rather a large matter to be disposed of in the ward of a single hospital, and, as there is so much at stake, both parties ought to be well agreed as to the fairness of the experiment.

It is to be remembered, to begin with, that a proposition of this kind could not possibly come from a man who, conscious of his own unworthiness, and humbly subordinating his will to that of God, expresses his earnest desires in prayer. No Christian and no body of Christians—not even "the whole body of the faithful"—would consent to have the question of God's providential interference in human affairs decided for the world by the strength of their hold upon the Almighty arm, through the medium of their prayers. The experiment would be preposterous, and almost blasphemously presumptuous. No body of reverent Christian physicians would engage in such a competition. With all the fair seeming of the proposition, it is evidently impossible to be acted upon. The issue is tremendous. The whole question of the supernatural in human affairs, and the whole question of Christianity based upon it, would be involved in that issue; and every Christian would shrink in terror from the presumption that the power of his poor petitions was relied upon to decide so vital a matter. So, if the experiment were tried, it would be instituted and executed by men who believe neither in prayer nor Providence, and who would conduct it with reference to their own ends. The world would not trust them, and the world ought not to trust them.

But supposing the physicians were equally divided between Christian and unchristian, and that the two bodies were placed in watch of each other: would it be altogether fair to give the ward or hospital subjected to the experiment any medical treatment whatever? Physicians make mistakes sometimes, and thwart the God of nature, who happens at the same time to be the God of Providence. Evidently a hospital without, would offer a fairer chance for experiment than one with, physicians. Then, if the result were not on the side of the skeptics, would they admit that the God of Providence cured the patients in answer to prayer, or would they claim that the unaided power of nature was the healing agent? Who knows, in this world of medical empiricism, whether the great obstacle to the efficacy of the prayers of the faithful is not the medical profession itself? And who knows that Providence does not withhold its cures that the world may learn, in the long years, that it is best to do without the medical profession altogether?

We take it for granted that the writer of the strange proposition we are considering belongs to what is denominated "the regular profession." Now if there is anything thoroughly well known among the people, it is that "the regular profession" object to any system of treatment not "regular," and doubt the reality of any cure not wrought by "regular" means. Is there any medical society that would permit its members to co-operate with irregular measures like those which this man proposes? Would not this be equivalent to a consultation with Providence—a practitioner not recognized by the societies generally? Is prayer regarded as an article of the materia medica? Is not this whole proposition grossly irregular, and does it not become the profession to set upon this writer who thus proposes to compromise his position and make an example of him? If not, then we have a proposition to make which is entirely practicable. It is one in which a great multitude of people would be much interested. Let us institute an experiment to see what system of medicine Providence favors. Our doctor of the *Contemporary Review* is utterly impracticable, but he manifests a disposition to try experiments, and shows a healthy fearlessness of professional proscription. We propose, therefore, that a hospital be run three years by the regular profession, then three years by, say, the hydropathists, and then three years by the homœopathists. Let each body of practitioners have the benefit not only of the "general prayer," or prayer for "all men," but of special prayer. Thus the moral effect of the use of material remedies would be secured to all, and we should learn what system of medicine Providence favors, or the one which interferes least with its laws. Here now is something entirely practical, and there are many people interested in the decision of this question where one is seriously in doubt about the other. The world is immensely, nay vitally, concerned in the decision to be arrived at through an experiment like this? Shall we have it?

We rather think not. We should really like to know which system of medical treatment the God of Providence or the God of Nature favors. Christendom must give up its Christianity or believe in prayer—prayer for the sick—prayer for the well. It will not consent that that system of religion on which is based the highest civilization of the world shall be decided for or against by the power of its prayers over Providence. No candid man would ever ask, and no sane man expect, it to do so. So we will leave the scientist to his Nature and the Christian to his Providence in the practical and most desirable experiment which we propose. Let us get at the truth. If it is not "irregular" to try an experiment with Providence, it ought not to be irregular to try one with less considerable personages. But that would put the medical profession on trial, which is so much more important an institution than Christianity that it will not be considered for a moment.

REVIVALS AND REFORMS.

The Philosophy of Reform.

It is the habit of men who regard themselves as "radicals," in matters relating to reform, to look upon the Christian and the Christian church as "conservative," when, in truth, the Christian is the only reformer in the world who can lay a sound claim to radicalism. The church has lived for eighteen hundred years, and will live until the end of time, because it holds the only radical system of reform in existence, if for no other reason. The greatness of the founder of Christianity is conspicuously shown in his passing by social institutions as of minor and inconsiderable importance, and fastening his claims upon the individual. The reform of personal character was his one aim. With him, the man was great and the institution small. There was but one way with him for making a good society, and that was by the purification of its individual materials. There can be nothing more radical than this; and there never was anything—there never will be anything—to take the place of it. It is most interesting and instructive to notice how, one by one, every system of reform that has attempted to "cut under" Christianity has died out, leaving it a permanent possessor of the field. The reason is that Christianity is radical. There is no such thing as getting below it. It is at the root of all reform, because it deals with men individually.

We suppose that it is a matter of great wonder to some of our skeptical scientists that Christianity can live for a day. To them it is all a fable, and they look with either contempt or pity upon those who give it their faith and their devoted support. If they had only a little of the philosophy of which they believe themselves to possess a great deal, they would see that no system of religion can die which holds within itself the only philosophical basis of reform. A system of religion which carries motives within it for the translation of bad or imperfect character into a form and quality as divine as anything we can conceive, and which relies upon this translation for the improvement of social and political institutions, is a system which bears its credentials of authority, graven upon the palms of its hands. There can be nothing better. Nothing can take the place of it. Until all sorts of reformers are personally reformed by it, they are only pretenders or mountebanks. They are all at work upon the surface, dealing with matters that are not radical.

It is most interesting and instructive, we repeat, to observe how all the patent methods that have been adopted outside of, or in opposition to, Christianity, for the reformation of society, have, one after another, gone to the wall, or gone to the dogs. A dream, and a few futile or disastrous experiments, are all that ever comes of them. Societies, communities, organizations, melt away and are lost; and all that remains of them is their history. Yet the men who originated them fancied that they were radicals, while they never touched the roots either of human nature or human society. The most intelligent of those who abjure Christianity have seen all this, and have been wise enough not to undertake to put anything in its place. They content themselves with their negations, and leave the race to flounder along as it will.

We suppose it is a matter of wonder to such men as these that Mr. Moody and Mr. Sankey can obtain such a following as they do. They undoubtedly attribute it to superstition and ignorance, but these reformers are simply eminent radicals after the Christian pattern, who deal with the motives and means furnished them by the one great radical reformer of the world—Jesus Christ himself. They are at work at the basis of things. To them, politics are nothing, denominations are nothing, organizations are nothing, or entirely subordinate. Individual reform is everything. After this, organizations will take care of themselves. No good society can possibly be made out of bad materials, and when the materials are made good, the society takes a good form naturally, as a pure salt makes its perfect crystal without superintendence. They are proving, day by day, what all Christian reformers have been proving for eighteen centuries, viz.: that Christian reform, as it relates to individual life and character, possesses the only sound philosophical basis that can be found among reforms. Christian reform, with all its motives and methods, is found to be just as vital to-day as it ever was. It is the same yesterday, to-day, and forever. There are a great many dogmas of the church whose truth, or whose importance, even if true, it would be difficult to prove; but the great truths, that humanity is degraded, and can only be elevated and purified by the elevation and purification of its individual constituents, are evident to the simplest mind. Men know that they are bad, and ought to be better; and a motive,—or a series of motives to reformation, addressed directly to this consciousness,—is not long in achieving results. The radicalism of Christianity holds the secret of revivals, of the stability of the church, of the growth and improvement of Christian communities. All things that are true are divine. There can be no one thing that is more divinely true than any other thing that is true. Christianity is divine, if for no other reason than that it holds and monopolizes the only radical and philosophical basis of reform. The criticisms of all those who ignore these facts are necessarily shallow and unworthy of consideration—just as shallow and just as worthless, as the dogmatism inside the church which attributes the power of Christianity to those things which are not sources of power at all. Christianity must live and triumph as a system of reform, because it goes to the roots of things, and, because, by so doing, it proves itself to be divinely and eternally true.

Mr. Moody and his Work.

We suppose there is no question that Mr. Moody has done a marvelous work, both in Great Britain and America. There is a great deal of popular curiosity to know exactly what it was, and how it was done. The remarkable thing about it seems to be that there was no remarkable thing about it, save in its results. Not a revivalist, but an evangelist; not a stirrer up of excitement, but a calm preacher of Jesus Christ, Mr. Moody has talked in his earnest, homely way upon those truths which he deemed essential to spiritual welfare, in this world and the next. Men went to hear him not only by thousands, but by tens of thousands. Not only the common people "heard him gladly," but very uncommon people—Prime Ministers, Earls, Duchesses, Members of Parliament, Members of Congress, Doctors of the Law, Doctors of Divinity, and clergymen by the hundred. All testified to the power of his preaching. The doubters were convinced, the wicked were converted, weary teachers of religion were filled with fresh courage and hopefulness, and there was a great turning of thoughts and hearts Godward. Mr. Tyndall and Mr. Huxley and Mr. Herbert Spencer were not very much in men's minds while Mr. Moody was around. One thing was very certain, viz.: the people wanted something that Mr. Moody had to bestow, and they "went for it."

Mr. Moody and Mr. Sankey think that the work they have seemed to do has not been done by them at all, but by the Spirit of the Almighty. It looks like it, we confess. Either the truth which Mr. Moody preached was wonderfully needed, and wonderfully adapted to human want; either the multitudes were starving for the bread of their souls' life, or there was some force above Mr. Moody's modest means which must be held accountable for the stupendous results. This is a scientific age. The great men of science now engaged in uprooting the popular faith in Christianity have a new problem in science. Was there enough in Mr. Moody's eloquence, or personal influence, to account for the effect produced? Would it not be very unscientific to regard these little means sufficient to account for these results? It is a fair question, and it deserves a candid answer. Until we get this answer, people who have nothing but common sense to guide them must repose upon the conviction that the power which Mr. Moody seemed to wield was in the truth he promulgated, or that it emanated from a source which he recognized as the Spirit of God.

But not alone have the scientists received a lesson from the wonderful results of Mr. Moody's simple preaching. The Christian ministry, all over the world, have found instruction in it which ought to last them during their life-time. As nearly as we can ascertain, Mr. Moody has not paid very much attention to the preaching of Judaism—involving a theism and a system of doctrine which Christ came to set aside and supersede. Paul resolved that he wouldn't know anything but Jesus Christ, and we are inclined to think that Mr. Moody doesn't know anything but Jesus Christ. It is a fortunate ignorance for him, and for the world. Our preachers, as a rule, know so many things besides the Master; they have wrought up such a complicated scheme, based on a thousand other things besides Jesus Christ, that they confess they don't understand it themselves. The man who offered a pair of skates to the boy who would learn the catechism, and a four-story house, with a brown stone front, if he could understand it, risked nothing beyond the fancy hardware; and yet we are assured that the path of life is so plain, that a wayfaring man, though a fool, need not err therein. And, considering the fact that Christ is the veritable "Word of God"—that he is, in himself alone, "*the* Way, *the* Truth, and *the* Life," and considering also the use that has been made of the Bible in complicating and loading down his simple religion with the theological inventions of men, it may legitimately be questioned whether the progress of Christianity has not been hindered by our possession of all the sacred books outside of the evangelical histories.

At any rate, we see what has come to Mr. Moody from preaching without much learning, without much theology, and without much complicated machinery, the truth as it is in Jesus Christ. A salvation and a cure he has somehow and somewhere found in the life, death, and teachings of this wonderful historical personage. For the simple story of this personage, he has found more listeners than could count his words—attentive, breathless, hungry, thirsty, believing. They have flocked to the refuge he has opened for them like doves to their windows. He has helped to start tens of thousands in the true way of life. He has done well not to be proud of his work. He has done well to refuse the wealth ready to be bestowed upon him. In this, he has exemplified the religion of his Master, and shown a just appreciation of the real sources of the power which he has been enabled to exert.

Against such demonstrations of the power of Christ and Christianity as are afforded by the London and New York meetings, infidelity can make no headway. They prove that man wants religion, and that when he finds what he wants, in its purity and simplicity, he will get it. They prove that Christianity only needs to be preached in purity and simplicity to win the triumphs for which the Church has looked and prayed so long. The cure for the moral evils of the world is just as demonstrably in the Christian religion as the elements of vegetable life are in the soil. Penitence, forgiveness, reformation, the substitution of love for selfishness as the governing principle of life, piety toward God, and good-will to men—in short, the adoption of Christ as Saviour, King, exemplar, teacher—this is Christianity—the whole of it. Christianity reveals the fatherhood of God, and men want a father. Christianity reforms society and government by reforming their constituents, and there is not a moral evil from which the world suffers that is not demonstrably curable by it. If there is any man who cannot find its divinity and its authority in this fact, we pity his blindness.

We believe that Mr. Moody has done a great deal of good directly to those who have come to him for impulse and instruction; but the indirect results of his preaching, upon the Christian teachers of the world, ought to multiply his influence a hundred fold. The simple, vital truth as it is in Jesus Christ, and not as it is in Moses, or Daniel, or Jeremiah, or anybody else, for that matter, is what the world wants. And when the Christian world gets down to that, it will get so near together that it will be ashamed of, and laugh at, its own divisions. It is nonsense to suppose that the Divine Spirit is any more willing to bless Mr. Moody's work than that of any other man, provided the work done is the same. The fact that his work has prospered more than that of others, proves simply that it is better,—that Christianity is preached more purely by him than by others. It becomes religious teachers, then, to find out what he does preach, and how he preaches it.

Revivals and Evangelists.

Revivals seem to have become a part of the established policy of nearly the whole Christian Church. The Catholics have their "Missions," the Episcopalians have their regular special seasons of religious devotion and effort, while the other forms of Protestantism look to revivals, occasionally appearing, as the times of general awakening and general in-gathering. Regular church life, family culture, Sunday-schools and even regular Mission work seem quite insufficient for aggressive purposes upon the world. We do not propose to question this policy, though the time will doubtless come, in the progress of Christianity, when it will be forgotten. We have only to say a word in regard to the association of evangelists with revivals, and the two principal modes of their operation. With one, we have very little sympathy; with the other, a great deal.

There is a class of evangelists who go from church to church, of whom most clergymen are afraid; and their fears are thoroughly well grounded. There arises, we will say, a strong religious interest in a church. Everything seems favorable to what is called a "revival." Some well-meaning member thinks that if Mr. Bedlow could only come and help the fatigued pastor, wonderful results would follow. The pastor does not wish to stand in the way—is suspicious that he has unworthy prejudices against Mr. Bedlow—tries to overcome them, and Mr. Bedlow appears. But Mr. Bedlow utterly ignores the condition of the church, and, instead of sensitively apprehending it and adapting himself to the line of influences already in progress, arrests everything by an attempt to start anew, and carry on operations by his own patent method. The first movement is to get the pastor and the pastor's wife and all the prominent members upon their knees, in a confession that they have been all wrong—miserably unfaithful to their duties and their trust. This is the first step, and, of course, it establishes Mr. Bedlow in the supreme position, which is precisely what he deems essential. The methods and controlling influences of the church are uprooted, and, for the time, Mr. Bedlow has everything his own way. Some are disgusted, some are disheartened, a great many are excited, and the good results, whatever they may seem to be, are ephemeral. There inevitably follows a reaction, and in a year the church acknowledges to itself that it is left in a worse condition than that in which Mr. Bedlow found it. The minister has been shaken from his poise, the church is dead, and, whatever happens, Mr. Bedlow, still going through his process elsewhere, will not be invited there again.

We will deny nothing to the motives of these itinerants. They seem to thrive personally and financially. They undoubtedly do good under peculiar circumstances, but, that they are dangerous men we do not question. If neighboring clergymen, in a brotherly way, were to come to the help of one seriously overworked, and enter into his spirit and his method of labor, it would be a great deal better than to bring in a foreign power that will work by its own methods or not work at all,—that will rule or do nothing. If the writer has seemed to be against revivals, he has only been against revivals of this sort, initiated and carried on by these men. We question very sincerely whether they have not done more harm to the Church than they have done good. That they have injured many churches very seriously there can be no question. The mere idea that the coming of Mr. Bedlow into a church will bring a revival which would be denied to a conscientious, devoted pastor and people, is enough, of itself, to shake the popular faith in Christianity and its divine and gracious founder. Even if it fails to do this, it may well shake the popular faith in the character of the revival and its results.

There is another class of evangelists who work in a very different way. It is very small at present, but it is destined to grow larger. It works, not inside of churches, but outside of them. It has a mission, not to the churches, but to the people who are outside of them. It works in public halls with no sectarian ideas to push, no party to build up, no special church to benefit. It aims at a popular awakening, and, when it gains a man, it sends him to the church of his choice, to be educated in Christian living. To this class belong Messrs. Moody and Sankey, whose efforts we have approved from the first, because they have done their work in this way. That it is a better work than the other class of evangelists have ever done, we have the evidence on every hand. The churches are all quickened by it to go on with their own work in their own way. There is no usurpation of pastoral authority and influence. There is no interference with methods that have had a natural growth and development out of the individualities of the membership, and out of the individual circumstances of each church.

There is another good result which grows naturally out of the labors of this class of men. It brings all the churches together upon common ground. The Presbyterian, the Baptist, the Methodist, the Episcopalian, sit on the same platform, and, together, learn that, after all, the beginning and the essence of a Christian life and character are the same in every church. They learn toleration for one another. More than this: they learn friendliness and love for one another. They light their torches at a common fire, and kindle the flame upon their own separate altars in a common sympathy. They all feel that the evangelist has to do mainly with the beginnings of Christian life, and that it is their work to gather in and perfect the results. Hence, all have an interest in that work and help it on with united heart and voice. The more of this kind of evangelism we have, the better.

CHRISTIAN PRACTICE.

The Average Prayer-Meeting.

The prayer-meeting constitutes so important a part of the Christian social life of this country, and is so much a thing of the people that it is legitimately a topic for the examination and discussion of laymen. We approach the subject with abundant reverence for the time-honored estimate of its usefulness, and only with a wish for the advancement of its efficiency as an agency in spiritual culture. That it is in any respect the boon that it should be, to the hundreds of thousands who attend upon and participate in its exercises, no one pretends. That it is the lamest and most nearly impotent of any of the agencies employed by the church, in perhaps two cases out of every three, is evident to all. Let us see if we can present a fair picture of the average prayer-meeting.

In a church of, say two hundred and fifty members, there is an average attendance of fifty persons. These are made up, so far as the men are concerned, of the principal church officials—the deacons, elders, etc. The remainder are women—the best women of the church, and such of their families as they can induce to accompany them. The clergyman, overworked, and discouraged by the small number in attendance, is there to lead. He gives out his hymn, prays, reads the Scriptures, and, with a few remarks, "throws open the meeting" to the laymen for prayer or exhortation. There is a long period of silence. The deacons, who suspect that their voices have been heard too often, or that they may be in the way of others, remain silent. At last, either one of them is called upon by the pastor, or some poor man, under the spur of a sense of duty, rises and utters, as well as he can, the words of a prayer. Everybody sees that he is in a struggle, and that he is so little at home that he is only anxious to get through without breaking down. The audience is, of course, sympathetic, and, instead of being led in prayer, become as anxious for him as he is for himself. And so, with long patches of embarrassing and painful silence, interspersed with dreary platitudes of prayer and speech, unrefreshing and lacking spontaneity to a sad degree, the meeting goes on to the end, which comes when the chapel clock shows that an hour has been spent in the service. To suppose that any great good comes from the spending of an hour in this way, is to offer an insult to common sense.

It would be instructive, if the facts could be ascertained, to know how many of those who attend the average prayer-meeting do so because they truly delight in it, how many because they wish to stand by and encourage their pastor, and how many because they think it is, or may be, their duty. It would also be instructive, if the facts could be ascertained, to know how many men are kept away by the fear of being called upon to engage actively in the exercises, and how many remain at home because they have learned by experience that the average prayer-meeting is a dreary place to weary men—one which bores without benefiting them. We fear that, if the facts were known as they relate to these two points, the average prayer-meeting would find itself in very sorry standing. When men go to a religious meeting, of any sort, they go to be reinforced, or refreshed, or instructed. How much of any one of these objects can be realized in such a meeting as we have described? How much of the still higher object of spontaneous, joyous worship can be secured, by listening to the painful blundering of some pious and conscientious layman? Is it not the truth that the average prayer-meeting is a sad mockery of both God and man?

Can it be possible that the Almighty Father of us all is pleased with an offering so little spontaneous, so far from joyous, so painful in its exercises, and so unprofitable in its counsels as this? If, once a week, a whole church would come together joyfully, and sing their songs, and pray their prayers, and speak their thoughts, and commune with one another on the great topic which absorbs them, that would be a meeting worth having. But how would such a meeting compare with the dead drag of the average prayer-meeting? It would compare as life compares with death, as beauty with deformity. So utterly valueless, to all human apprehension, are the prayer-meetings carried on by some churches, that it may well be questioned whether they are not rather a detriment than an advantage, a harm rather than a help, to the regular work of the pastors, and the spiritual prosperity of those whom they lead and teach.

There is something to be said for the layman in this connection, which will leave his piety unimpugned. In the first place he labors at an absorbing employment. He goes to the meeting utterly weary, and without the slightest preparation of heart or brain for any active participation in its exercises. He needs help, and does not feel capable of offering any. He is empty of his vitality, and needs to be refreshed, and diverted from the currents of thought in which his trade or profession holds him. Again, as a rule, he is unused to public speech of any sort. It is impossible for him to lose the consciousness that he is speaking; and, becoming critical upon himself, his spontaneity, and all the good that comes of it, are lost. He sinks to his seat at last, humbled into the dust in the conviction that he has been engaged in a performance, in regard to whose success or failure he feels either gratification or mortified pride. It does him no good, and what is thus fruitless to him is, by force of its nature, fruitless of good to others.

Shall the prayer-meeting be dropped when it ceases hopelessly to be the vivifying, spontaneous agency of worship and communion that it ought to be? Can any change be made in its methods that will work a reformation? Can it be modified so as to avoid the evils we have indicated? These are questions that we cannot answer, but it is not hard to see that a meeting conducted entirely by the pastor is a thousand times better than a poor prayer-meeting, and that, if a prayer-meeting must be had, it is better to conduct it after some liturgical form than to trust to the blind and blinding leadings of ignorant and half distracted men. Spontaneous lay prayers in public are very nice in theory, but in practice, in the main, they are apples that break into ashes on the tongue. The opinion seems reasonable to us that any pastor, or body of pastors, who will present to the American churches a liturgy for social use, so genial, so hearty, so full of the detail of common wants, and so appreciative of the aspirations of the people, as to be the best possible expression of social worship and common petitions, will do more to lift the average prayer-meeting out of decrepitude, not to say disgrace, than can be done by any other means. If non-Episcopal Protestants wish to learn why it is that the Episcopal Church makes converts with such comparative ease, they need not go outside of our suggestion for their information.

SPEAKING DISRESPECTFULLY OF THE EQUATOR.

We heard a sermon recently on the subject of irrational reverence. It was suggestive and stimulating. It recalled to us the fact that one of the principal objects of American reverence is the Devil. There are multitudes who are shocked to hear his name mentioned lightly, and who esteem such mention profanity. We believe we do no injustice to millions of American people in saying that they have a genuine reverence for the being whom they believe to be the grand source and supreme impersonation of all evil. Of course this respectful feeling has grown out of the association of this being with religion, and is strong just in the proportion that the religion is irrational or superstitious. Now we confess to a lack of respect for the being who played our great grandmother a scurvy trick in the garden, and has always been the enemy of the human race; and we have persistently endeavored to bring him into contempt. It is harmful to the soul to entertain reverence for any being, real or imaginary, who is recognized to be wholly bad. That attitude of the man which defies, rather than deprecates, is a healthy one. If we have an incorrigible devil, who is not fit to live in the society of pure beings, let's hate him, and do what we can to ruin his influence. Let us, at least, do away with all irrational reverence for him and his name.

There is a good deal of irrational reverence for the Bible. There are men who carry a Bible with them wherever they go, as a sort of protection to them. There are men who read it daily, not because they are truth-seekers, but because they are favor-seekers. To read it is a part of their duty. To neglect to read it would be to court adversity. There are men who open it at random to see what special message God has for them through the ministry of chance or miracle. There are men who hold it as a sort of fetich, and bear it about with them as if it were an idol. There are men who see God in it, and see Him nowhere else. The wonderful words printed upon the starry heavens; the music of the ministry that comes to them in winds and waves and the songs of birds; the multiplied forms of beauty that smile upon them from streams and flowers, and lakes and landscapes; the great scheme of beneficent service by which they receive their daily bread and their clothing and shelter,—all these are unobserved, or fail to be recognized as divine. In short, there is to them no expression of God except what they find in a book. And this book is so sacred that even the form of language into which it has been imperfectly translated is sacred. They would not have a word changed. They would frown upon any attempt to examine critically into the sources of the book, forgetting that they are rational beings, and that one of the uses of their rational faculties is to know whereof they affirm, and to give a reason for the hope and faith that are in them. It is precisely the same irrational reverence that the Catholic has for his church and his priest.

The irrational reverence for things that are old is standing all the time in the path of progress. Old forms that are outlived, old habits that new circumstances have outlawed, old creeds which cannot possibly contain the present life and thought and opinion, old ideas whose vitality has long been expended—these are stumbling-blocks in the way of the world, yet they are cherished and adhered to with a reverential tenderness that is due only to God. A worn out creed is good for nothing but historical purposes, and, when those are answered, it ought to go into the rag-bag. Forgetting those things which are behind, the wise man will constantly reach toward those that are before. The past is small; the future is large. We travel toward the dawn, and every man who reverences the past, simply because it is the past, worships toward the setting sun, and will find himself in darkness before he is aware. Of all the bondage that this world knows, there is none so chilling or so killing as that which ties us to the past and the old. We wear out our coats and drop them; we wear out our creeds and hold to them, glorying in our tatters.

There is even an irrational reverence for the Almighty Father of us all. We can, and many of us do, place Him so far away from us in His inaccessible Majesty, we clothe Him with such awful attributes, we mingle so much fear with our love, that we lose sight entirely of our filial relation to Him—lose sight entirely of the tender, loving, sympathetic, Fatherly Being, whom the Master has revealed to us.

In the sermon to which we have alluded, the preacher quoted Coleridge's definition of reverence, which makes it a sentiment formed of the combination of love and fear. We doubt the completeness of the definition. Certainly, fear has altogether too much to do with our reverence, but if perfect love casteth out fear, where is the reverence? That is an irrational reverence which lies prostrate before a greatness that it cannot comprehend, and forgets the goodness, the nature of which, at least, it can understand. That is an irrational reverence which always looks up, and never around—which is always in awe, and never in delight—which exceedingly fears and quakes, and has no tender raptures—which places God at a distance, and fails to recognize Him in the thousand forms that appeal to our sense of beauty, and the thousand small voices that speak of His immediate presence.

Christianity and Color.

No American of ordinary habits of observation have failed to notice that in those sects in which much is made of religious emotion, and the policy of powerful public appeals to feeling is pursued, the moralities of life are at a discount. The same fact is evident in those communities where dogma and doctrine form the staple of religious teaching and religious life. If any one will take up the early colonial records of New England, he will be surprised and shocked at the amount of gross immorality which he will find recorded there. Rigidity of doctrine, the fulmination of the most terrific punishments in the future life, the passage and the execution of the most searching and definitive laws against every form of social vice, go hand in hand with every form of vice. There was adultery in high places and adultery in low. Slander held high carnival. Common scolds were almost too common to be noteworthy. In brief, it seems that a religion which makes most of its orthodoxy, or most of its frames and emotions of mind, is a religion most divorced from morality. A man who is told that the genuineness of his religion depends mainly upon the orthodoxy of his faith, or mainly upon the raptures of his mental experience, is either partly demoralized by his reception of the statement, or specially unfitted to meet the temptations of his life.

The negro has been supposed to be particularly susceptible to religious influences. He is as fond of religion as he is of music; and we fear that he is fond of it in very much the same way. It is no slander to say that a large proportion of the religious life of the negro is purely emotional, and that a large proportion of the negroes of the United States have never thoroughly associated, either in their theories or their practical life, religion with morality. The typical negro preacher is a "tonguey," loud-mouthed man, who appeals in his own fashion to the crowd before him; and the more he can work them up to great excitement, and wild and noisy demonstrations of feeling, the better he is pleased. In portions of the South there are orgies connected with the religious meetings of the negroes which are too absurd, too ridiculous, too heathenish, to be mentioned by one who reverently remembers in whose sacred name they are performed. The yelling, dancing, pounding of backs and insane contortions of these worshipers, are the same, in every essential respect, as they would be in the worship of a fetich. It is an amusement—a superstitious amusement—which leaves no good result whatever, and does no more toward nourishing their morality than the music of the fiddle to which they dance away the next night with equal enthusiasm.

In a recent conversation with an intelligent clergyman, who has spent many years at the South—though a Northern man—we heard him declare, without reserve, that he did not know a negro in the whole Southern country whom he regarded as thoroughly trustworthy in matters of practical morality. Moreover, he declared that the worst men, as a class, among them, were the preachers themselves. By these latter he intended to indicate specially the self-appointed preachers—ignorant, but bright men—who had secured the admiration and support of the masses. We asked him if he could not except from his very sweeping condemnation such among them as had been educated at the North. He shook his head, and replied that he knew some among those, whose superb intellectual culture would grace the proudest race in the world, but never knew one of them whom he could trust—particularly with his neighbor's wife. Now, this man had had abundant opportunities of observation, and spoke with candor and conscience. On a recent Sunday the writer listened to the out-door preaching, on Boston Common, of one of the finest and most amiable-looking specimens of the African race he ever saw, and what was he preaching about? Not purity of character and life, not love of God and love of man, not duty to family and neighbor, but the theological machinery of salvation. It was the natural reaction from the emotional religion of his race, but it had no more in it for his race, in its moralities, than the fiery nonsense of his less educated brethren.

Let us allow something for mistakes in the judgment and observation of the man whom we have quoted, and still we shall have sufficient ground for the declaration, that the negro in America, as a rule, holds his religion independent of morality —as something which either takes the place of it, or has nothing whatever to do with it, in his practical, every-day life. The fact is one full of grave suggestion, not only as it regards the future welfare of the race, but as regards the country in whose political fortunes he has become so important a factor. Much as the negro needs intellectual education, he needs moral education more. To learn to read will do little for him if, at the same time, his sense of right and wrong, his personal purity, his regard for the rights of others, his conscience, are not improved. If he cannot more fully perceive than he does to-day the relations of Christianity to character and conduct, his Christianity will rather debase than elevate him. In an enormous multitude of instances, all over the South, his religious rites are a travesty of Christian observances, and a libel on Christianity itself—a travesty and a libel that bring religion into contempt among thousands of observers.

It will be said that the loose notions of marriage that prevailed during the negro's bondage, and the thefts in which he then justified himself, have a great deal to do with his present lack of moral sense. It is claimed that his education will lift him above his present religious teaching. Granted, and still we have the emotional nature of the negro left, and his natural tendency to emotional Christianity. It is one of the great problems with which we have to deal—to educate the conscience of the negro. To give him intelligence without this, is to make him more dangerous to himself and us than he is. Either a white man or a black man, with rights and no sense of righteousness, is a dangerous man. His political power is easily bought and readily sold in the market, he is led with awful facility into unlawful combinations, he becomes a social curse in every community. The first special aim, in all our efforts to raise the negro from his degradation, should be directed to his morals. This must be mainly done among the young, and in schools; and any teacher who is not competent to this work has no calling among the Africans, and, if he belongs to the North, he had better come home.

Sunday in Great Cities.

Of the importance of the observance of Sunday, in the vital economy of the American people, there is no longer any doubt. With all the periodical rest it brings us, we still find ourselves overworked; and the wrecks of paralysis are strewn around us on every hand. Without it, we should find ourselves despoiled of our most efficient and reliable safeguard in the dangers which beset the paths of business enterprise. As a matter of economy, therefore—as a conservator of health and life and the power to work—the Sunday, observed strictly as a day of rest from secular labor, is of the utmost importance. We cannot afford to-day, and we shall never be able to afford, to give it up to labor, either in city or country. Experience has settled this point, and yielded upon every hand its testimonies to the wisdom of the divine institution. As a measure of social, moral and physical health—as a measure of industrial economy—the ordination of a day of periodical rest like that which Sunday brings us would come legitimately within the scope of legislation. If we had no Sunday, it would be the duty of the State to ordain one; and as we have it, it is equally the duty of the State to protect it, and confirm to the people the material and vital benefits which it is so well calculated to secure.

There are certain other facts connected with the observance of Sunday in America which are quite as well established as the one to which we have alluded, the most prominent of which is, that the high morality and spirituality of any community depends uniformly on its observance of Sunday. We do not believe there is a deeply religious community in America, of any name, that does not observe one day in seven as a day specially devoted to religion. The earnest Christian or Jewish workers everywhere are Sabbath-keepers, in their separate ways and days. It is very well to talk about an "every-day Christianity," and better to possess and practice it; but there certainly is precious little of it where Sunday is not observed. The religious faculties, sentiments, and susceptibilities, under all schemes and systems of religion, are the subjects of culture, and imperatively need the periodical food and stimulus which come with Sunday institutions and ministries. The prevalence and permanence of a pure Christianity in this country depend mainly on what can be done for them on Sunday. If the enemies of Christianity could wipe it out, they would do more to destroy the power of the religion they contemn than all the Renans and Strausses have ever done, or can do. They understand this, and their efforts will be directed to this end, through every specious protest, plea, and plan.

The most religious and earnest of the Catholic clergy of Europe lament the fact that the Sunday of their church and their several countries is a day of amusement. They see, and they publicly acknowledge, that without the English and American Sunday they work for the spiritual benefit of their people at a sad disadvantage. It is this European Sunday, which we are told is to come to America at last through her foreign population. We hope not. We would like to ask those who would rejoice in its advent, how much it has done for the countries where it exists. Go to Italy, France, Spain, Ireland—to any part of Germany, Catholic or Infidel, and find if possible any people so temperate, pure, chaste, truthful and benevolent as the Sunday-keeping communities of America. It cannot be done. The theatre, the horse-race, the ball, the cricket-ground, the lager-beer saloon, have nothing in them that can take the place of the institutions of religion. They are established and practiced in the interest of the animal, and not at all in the interest of the moral and intellectual side of humanity. They can neither build up nor purify. They minister only to thoughtlessness and brutality. So much, then, seems obvious: 1st.—That we cannot do without Sunday as a day of physical and mental rest; 2d.—That either as a consequence or a concomitant, moral and spiritual improvement goes always with the observance of Sunday as a religious day; and, 3d.—That Sunday, as a day of amusement simply, is profitless to the better and nobler side of human nature and human life.

Now the questions relating to the opening of parks, libraries, reading-rooms, etc., in great cities on Sunday, are not moral or religious questions at all,—they are prudential, and are to be settled by experiment. It is to be remembered that there are large numbers of the young in all great cities who have no home. They sleep in little rooms, in which in winter they have no fire, and can never sit with comfort. They are without congenial society. They have not the *entrée* of other homes; and they must go somewhere, and really need to go somewhere. Christian courtesy does much to bring them into Christian association, and ought to do a thousand times more. The least it can do is to open all those doors which lead to pure influences and to the entertainment of the better side of human nature. A man who seeks the society of good books, or the society of those who love good books, or chooses to wander out for the one look at nature and the one feast of pure air which the week can give him, is not to be met by bar or ban. Whatever feeds the man and ignores or starves the brute is to be fostered as a Christian agency. The Sabbath was made for man, and not man for the Sabbath. That is not religion, but pagan slavery, which makes of Sunday a penance and a sacrifice. It is better that a man be in a library than alone all the time. It is better that he wander in the park than even feel the temptation to enter a drinking-saloon or a brothel. The Sunday horse-car is justified in that it takes thousands to church who could hardly go otherwise. The open library is justified in that it is a road which leads in a good direction. The roads devoted to Sunday amusement lead directly away from the Christian church. All pure ways are ways that tend upward, toward God and heaven.

American Sunday-schools.

Let us have some honest talk about our Sunday-schools. Admitting that they are useful beyond our finite calculation, and that, as an agency in Christian civilization, they stand in one of the places of highest importance, it will not be amiss to inquire whether there may not be in them some tendencies to evil, some wrong ideas, some misconceptions of the highest end to be sought in their operation and management.

Let us touch the heart of the matter in our opening statement. We know of no good reason for sending a child to a Sunday-school, or of seeking to bring a child into a Sunday-school, except to make a Christian of him. We are in the habit of speaking of Sunday-schools as "nurseries of the Church;" and no phrase could be happier in defining that which is undeniably the first object of a Sunday-school—namely, Christian nurture. There is a class of Sunday-schools, in large cities mainly, that need instruction in the facts of Christianity, but it is true that the great mass of children in the Sunday-schools of the United States know the story familiarly, and need nothing so much as to be religiously impressed and brought consciously and by a sweet and solemn choice into direct relation with the great object of worship, and into a voluntary and loving allegiance to Him. The observations of a life of observation have taught us that the principal good results of Sunday-schools come not from enterprising and gifted superintendents, come not from interesting and funny story-tellers, who are known technically as "Sunday-school men," come not from singing sacred words to Yankee Doodle, or of frivolous words to still more frivolous tunes, come not from huge feats of memory in the rehearsal of long chapters of Holy Writ, come from none of the numberless tricks resorted to for enthralling juvenile interest and exciting juvenile ambition and love of praise, but from the personal influence of Christian teachers, who, knowing their scholars intimately and loving them tenderly, lead them by the power of their love and the light of their own Christian character into the adoption of a Christian life.

Nothing is more notorious than the fact that a man may carry the whole scheme of Christian truth in his mind from boyhood to old age without the slightest effect upon his character and aims. It is there, but it fructifies nothing. It has less influence than the multiplication table. A community may be—and often is—thoroughly intelligent in everything relating to the facts and claims of Christianity, and, at the same time, almost hopelessly frivolous or vicious. It follows, then, that a Sunday-school which does no more than teach fails to do that thing without which teaching is of very little account. The power of a Sunday-school to make Christians of its scholars resides almost entirely in its teachers. If they are Christians indeed, and are possessed by the Christian's love of the young natures committed to their keeping and leading, they will never rest until, by all practical means, they have endeavored to lead them to the adoption of that life which is the highest placed before the choice of humanity. The best minds and finest spirits of a church ought always to be in the Sunday-school. The highest office of this age, or of any age, is that of a Christian teacher; and a man who can look with contempt upon the office of Sunday-school teacher, or regard it as detracting in any degree from his personal dignity, betrays inevitably the feebleness of his conceptions and the shallowness of his piety. How many churches are there in which there are not men and women who look upon Sunday-school teaching as a burden and a bore? How many Sunday-schools are there in which there are not teachers who stand week after week before their classes, refusing themselves to receive and profess the religion whose truths they undertake to impart?

With such views as these—stated or indicated—our readers will conclude that we have not a very favorable opinion of much of the machinery used in Sunday-schools. The children are not to blame for demanding excitement and amusement, because these have been the means resorted to for bringing them into Sunday-school and keeping them there. Indeed, the impression is quite prevalent among the children of some schools that they are conferring a great favor on superintendent and teachers by their attendance. If they cannot get funny books, or premiums, or hear funny stories, or have picnics, or Christmas presents, or some visible reward, they threaten to leave the school,—either to stay out entirely, or go to some other school where they can obtain what they demand. So all sorts of means are resorted to to keep up excitement, and, in the mean time, they get no religious impression whatever. The tunes they sing amuse them, but nurse no spirit of devotion. The books they read and the stories they hear interest them, but leave no result except hunger for more excitement of the same kind. The premiums they win inspire their pride in a sort of excellence which spares little room for Christian humility. In one way and another, the opportunities of making a deep and good impression upon character and life are frittered away, and the children are no better prepared to enter upon life and the resistance of its multiplied temptations to evil than if they had never seen a Sunday-school.

In our judgment there is a vast amount of machinery instituted by professional Sunday-school men that is the veriest humbug. They have complicated that which is unspeakably simple. They have undertaken to do that by artificial processes and by ingenious contrivances which can only be done well through the instincts of a loving heart and a heaven-enkindled zeal. The touch of a gentle hand in the exhibition of a personal affection and interest is worth ten thousand times more than the most elaborate exposition of Bible truth on a black-board. If superintendents and teachers possess common sense, and know exactly what they wish to do, and wish first and most to make Christians of their children, let them follow their own methods, and leave the professional methods to those who need them.

SHAKERISM.

Something has been written recently on the public worship of the Shakers, which has not been relished by that eccentric sect; and we hear that they have shut out the world from their social religious gatherings. We are glad they have taken this step. No poorer way of spending Sunday was probably ever found than that of attending a Shaker meeting; and when it is remembered that no one from "the world" ever looked in upon such a gathering with any motive but that of curiosity, it will be seen that the Shakers themselves have lost nothing by the change. They probably never made a convert by their exhibition, or excited in the minds of the strange witnesses of their worship any feelings but those of mingled wonder and pity. If other sentiments than these were ever roused, we fear they were not in consonance with the spirit of the day. But they have a right to worship as they will, and to do it without intrusion and disturbance. If they find their way to the Good Father by a road that seems so very strange to us, it is entirely their business, or a business between them and their Maker. If a worldly man is moved to mirth by their methods, why, they must wonder and pity too, and not get angry about it. This thin-skinned sensitiveness to frank and honest comment will never do. It is not only a sign of weakness, but a proof of the consciousness of it.

It is curious to see how quickly the marriage relation begins to be tampered with when any body of religionists begins to get new light, or light additional to, or independent of, the Christian revelation. The Mormon gets new light, and forthwith he gets new wives. The Shaker gets new light, and straightway he divorces himself from womankind. The Spiritualists of the baser sort get new light, and adopt the most free and easy policy of "touch and go." Always with new light this institution of Christian marriage shows, by its perturbations, how central and vital it is in our social system. To the observant philosopher this matter of marriage has become a sort of test or touchstone in the examination of every new scheme of social and religious life; and it may safely be calculated that any scheme which interferes with Christian marriage —any scheme which interferes with its prevalence and freedom, or reflects upon its honor and purity, or undermines its sacredness, or cheapens its obligations—is either intentionally or mistakenly unchristian; sometimes the former, often the latter.

The assumption of the Shaker is that he leads a purer life than the world around him, in consequence of the fact that none marry or are given in marriage within the circle of his sect. He acknowledges that the society of woman in the intimate relations of a wife would be inexpressibly sweet to him. He acknowledges that it would be delightful to be surrounded by his own children, and that the loves of wife and children would be full of pleasure and satisfaction to him. All this he sees and talks about with candid and respectful outsiders. Indeed, it is this fact that gives the great significance to his life and his religion. Destroy the idea lying in the representative Shaker's mind, that he merits something for the voluntary surrender of these loves and satisfactions, and his Shakerism has gone to ruin. He is to get something for his self-denial. He is to win the favor of Heaven, and a high seat in heaven itself, as a reward for his hardships. He lays up treasure by his sacrifices. That is Shakerism, pure and simple. That is Shakerism in the kernel. It is the central, vitalizing idea of the system. Modes of worship, and supplementary revelations, and industrial policies, do not make Shakers. It is the thought that by surrendering the sweet sinfulness of marriage, and undertaking the "angel life" in this world, he achieves pre-eminence among the saints, that makes the Shaker, and replenishes his little sect from year to year.

In this assumption of the Shaker lies a gross insult to his own father and mother, and to all fatherhood and motherhood in the world. Even the virgin mother of our Lord and Saviour Jesus Christ was not set apart from marriage, and all that came of marriage, by the divine office to which she was appointed; and He Himself ministered to the pleasures of a marriage feast which he attended with his married Mother. Many, many times he called himself the "bridegroom," and the marriage relation was the favorite among his figures for illustrating the pure and loving intimacy and sympathy between Himself and his church. The Shaker is horribly mistaken. Men and women were made to live together in Christian marriage; and the experience of the world has proved that it is not those who live out of wedlock who live purely. The unnatural position of the Shaker concentrates his thoughts upon this subject, and we venture to say that it occupies more thought, and more damaging thought, among Shakers, and celibate priests, and monks and nuns, than among any other people of equal education and equally good principles in the world. Human nature is human nature, and the strongest human passion cannot be denied its legitimate object without a constant protest that destroys personal peace, and wars perpetually upon the purity of the mind. It is useless for the Shaker to say that he lives more purely for his celibacy. We know better, and the world knows better. He lives a life of torture and of meagre satisfaction, and he knows it; and if he did not think that he was in some way making something by it, he would, save for his sensitive personal pride, forsake it. As it is, he simply starves himself and his dupes, and shuts himself off from personal happiness and personal usefulness. Who is doing the Christian work of the world? Is it the Shaker? Not he. He draws the lines around him, and selfishly takes care of his own. His scheme of self-denial proves itself utterly selfish, in that it gives birth to no self-denying enthusiasms. He does not go out where men and women live, and work for the world, but he stays at home and works for himself. He has neither part nor lot in the great schemes for Christianizing mankind. This work, which he shuns, is done by those gross men and women who marry and are given in marriage. Why, there is more Christian heroism in the humble little household of the Methodist pioneer minister and his devoted wife, surrounded by their children and their humble flock, than all the Shaker establishments of the United States ever dreamed of. Are we to talk about such a family as being more impure and less saintly than those who hold themselves apart from each other, and spend their lives in fighting a passion which God made strong that his institution of the family life might be well-nigh compulsory? Out upon such nonsense! The truth is, that the doctrines of these people are an insult to the Christian world, and nothing but their failure to secure a wide adoption has kept them from being denounced. They have little influence in the world, and will have less as the world grows wiser and better. The best thing the Shakers can do is to pair off, and go to separate housekeeping. In their long association they have had rare opportunities for studying each other, and they must by this time understand their "affinities." There is no good reason why a Shaker should not have a wife, and there are ten thousand good reasons why he should, including those which concern his own personal purity, and the pleasure with which the Good Father regards the peace and the heart-satisfactions of his children.

THE CHURCH OF THE FUTURE.

The Outlook.

If any of our thoughtful readers have omitted the perusal of Dr. Blauvelt's articles on "Modern Skepticism," we beg them to go back and read every word of them. They will there obtain a view of the infidelity of the day which will give them food for reflection, and suggestions for action. No papers published during the last five years have presented the extent and nature of modern skepticism with such faithfulness as these. They ought to attract universal attention, and summon the whole Christian host to battle under leaders who know something about the basis of Christianity besides the traditional "apologies." It is not a form of Christianity that is now in question. It is not a question between sects. It is a question which involves Christianity itself, and the authority of the Bible. Have we a divine religion at all? Is Christianity anything better than Buddhism, or of any higher authority? If the Christian optimist supposes that these questions are to be met and decided by the "pooh-pooh" of sectaries, or the dicta of professional teachers, or the resolutions of conferences and councils, he is very much mistaken. We are inclined to think that the pulpit and the distinctively religious press will have very little to do with the matter, and that the question will at last be settled where it has been unsettled. The pulpit can do very little in any direct struggle with infidelity, because—not to mention other reasons—infidelity does not come within its reach. The religious press can do very little, because infidelity does not and will not read it. Both these powers must be content to preach Christianity as well as they can, and leave the struggle to be decided among those who have a common desire to get at the truth, whatever that may be.

It may as well be understood among Christian men and women that they are every day doing that which brings their religion under suspicion with the unbelieving world. The world does not see the fruits of that divine influence which is claimed for the Christian religion by its professors. Nothing is more notorious than that the educated men of France, Italy and Spain are infidel; and nothing has been better calculated to make them so than the whole policy of the Catholic Church in those countries. They have seen a populace kept in ignorance and poverty through many generations by a Christian Church. They have seen that populace fed with traditions, machine-miracles, shows, processions, humbugs, by a priesthood that is foolish if it knows no better, and knavish if it does know better; they have seen that priesthood taking side with tyranny against every popular struggle for liberty and liberal institutions; they have seen that priesthood grasping at wealth and power, and intriguing for temporal influence all over the world. This is the Christianity they have seen; it is all they have seen; and their conclusions, when made against the Catholic Church, are made against Christianity itself. Does anybody blame them? Not we.

The influences of the prevalent form of Christianity in England are very little better than in the nations mentioned. The world looks on and sees livings bought and sold like commissions in the army—places made in the church for younger sons—wine-drinking, pleasure-loving men in the pulpit; and then, when it sees any action, it is with regard to candles, and vestments, and rites and ceremonies that have no more vital relation to the redemption of mankind and the service of God than they have to the policy of the Czar in Turkey. Is it supposed that men of common sense do not and cannot see through all this stuff and nonsense? Four hundred of these clergymen have just petitioned for what they call "sacramental confession." Drifting toward Romanism, grasping after new and old machinery, busied only with husks and human inventions, quarreling over baubles, excommunicating their own free thinkers and free speakers, obsequious to worldly grandeurs, mingling in politics, frowning upon nonconformists as social inferiors, the great majority of the English clergy are doing what they can to manufacture infidels out of all Englishmen who do their own thinking.

And here in America, how much better are we doing? We fritter away our energies and waste our substance in building costly churches for the rich, in multiplying sects and keeping up the differences between them, and in aping the wretched religious fooleries of the Old World. Our organization into a hundred religious sects amounts to the disorganization of Christianity. There are thousands of towns lying religiously dead to-day because there is not Christianity enough in them to unite in obtaining the services of a minister who has brains enough to teach them; and, as a rule, there are from three to six religious societies in all these towns—starveling churches—monuments only to the ambition of the sects which they represent. The world looks on and scoffs. The world looks on and recognizes the lack of power in Christianity, or of such Christianity as it sees, to unify the church in feeling and effort;

and it learns only contempt for it. Every pulpit, as a rule, is a party pulpit. Every religious press is a party press—published in the interest of a sect and supported by it. So unusual is the spectacle of various bodies of Christians coming together for the accomplishment of a common Christian purpose, that it is noted as something remarkable, and pointed at with self-complacent boasting. We have fashionable churches, and churches made attractive by music that costs enough to support Christian teachers in half a dozen barren districts, and enough of the exhibition of a worldly spirit to show to keenly-observing outsiders that the Christian spirit of self-sacrifice and the Christian faith in the hereafter are not in us—are hardly in the best of us.

We would not be harsh, but we ask, in all candor, if there is not in every Christian country enough in the aspect of Christian people to make their religion seem a hollow pretense, a thing without vital power, a system not half believed in by those who profess it. Does not the world find us quarreling about non-essential things, striving for sectarian precedence, and practically ignoring the fact that the world needs to be saved through simple faith in and following of Jesus Christ? Really, when the scientist and the naturalist come, with their scalpels and crucibles and blow-pipes, and tell us they will believe in nothing they cannot see and weigh and measure, there is but little left for them to do. Whose fault is it that they find their work so easy? Why is it that there is such a flutter when they speak, except that those who profess to be Christians do not half believe in Christianity, and have no rational comprehension of the basis of such belief as they possess?

Two things must come before skepticism will be overthrown, viz.: 1st. A perfect willingness to go into an examination of Christianity for the truth's sake alone. Any man who is interested as a partisan, either for Christianity or against it, is unfit for the investigation. So far as the claims of Christianity are to be settled by investigation, *they are to be settled by men whose supreme desire is to find the truth, wherever it may lead or land them.* 2d. Christianity must be better illustrated in life by those who profess it. When Christians everywhere are controlled by a love that takes in God and every human being; when "divine service" consists of ministry to the poor and the suffering and not of clothes and candles; when the Christian name is greater than all sectarian names and obliterates them all; when benevolence is law, and humblest service is highest honor, and life becomes divine, then skepticism will cease, and not till then.

A Time to Speak: A Time to Keep Silence.

The introductory words of the preface to Matthew Arnold's "Literature and Dogma" are these: "An inevitable revolution, of which we all recognize the beginnings and signs, but which has already spread further than the most of us think, is befalling the religion in which we have been brought up." We wonder how far the American clergy have recognized these beginnings and signs. We wonder how far they are recognized in the theological schools, where the young men of the present day are trained for the Christian ministry. We wonder if, when they are recognized, they are published, or in any way prepared for. We wonder if the pulpit anywhere openly recognizes them, undertakes to lead the people safely through them, tries to occupy the new stand-point, and, while tossing aside the lumber of the old theologies, grasps firmly the vital truths of religion and proclaims them.

If we were to judge by the hue-and-cry raised about certain articles that have appeared in this magazine, these beginnings and signs have not been recognized at all; yet it is just as true in this country as in England, and just as true in England as for twenty-five years it has been in Germany, that this revolution is in progress. The old orthodox view of the Bible, as a plenarily inspired book, from the first word of Genesis to the last of St. John's Revelation, is already forsaken by more minds than can be counted; and, by necessity, with the relinquishment of this view, goes by the board a great mass of theology entirely dependent upon it for existence. The current popular theology cannot possibly be saved without saving the current and popular view of the Bible. They stand and fall together; and it would be interesting to know how many of our theologians are shaping their systems and teachings by their new views of inspiration, and of the relative importance and authority of the different books that make up our sacred volume. Are we to go on, as a Christian people, until criticism has undermined our elaborate systems, and those systems fall, carrying with them those simple, vital truths which the Bible most indubitably holds, and upon which depend the moral health and the salvation of the race?

Mr Arnold says, "there is no surer proof of a narrow and ill-instructed mind than to think and uphold that what a man takes to be truth upon religious matters is always to be proclaimed." Mr. Greg, in one of his "Judgments," finds serious fault with this proposition; but in one respect, at least, it is sound. For instance, we find that the Christian religion, as it is taught to-day, and has for many years been taught, is a purifying, elevating, saving influence among all men who in faith receive, and, in life, practice it. So much we know—that, however false our theologies may be, and however incorrect our views of all that relates to God and man in their nature and relations, we hold enough of pure and vital truth to bring the hearts of men into sympathy with Jesus Christ, and their lives into consonance with his. Now, until a man has something as good to say,—something more sound, simple, saving,—better based, more easily comprehended, working larger and better results—let him keep silence with his doubts, and withhold his hand from destruction. Nothing is more basely cruel than the destruction of any system of religious life that has good in it, without having in hand something better to put in its place. The time for keeping silence is when one has nothing to put in place of that which his words are intended to destroy. We may not hold the truth in its purity, but we hold enough of it to make it invaluable, and until we can present it in a purer and a more fruitful form, so that those who may cut loose from their old belief shall have something to grasp that is better, it is well to hold the tongue and restrain the pen.

The facts are, however, that the revolution is going on independent of the theologians and the religious teachers, and if they are doing anything about it they are fighting it. The result will probably, and most naturally, be a reign of infidelity, out of which, after weary, wretched years, we shall slowly emerge, with our Christianity purged of its extraneous doctrines, and with a new class of religious teachers, who will look back upon the present position as one of gross blindness and fatal fatuity.

What we want to-day is teachers who are capable of comprehending the situation; who have learned what irreparable havoc has been made in some of their old beliefs; who, casting out all those superstitious notions of the Bible that have made it half-talisman, half-fetich to millions of men, women and children, can grasp the history, meanings and uses of the book, get at its central, saving truths, and proclaim them.

There is no question that Christianity is as independent of our old ideas of the Bible as it is independent of our ideas of the Koran, or our ideas of any book or anything whatsoever. We have in the Bible, when we find it, the true religion; but, when we make the existence of that religion dependent upon our ideas of the Bible, we do it the cruelest wrong that we can inflict upon it.

And that, precisely, is the danger to-day. The people, having been taught to associate the religion of the Bible with a certain view of inspiration, imagine that religion stands or falls with that view. There could not be a more natural or logical result of the teachings of the last three hundred years than this; and if religious teachers are not ready with their answer when the time comes to speak,—and that time in a great many communities is now,—a crop of infidels will be the result. The growing inattention to religion among the more intelligent masses, the lack of religious faith in the literary class, the enmity,—sometimes coarse and always aggressive,—of the scientists, show that the time to speak, and to speak in earnest, has come. But the speaking must be done from the new stand-point, and with a thorough recognition of the modifications that science and criticism have wrought in the materials and combinations that have entered into the structure of our old systems of faith and opinion. The old machinery and the old doctrine will not avail in this fight. It is precisely those that are the subjects of dissent. A teacher who has nothing but these with which to meet the foes of religion may as well retire from the field of conflict.

Why Not?

In a little book, by Rev. Dr. Dorus Clarke, we find the sentiment of Christian unity, so popular during the late meetings of the Evangelical Alliance in New York—so frequently expressed, and so cordially responded to by those in attendance—supplemented by a practical proposition which demands from the Christian public a candid consideration. Dr. Clarke declares the existence of sects to be a reproach and not a commendation of Christianity—that "it was not so in the beginning, will not be so in the end, and ought not to be so now." Then, after disposing of the usual apologies made for the creation and preservation of sects, he declares that Christ founded a church, and not a sect, and that the unity for which He prayed was an open and organic one, as well as a spiritual one—that the world might know that the Father had sent Him.

The larger part of Dr. Clarke's book is devoted to an effort to show how all sects may resolve themselves into one,—or, rather, how all the sects may become one church,—at least, all those who accept the Bible as the authentic and authoritative Word of God. We should mar his work by undertaking to condense it; so we leave our readers to examine it in detail in the book itself, while we allude to the obstacles that stand in the way of the consummation so devoutly to be desired.

Christianity itself is not responsible for one of these obstacles. They exist entirely in the minds of men. As we have declared elsewhere and often, the simple facts that the different evangelical sects recognize each other as Christians, and rejoice in unity of spirit, make every possible apology for sectarianism an absurdity. They are an open confession that nothing essential to Christianity divides them, and keeps them divided,—an open confession that sectarian divisions are based upon non-essential differences of belief, policy, and practice. The day is past for defending sectarianism from the divine or Christian side of the question. Christianity will have nothing to do with such a defense. The founder of our religion never founded a sect, and the religion itself is not responsible for one that exists. So far as the church exists it is spiritually a unit in the eye of Him who founded it. That it is divided into parties which compete with one another, and quarrel with one another, and regard one another with jealousy, and are full of party spirit, is man's affair entirely, for which he is to be held responsible, and for which he is most indubitably blameworthy.

The grand obstacles that stand in the way of organic union are, first, a failure to appreciate the necessity and desirableness of such a union, and, second, the established sectarian organizations and interests. Now in our political affairs we accept the adage: "In union there is strength," as our axiom. No one thinks of questioning it. A number of free and independent States could gather, as the Evangelical Alliance did, in a representative assembly, on a common basis of love of, and devotion to, liberty. The members could be one in spirit, and every time they spoke of liberty they would meet the applause of the multitude. Yet, when these members should separate, each would go to his own, and exercise his liberty in building up his own, even at the expense of his neighbor. The fact that all believe in liberty forms no practical union. A union which lives alone on a sympathy of this sort would not make a nation, and would not be considered of any practical value among the nations of the world. The fact that all these States are founded on the principle of liberty and that all can sympathize in the love, and praise, and enjoyment of liberty, does not save them from selfishness and jealousy, and competition and quarrel; while against a common foe they present no united front, and no concentration of united power.

The analogy between the position of such States and the Protestant Christian sects, in the aspect in which we present them, is perfect. The fact that these sects have a common basis of sympathy, in that love of the Master on which they are founded, does not make them an organic Christian church, in any open, appreciable, practical sense. It does not restrain them from controversies, quarrels, and competitions, or the outlay of that power upon and against each other which ought to be united, and brought to bear upon the common enemy. All sectarian and party spirit in the church is of the earth, earthy; and is not only contemptible as a matter of policy, but criminal as a matter of principle. When all Christians become able to see it in this light,—and they are thus regarding it more and more,—the first grand obstacle to the obliteration of sects, and the organic union of the church, will have been removed.

The established sectarian organizations and interests will prove, we suppose, the most serious obstacles in the way of reform. The absolute abolition of all sectarian machinery, of all sectarian schools of theology, of all sectarian newspapers and magazines, the amalgamation of diverse habits and policies, the remanding of sectarian officials into the Christian ranks,—officials many of whom have found their only possibility of prominence through their adaptation to sectarian service,—all this will involve a revolution so radical, will call for so much self-denial for the sake of a great, common cause, that the Christian world may well tremble before it, particularly when it sees in these obstacles something of the horrible pit of selfishness into which sectarianism has plunged it. But this revolution can be effected, and it must be. It is foolish to say that the world is not ready for it. The laity are already far in advance of the clergy on this subject; and if the clergy, who are their recognized leaders, do not move soon in the right direction,—soon and heartily,—they will find a clamor about their ears which it will be well for them to heed. Through whatever necessary convulsions, Protestant church unity will come. Men who have come to see that they are kept apart by no difference that touches vital Christianity, will not consent to remain divided.

A free, enlightened, united, Protestant Christianity, arrayed against the repressive despotism, and the corrupting superstition of the Church of Rome, and against an unbelieving world,—now puzzled and repelled by the differences among Christians,—would be the grandest sight the world ever saw; and men may as well stop praying for the millennium until they are ready to pray for that which must precede it. This first, and then purified, reformed, and enlightened Rome; and then, the grand and crowning union of all!

How Much has been Gained?

Among the various important topics discussed by the Evangelical Alliance, which lately met in this city, there was none that awoke more interest or more genuine feeling than "Christian Unity." It was a topic which, under the circumstances, naturally came first to hand, and which accompanied the other topics all through the programme. It was recognized, indeed, as the root of the whole enterprise, and it gave occasion for the expression and demonstration of a great deal of true Christian feeling. More than that, the vast numbers of people who listened to these expressions, and the still larger numbers who read the report of them in the newspapers, gave a hearty "amen" to them all.

Now, there ought to come out of all this some high practical result; but we fear that it will be a long time coming.

The first conclusion that the outside world arrives at, is, that the recognition of all the sects by each, as Christian, and as possessing real unity of spirit and life, is an open confession that nothing but non-essential questions and opinions keep the sects from actual unity. It is a declaration, emphasized in many notable ways, that all the sectarian quarrels of the past, and all the sectarian differences of the present, relate to matters that do not touch the essentials of Christian salvation and Christian character. If it does not mean exactly this, it does not mean anything. If it does mean exactly this then all the words that were uttered with such a show of earnestness, and endorsed with such rounds of applause, were a cheat. So much has been gained; and, this gained, we have a right to ask that the natural consequences of the step shall not be hindered or set aside. The first natural consequence is that no sect can claim the right to make a creed that shuts out a Christian from its fellowship, and that every sect is bound to give the same latitude of opinion within its communion, on all non-essential questions, that it yields to other sects. Now let us see how much real sincerity there has been in the declarations so eloquently made and reiterated and popularly responded to in the meetings of the Alliance!

Another natural consequence is the consolidation of all the sects in those localities where, by multiplication of sectarian churches, Christian work is feeble, and Christian enterprise is burdened with poverty and poisoned by jealousies and competitions. We spent the last summer in a country town containing many families of intelligence and culture, supported by an interesting and thrifty husbandry. It had two Presbyterian churches, two meetings of Friends,—the progressive and the orthodox,—one Methodist church, and one Episcopal. With all this machinery, it could hardly be claimed, that there was an active interest in religious affairs in the town, and the fact was patent that not one of those churches was either well attended or well supported. They were feeble, struggling churches, every one of them; and at least one of them went outside for funds to keep itself alive. There are ten thousand just such towns in America—sect-ridden, with feeble churches, usually a feeble and discouraged ministry, and a population grown dead for lack of unity in the church, and brains and culture and fervor in the pulpit. To build a large church in such a town as we have described, to fill its pulpit with a first-rate man, to bring all those churches together in a union that is actual and not sentimental, would be like bringing life to the dead. If so simple a thing as this cannot be done, for reasons that no sane man can dispute, then let the talk about Christian unity cease until we get a little further along.

It is claimed by those who represent the various sectarian organizations that the people are not ready for changes so radical as this would be. We know something of the views and feelings of the people on this subject, and we declare our conviction that they are half a century in advance of the clergy. It is not the people who are against actual Christian unity, where such unity is absolutely essential to Christian success. The sectarian organizations oppose it. The sectarian newspapers oppose it. The sectarian colleges and theological institutions oppose it. The sectarian clergy oppose it. It is from the church leaders that the opposition comes. The entire sectarian machinery and policy of the various churches are against it. Can an instance be given where the governing sectarian influences have combined to reduce to harmony the denominational differences in a town, and bring all into one fold, under one shepherd? We shall be glad to hear of such an instance; we certainly never heard of one.

The question may legitimately be asked of those who declare that the people are not ready for this change, whether they are doing anything to prepare them for it. Do they propose to do anything in the future? If not, then we can arrive at a just estimate of the importance which actual Christian unity and sectarian success relatively obtain in their judgments and hearts.

But it is claimed that there can be true unity of spirit among various denominations. We do not deny it. We believe there has been this among those who have constituted the membership of the Alliance, to a very great extent. We do not expect the destruction of denominationalism for many years. With its present machinery, it can do much for Christianity in many places, particularly in large towns and cities; but there is a multitude of places where it is a constant curse. Is denominationalism willing to sink itself there? If not, then there is no use in talking about Christian unity, or about the love of it, or about devotion to it. The people desire to see a practical embodiment of all this pleasantness between the sects, in our own home affairs, as well as on foreign ground; and they have a right to expect it. If they do not get it, we trust they will undertake the matter for themselves. They have done this thing more than once, and they can do it again.

Church-Debts.

The way in which church edifices are built nowadays really necessitates a new formula of dedication. How would this read? "We dedicate this edifice to Thee, our Lord and Master; we give it to Thee and Thy cause and kingdom, subject to a mortgage of one hundred and fifty thousand dollars ($150,000). We bequeath it to our children and our children's children, as the greatest boon we can confer on them (subject to the mortgage aforesaid), and we trust that they will have the grace and the money to pay the interest and lift the mortgage. Preserve it from fire and foreclosure, we pray Thee, and make it abundantly useful to Thyself,—subject, of course, to the aforesaid mortgage."

The offering of a structure to the Almighty, as the gift of an organization of devotees who have not paid for it, and do not own it, strikes the ordinary mind as a very strange thing, yet it is safe to say that not one church in twenty is built in America without incurring a debt, larger or smaller. A more commodious and a more elegant building is wanted. A subscription is made that will not more than half cover its cost, and money enough is borrowed to complete it. The whole property is mortgaged for all that it will carry, the financial authorities are saddled with a floating debt which they can only handle on their personal responsibility, and then comes taxation for interest, sufficient to keep the church always in distress. This sort of church enterprise is so common that it has become commonplace. The children of this world do not build railroads with capital stock paid in, but they build them with bonds. The children of light really do not seem to be less wise in their generation, in the way in which they build their churches. Indeed, we think the latter can give the former several points and beat them; for the paying success of a church depends upon more contingencies than the success of a railroad, and i s bonds really ought not to sell for more than fifty cents on the dollar "flat."

If we seem to make light of this subject, it is only for the purpose of showing how absurd a position the churches have assumed in relation to it. It is not a light subject; it is a very grave one, and one which demands the immediate and persistent attention of all the churches until it shall be properly disposed of. In the first place, it is not exactly a Christian act for a body of men to contract a debt which they are not able to pay. It is hardly more Christian to refuse to pay a debt which they know they are able to discharge. It can hardly be regarded as a generous deed to bequeath a debt to succeeding generations. The very foundations of the ordinary church-debt are rotten. They are rotten with poor morality, poor financial policy, and personal and sectarian vanity. Does any one suppose that these expensive and debt-laden churches were erected simply for the honor of the Master, and given to Him, subject to mortgage?

The results of building churches upon such an unsound basis are bad enough. The first result, perhaps, is the extinguishment of all church beneficence. The church-debt is the apology for denying all appeals for aid, from all the greater and smaller charities. A church sitting in the shadow of a great debt, is "not at home" to callers. They do not pay the debt, but they owe the money, and they are afraid they shall be obliged to pay it. The heathen must take care of themselves, the starving must go without bread, the widow and the fatherless must look to the God of the widow and the fatherless, the sick must pine, and the poor children grow up in vagabondage, because of this awful church-debt. All the meanness in a church skulks behind the debt, of which it intends to pay very little, while all the nobleness feels really poor, because it is conscious that the debt is to be paid, if paid at all, by itself.

Again, a church-debt is a scare-crow to all new-comers. A stranger, taking up his residence in any town, looks naturally for the church without a debt. He has a horror of debt of any sort, perhaps, and, as he had no responsibility for the church-debts he finds, he does not propose voluntarily to assume any. So he stays away from the debt-ridden church, and the very means that were adopted to make the edifice attractive, become, naturally and inevitably, the agents of repulsion. Debt-ridden churches, with good preachers, do not need to look beyond their debts for the reason which prevents more frequent and remunerative accessions to their number.

Still again, church-debts are intolerable burdens to their ministers. They must "draw," in order that the debt may be paid. If they do not "draw," they must leave, to make place for a man who will. The yearly deficit is an awful thing for a sensitive minister to contemplate, and puts him under a constant and cruel spur, which, sometimes swiftly and sometimes slowly, wears out his life. The feverish desire, on the part of churches, for brilliant or sensational preaching, is more frequently generated by the debt than by any other cause. In many instances the minister is forced into being a politician, a manager, an intriguer, a society-hunter, rather than a soul-seeker. This latter point is a painful one, and we do not propose to dwell upon it; but the deference to the man of money, shown in some churches, is certainly very pitiful, when its cause is fully understood.

Now isn't it about time to make a new departure? Isn't it about time for the debtor churches to take up their debts like men, and discharge them? Isn't it about time to stop dedicating church edifices to Jehovah, subject to a mortgage of one hundred and fifty thousand dollars? Isn't it about time that churches become sound in their moralities, as they relate to the contraction of debts which they either will not, or cannot, pay? We say "yes" to all these questions, and we know that the good sense and Christian feeling of the country will respond Amen! Let that "Amen" be put into practical shape at once, so that a thousand churches, now groaning under their debt, may go into the next year with shoulders light, and hearts not only lighter, but ready for all the good work that is going on around them.

Temporal and Spiritual.

Great public interest is concentrated upon the present struggle of Germany with the Papal power, and the free discussion of the relations of that power to the allegiance of the citizen to his own Government, now in progress in England. Mr. Gladstone's manifesto has placed the vital question involved squarely before the English people, and not less plainly before all the people of Europe. The ingenious protest and denial of Archbishop Manning and other adherents of His Holiness, have failed to do away with the charge of the ex-Premier, simply because it cannot be done away with. The assumption of supreme authority over the consciences of men by a man who claims infallibility, is one which no Government constituted like the British can tolerate with either dignity or safety. The German Government is right in principle on this question, whether it be just and wise in its measures or not; and Mr. Gladstone occupies a position that is impregnable. The dogma of Papal infallibility is an offense to the common sense of the world, and the doctrine of supremacy which grows out of it as naturally as a tree grows out of the soil, is a challenge and an insult to every Government that holds and protects a Catholic subject within its limits.

This would seem to be too plain a matter to call for argumentation. To claim supremacy in matters of conscience, and to hold, at the same time, the power of deciding on questions of conscience—of declaring what is right and what is wrong, in all things, civil as well as religious—is to claim the supreme and all-subordinating allegiance of every man who belongs to the Catholic communion in every country of the world. How any fair-minded man can deny this is beyond our comprehension; and the only reason why the matter does not make as great a commotion in America as it does in Great Britain and Germany, is that, as a State, we have no connection with the Church. Practically, the matter is of very little importance to us. The Catholic Church has the same toleration here that the Methodist Church has—no more, no less. Our Government simply protects it in its liberty, and sees that its own laws are obeyed, irrespective of all church communions. We come into no collision with it, because we assume no church prerogatives and functions. England has a State Church, and it cannot tolerate the existence of two authorities that assume supremacy within the same kingdom; but England is weak in its position, because itself assumes to be an authority in matters of religion.

Theoretically, the Sovereign of Great Britain "can do no wrong." Here is a doctrine of "infallibility;" and though it has no such range as that of the Papacy, and is applied rather to the breaking than the making of law, it is just as absurd as that against which Mr. Gladstone inveighs so mightily. There the State undertakes to meddle with the Church. It supports and in many ways directs it, and exercises functions that are just as illegitimate and presumptuous as those assumed by the Pope with relation to the different States. The same may be said of Prussia; and the Pope has good right to say, if he chooses to do so: "Take your hand from religion, and I will take mine from the State. So long as you choose to make a State affair of religion you must not blame me for doing the same. Give me back my kingdom and my temporalities. Shape your policy to the necessities of my Church. Until you do so, I will define the limits of your power, and of my own, as it seems best to me, and best for the interests I have in charge."

For ourselves, we rejoice to witness the present struggle. In the progress of the world, and in the free development of the power of Christianity, it was necessary that it should come; and its coming marks an epoch and demonstrates an advance. Just so soon as the nations of the world can comprehend the fact that the Kingdom of Christ is not a kingdom of this world; that it is within men, and is not in any way complicated with civil organization and administration,—just so soon will all strife between the State and the Church cease. The Pope, if report be true, has recently said that the only country where he is truly and practically respected is the United States. The reason is, that the State simply minds its own business, and lets him alone. When other States attend only to their civil functions, and let the Church, in all its denominations, take care of itself, they will care no more about the dogma of Papal infallibility than they do about the civil dogma of regal infallibility. They will not even take the trouble to "speak disrespectfully of the equator." It is now essentially a fight between the head of the greatest of the churches and the civil heads of the smaller churches. We have no such head in America, and therefore we don't care. Particularly, we do not care how soon the fight proceeds to its predestined end—the disestablishment of all the churches of Europe. That is the natural solution of the difficulty, and the only possible one. It may come through "a great religious war," which the wise are foretelling, but which real wisdom will avoid, by putting away, at once and forever, its cause.

The ox is a strong and excellent beast, but he cannot be yoked with the horse, who is equally strong and excellent. The horse cannot work according to his law without wearing out the ox, and the ox cannot work according to his law without degrading the horse, and cheating him of his power. The Church and the State can no more be yoked together with natural advantage than the ox and the horse. Their nature, wants, modes of action, drift of power are utterly different, and in the long run the ox will drag down and degrade the horse. To undertake to unite the machinery of the State and the Church is, in the end, to degrade the latter. To make the Church in any way subordinate to the shifting necessities and caprices of politics is a practical desecration of holy things. We believe that no State church ever existed, whether presided over by pope or king, that did not become corrupt, or so nearly dead as to lose its aggressiveness and healthfulness as a spiritual power. Mr. Gladstone and his friends have only to labor earnestly for the disestablishment of the Church of England, to lose all practical interest in the Papal dogmas and the Papal assumptions. By doing this, they will at least be in a position, as Englishmen, to oppose them with some show of consistency.

Organs.

Machine music is not as popular as it was. The old-fashioned hand-organ has become a bore, even to the children; and unless it be supplemented by a knowing monkey, with appeals to the eye, the grinding goes on without reward. This confinement of musical execution to certain tunes, for which the player is not responsible—this circumscription of the limits of emotion by a foreign manufacturer—this reiteration of the same jingle from street to street, at all times of the day and in all months of the year, to ears that are dainty and ears that are dull—all this conspires to make the organist an offense and the hand-organ a nuisance. There really was a time when things were different. When children heard no music in the school and none in the home, when brass bands were scarce and church-organs were supposed to be an invention of the devil, or one of the seductions of the Woman of Babylon, it was quite nice to be assured by a dirty Italian, who never had a home in his life, that there was no place like it, even when his reluctant instrument groaned and fainted away on the last syllable.

What has happened with regard to the hand-organ has also happened with regard to party organs of every kind, political and religious. The fact can be no longer ignored that the people are tired of organs. A newspaper, recognized as strictly a party organ, is regarded as a newspaper without any soul. A newspaper that is simply the exponent of a party policy, the defender of party measures, and the unvarying supporter of party men, is looked upon with a contempt in this country which may well make it tremble with the apprehension of its certain doom. Party organs were adapted to a simple, unintelligent condition of society. At a time when the few invariably led the many, when the great masses of the people pinned their faith to their leaders, and did not do their own thinking, the party organ was in its glory. It cracked its whip, and the whole team, however widely straggling, came into line. It blessed and blamed at will. When it declared one man to be a patriot, and another to be a traitor, the people believed it. It led unquestioning hosts to battle for measures and against measures, for men and against men, according to party policy, and did not even pretend to independence. Now, everything from a party organ is regarded with distrust; and it ought to be. The mouth-piece of a party is never the mouth-piece of a man. Its utterances are all shaped by the selfish policies and interests of party leaders; for the strictly party press is never its own. The people have learned that there is nothing which needs to be accepted with so much caution as any political statement uttered by a political organ. The chances are all against its being strictly true. In short, the people have outgrown the party press, and the day of independent thinking and independent "scratching" and bolting has come.

What we have said of the political party press, is quite true of the religious party press. It has come to be absolutely essential that, in order to the achievment of a large success in religious journalism, the journal shall be independent. The strictly sectarian newspapers are not regarded at all with the respect which was formerly accorded to them. It is only the independent religious press that wins subscribers by the hundred thousand. Men have ceased to be interested in the discussion of questions from a sectarian stand-point. Their sympathies have surpassed sectarian bounds, and their interest goes deeper than creeds. They want to know what the independent thinker thinks. They would read what he writes. They have learned that the organ of a sect is as much the slave as the organ of a party. They have learned to think little of the conflicting systems of theology, and are anxious to know something about religion. They are less anxious about any particular "ism," and more interested in Christianity. Orthodoxy and heterodoxy mean less to them, and truth, more. In brief, they have ceased to pin their faith to sectarian leaders, and are thinking for themselves.

Now, all this is undoubtedly true, and what is to be done about it? Is it a good thing, or a bad thing? Without any question it is a good thing. It marks an era in the development of American Christianity. Everything that looks toward Christian unity breaks the power of the religious party press. Whatever the late meeting of the Evangelical Alliance did to forward Christian unity drove a nail in the coffin of the sectarian organ; and more and more in the future the sectarian organ will cease to be a moral and religious power in the world, until it shall become simply a record of sectarian decadence.

Meantime, the great masses of the people will read only for instruction and inspiration such records of independent religious thought as emanate from those whose interest in Christianity is so deep and broad that they have no partisanship, and no party schemes to promulgate. All advance towards Christian unity—all advance towards vital Christianity—is an actual retirement from the influence of the sectarian organ; and one of the best signs of the times is the recognized necessity of urgent appeals to the people for the support of the organs representing the different sects.

Everything goes to prove that religious truth is to be formulated anew, in the interest of Christian unity, and it is proper to ask those clergymen who stand by their party organs, and hold themselves up as the representatives, conservators and defenders of orthodoxy, if it is not about time for them not only to recognize the signs of the day, but to begin to be true to their own convictions. There is no one of them who can express fully on paper his views of the Sabbath question, or the Bible question, or the question of future punishment, to say nothing of questions still higher, and get all his orthodox associates to sign that paper. There are numbers of them who do not choose to preach the doctrines which they profess, and who do not fully preach what they believe. And they call themselves orthodox, and they criticise the orthodoxy of others, and they dread the proscription of the sectarian press, from whose influence the people are becoming more and more free every year. Woe to a sectarian press that stands in the way of progress, and woe to those mistaken teachers who either bow to that press in front, or bolster it behind. The organ is worn out. It creaks and groans and whines with its old, old tunes, and they who turn the crank have lost their admirers, because the children have become men and women, and can do better with their time and money.

The Free-Church Problem.

There is one sad fact that stares the churches of this city, and of all other American cities, in the face, viz., that Christianity is not preached to the poor. If we step into almost any church on Fifth and Madison Avenues, on any Sunday, we shall find there a well-dressed crowd, or a thinly scattered company of fashionable people, and almost no poor people at all. These churches may carry on, and, as a rule, do carry on, a Mission Sunday-school in some part of the city, where a great deal of useful work is done. Under the circumstances, they do as well as they can; but the fact remains, that the people whose children are taught do not enter a church at all. It is in vain that they are invited to attend preaching; and the fact is demonstrated beyond all question, as it appears to us, that there must be a change effected in the basis and policy of church support before they can be induced to do so. We may attribute their non-attendance to indifference to religious subjects. This is an easy method of relieving ourselves of responsibility, but in view of the alarming fact that this indifference is steadily increasing, it becomes us to inquire whether the Church itself does not come in for a share of the blame, and to find, if possible, where that blame lies.

We have before us a book entitled "*Copy*," by Hugh Miller Thompson, Rector of Christ Church, in this city, consisting of between sixty and seventy brief editorial articles, which has, we may say in passing, more straightforward common sense in it than any book we have met with in a year, and which presents to us two articles respectively revealing the basis of our difficulty and the way of release from it. The first is entitled, "A Proprietary Christianity," and the second, "A lost Act of Worship." We do not propose to quote from them, for we have not the space, but if the reason for a change in the basis of church support, and the solution of the problem of a free church are not to be found in them, then they are hardly to be found in current literature. Our churches are houses of men, and not houses of God. They are largely owned by individuals, and not by the church, or by any body of men representing the church. Either this is the case, or they are sold every year to the highest bidder. Tremendous expenditures are made in building churches; great outlays of money are needed for carrying them on; in most of the churches there is absolute ownership of pews on the part of individuals; and by private sale or public auction the sittings are apportioned to those who have the money to pay for them. There are free sittings, of course, but the men for whom they are left will not take and occupy them, and thus publicly advertise themselves as paupers. It seems plain to us that some change must be made exactly here, before the first step can be taken toward reform. Indeed, this change must be the first step. Our houses of worship must be recognized as houses of God—houses in which there are no exclusive rights purchasable in any way by money—houses where the rich man and the beggar meet on common ground to worship a common Lord—houses to any seat in which any man, high or low, rich or poor, has equal right with any other man. We have tried the other plan long enough, and ought to be satisfied by this time that it is a failure, as it most lamentably is.

Now comes up the question of church support. A church cannot be "run" without money. It cannot be built or bought without money. Well, in the first place, churches need not cost half the money they do, either to build or to carry on. We pay immense sums to make churches attractive, and there are those in New York that are crammed every Sunday simply for the purpose of hearing expensive music. There is a very large attendance upon certain churches in this city that has not the first motive of worship in it—churches in which artistic music is made so prominent, indeed, as quite to put all ideas of worship out of the mind of those who are musically inclined. There is not only money enough for all necessary purposes, but money is absolutely wasted. Our churches are now built and run on the theory that men will pay for exclusive privileges for themselves, and will not pay for free privileges for all.

And here is where Dr. Thompson's article on "A lost Act of Worship" comes to its practical bearing. He claims that the Worship of God in Gifts has been lost, and ought to be recovered. The first worship offered to Christ on earth was a worship of gifts. Gifts were recognized acts of worship in the Jewish church from time immemorial. All that is necessary is to re-instate this act of worship, so that every Christian who goes to church shall bring with his tribute of prayer and praise his offering of money, as an act of worship, in order to solve the free church problem at once. Churches are to be built by gifts offered in worship—by a dedication of substance as well as of self; and they are to be carried on in the same way. We believe that if the solution of the free church problem is anywhere, it is here. We are to lay aside all ideas of the ownership of pews, in every sense, and to bring every Sunday our offering of gifts, according to our ability and our degree of prosperity, as an act of worship, just as conscientiously as we bring our petition and our praise. We believe in the theory and in the plan wholly, and thus believing we believe it to be wholly practicable. We have not a question that a living Christian church, thoroughly enlightened on this subject by a clergyman sympathetic with these views, would find the obstacles to the plan all removed, as well as the obstacles to its usefulness. Of course the church must go through a process of education to bring it to this high plane, but we are satisfied that it must be brought here before its triumphs will be great—before it will check in any considerable degree the tide of worldliness that threatens to engulf it, or bring its influence to bear upon those who persistently refuse to hear its voice.

The experiment will not be a new one of sustaining a church on the current gifts of its attendants, but this grand idea of incorporating acts of beneficence into the regular Sunday worship of the Christian church will be new to the great multitude, and, if adopted, will forever relieve the preacher from appearing before his people as a beggar. It will make the churches God's houses and not man's, and the ministry of the churches a universal ministry. It will at least secure the world's confidence in our sincerity, and, if it persists in its indifference, leave it without excuse.

Cheap Opinions.

There is probably nothing that so obstinately stands in the way of all sorts of progress as pride of opinion, while there is nothing so foolish and so baseless as that same pride. If men will look up the history of their opinions, learn where they came from, why they were adopted, and why they are maintained and defended, they will find, nine times in ten, that their opinions are not theirs at all,—that they have no property in them, save as gifts of parents, education, and circumstances. In short, they will learn that they did not form their own opinions,—that they were formed for them, and in them, by a series of influences, unmodified by their own reason and knowledge. A young man grows up to adult age in a Republican or Democratic family, and he becomes Republican or Democrat in accordance with the ruling influences of the household. Ninety-nine times in a hundred the rule holds good. Like father, like son. Children are reared in the Catholic Church, in the Episcopal, Unitarian, Presbyterian, Baptist, Methodist Churches, and they stand by the Church in whose faith and forms they were bred. They become partisans, wranglers, defenders, on behalf of opinions, every one of which they adopted without reason or choice. Touch them at any point, and they bristle with resistance, often with offense; yet they borrowed every opinion they hold! If they had all been changed about in their cradles, we should have the same number of partisans, only our present Republican would be a Democrat, our Roman Catholic would be a Methodist, and so on through all the possibilities of transformation.

Opinions acquired in the usual way are nothing but intellectual clothes, left over by expiring families. Some of them are very old-fashioned and look queerly to the modern tailor; but they have the recommendation of being only clothes. They do not touch the springs of life, like food or cordial. Certainly they are nothing to be proud of, and they are not often anything to be ashamed of. Multitudes would not be presentable without them, as they have no faculty for making clothes for themselves. The point we make is, that opinions acquired in this way have very little to do with character. The simple fact that we find God-fearing, God-loving, good, charitable, conscientious, Christian men and women living under all forms of Christian opinion and church organization, shows how little opinion has to do with the heart, the affections and the life. Yet all our strifes and all our partisanships relate to opinions which we never made, which we have uniformly borrowed, and which all Christian history has demonstrated to be of entirely subordinate import—opinions, often, which those who originally framed them had no reason to be proud of, because they had no vital significance.

When we find, coming squarely down upon the facts, what cheap stuff both our orthodoxy and our heterodoxy are made of; when we see how little they are the proper objects of personal and sectarian pride; when we apprehend how little they have to do with character, and how much they have to do with dissension and all uncharitableness; how childish they make us, how sensitive to fault-finding and criticism; how they narrow and dwarf us, how they pervert us from the grander and more vital issues, we may well be ashamed of ourselves, and trample our pride of opinion in the dust. We shall find, too, in this abandonment of our pride, a basis of universal charity,—cheap, and not the best, but broad enough for pinched feet and thin bodies to stand upon. If we inherit our opinions from parents and guardians and circumstances, and recognize the fact that the great world around us get their opinions in the same way, we shall naturally be more able to see the life that underlies opinion everywhere, and to find ourselves in sympathy with it. We heard from the pulpit recently the statement that when the various branches of the Christian Church shall become more careful to note the points of sympathy between each other than the points of difference, the cause of Christian unity will be incalculably advanced; and that statement was the inspiring word of which the present article was born.

We can never become careless, or comparatively careless, of our points of difference, until we learn what wretched stuff they are made of—that these points of difference reside in opinions acquired at no cost at all, and that they often rise no higher in the scale of value than borrowed prejudices. So long as "orthodoxy" of opinion is more elaborately insisted on in the pulpit than love and purity; so long as dogmatic theology has the lead of life; so long as Christianity is made so much a thing of the intellect and so subordinately a thing of the affections, the points of difference between the churches will be made of more importance than the points of sympathy. Pride of opinion must go out before sympathy can come in. So long as brains occupy the field, the heart cannot find standing room. When our creeds get to be longer than the moral law; when Christian men and women are taken into, or shut out of, churches on account of their opinions upon dogmas that do not touch the vitalities of Christian life and character; when men of brains are driven out of churches or shut away from them, because they cannot have liberty of opinion, and will not take a batch of opinions at second-hand, our pride of opinion becomes not only ridiculous, but criminal; and the consummation of Christian unity is put far off into the better future.

With the dropping of our pride of opinion—which never had a respectable basis to stand upon—our respect for those who are honestly trying to form an opinion for themselves should be greatly increased. There are men who are honestly trying to form an opinion of their own. They are engaged in a grand work. There are but few of us who are able to cut loose from our belongings. Alas! there are but few of us who are large enough to apprehend the fact that the opinions of these men are only worthy of respect, as opinions. We can look back and respect the opinions of our fathers and our grandfathers, formed under the light and among the circumstances of their time, but the authors of the coming opinions we regard with distrust and a degree of uncharitableness most heartily to be deplored.

THE COMMON MORALITIES.

The Popular Capacity for Scandal.

One of the most saddening and humiliating exhibitions which human nature ever makes of itself, is in its greedy credulity touching all reports of the misdemeanors of good men. If a man stand high as a moral force in the community; if he stand as the rebuker and denouncer of social and political sin; if he be looked up to by any considerable number of people as an example of virtue; if the whole trend and power of his life be in a high and pure direction; if his personality and influence render any allegation against his character most improbable, then most readily does any such allegation find eager believers. It matters not from what source the slander may come. Multitudes will be influenced by a report against a good man's character from one who would not be believed under oath in any matter involving the pecuniary interest of fifty cents. The slanderer may be notoriously base—may be a panderer to the worst passions and the lowest vices—may be a shameless sinner against social virtue—may be a thief, a notorious liar, a drunkard, a libertine, or a harlot—all this matters nothing. The engine that throws the mud is not regarded. The white object at which the foul discharges are aimed is only seen; and the delight of the by-standers and lookers-on is measured by the success of the stain sought to be inflicted.

As between the worldling and the man who professes to be guided and controlled by Christian motives, all this is natural enough. The man bound up in his selfish and sensual delights, who sees a Christian fall, or hears the report that he has fallen, is naturally comforted in the belief that, after all, men are alike—that no one of them, however much he may profess, is better than another. It is quite essential to his comfort that he cherish and fortify himself in this conviction. So, when any great scandal arises in quarters where he has found himself and his course of life condemned, he listens with ready ears, and is unmistakably glad. We say this is natural, however base and malignant it may be; but when people reputed good—nay, people professing to be Christian—shrug their virtuous shoulders and shake their feeble heads, while a foul scandal touches vitally the character of one of their own number, and menaces the extinguishment of an influence, higher or humbler, by which the world is made better, we hang our heads with shame, or raise them with indignation. If such a thing as this is natural, it proves just one thing, viz.: that these men are hypocrites. There is no man, Christian or Pagan, who can rejoice in the faintest degree over the reputed fall of any other man from recitude, without being at heart a scamp. All this readiness to believe evil of others, especially of those who have been reputed to be eminently good, is an evidence of conscious weakness under temptation, or of conscious proclivity to vice that finds comfort in eminent companionship.

There is no better test of purity and true goodness than reluctance to think evil of one's neighbor, and absolute incapacity to believe an evil report about good men except upon the most trustworthy testimony. Alas, that this large and lovely charity is so rare! But it is only with those who possess this charity that men accused of sins against society have an equal chance with those accused, under the forms of law, of crime. Every man brought to trial for crime is presumed to be innocent until he is proved to be guilty; but, with the world at large, every man slandered is presumed to be guilty until he proves himself to be innocent; and even then it takes the liberty of doubting the testimony. Every man who rejoices in a scandal thereby advertises the fact of his own untrustworthiness; and every man who is pained by it, and refuses to be impressed by it, unconsciously reveals his own purity. He cannot believe a bad thing done by one whom he regards as a good man, simply because he knows he would not do it himself. He gives credit to others for the virtue that is consciously in his own possession, while the base men around him, whether Christian in name or not, withhold that credit because they cannot believe in the existence of a virtue of which they are consciously empty. When the Master uttered the words, "Let him that is without sin among you first cast a stone at her," he knew that none but conscious delinquents would have the disposition to do so; and when, under this rebuke, every fierce accuser retired overwhelmed, He, the sinless, wrote the woman's crime in the sand for the heavenly rains to efface. If He could do this in a case of guilt not disputed, it certainly becomes his followers to stand together around every one of their number whom malice or revenge assails with slanders to which his or her whole life gives the lie.

In a world full of influences and tendencies to evil, where every good force is needed, and needs to be jealously cherished and guarded, there is no choicer treasure and no more beneficent power than a sound character. This is not only the highest result of all the best forces of our civilization, but it is the builder of those forces in society and the State. Society cannot afford to have it wasted or destroyed; and its instinct of self-preservation demands that it shall not be suffered. There is nothing so sensitive and nothing so sacred as character; and every tender charity, and loyal friendship, and chivalrous affection, and manly sentiment and impulse, ought to intrench themselves around every true character in the community so thoroughly that a breath of calumny shall be as harmless as an idle wind. If they cannot do this, then no man is safe who refuses to make terms with the devil, and he is at liberty to pick his victims where he will.

Professional Morals.

No man has a right to practice his profession in such a way as to encourage personal vice in those whom he serves, or wrong-doing towards individuals and the community. This is a very simple proposition, to which no respectable man in any profession will presume to make an objection. If there ever lived a professional villain of whom a professional vilifier could say: "This is he who made it safe to murder, and of whose health thieves inquired before they began to steal," he could only be saved from universal execration by a natural doubt of the justice of the sarcasm and the candor of its author. Theoretically, there are no differences among decent men on this subject, when it is placed before the mind in this way. It is one of those simple, self-evident propositions, about which no man would think of arguing for an instant. Up to the bar of this proposition one can bring every act of his professional life, and decide for himself whether it be legitimate and morally good. We repeat it,—*No man has a right to practice his profession in such a way as to encourage personal vice in those whom he serves, or wrong-doing towards individuals and the community.*

The great cities are full of men who have achieved remarkable skill in the treatment of a certain class of diseases, and other dangerous or inconvenient consequences of a bestial social vice. No matter how often their patients may approach them, or how vile they may be, or how successfully they may scheme against the peace and purity of society, or what form the consequences of their sin may assume, these professional men take their fee, and do what they can to shield the sinners from the effect of their crimes. Whatever they may be able to do professionally to make it safe for men and women to trample upon the laws of social purity, they do and constantly stand ready to do. Yet these men have a defense of themselves which enables them to hold their heads up. They are physicians. It is their business to treat disease in whatever form it may present itself. It would be impertinent in them to inquire into the life of those who come to them for advice. They are not the keepers of other men's consciences. They are men of science and not of morals. It is their business to cure disease by the speediest and best methods they know, and not to inquire into character, or be curious about the indirect results of their skill. Such would be their defense, or the line of their defense; yet, if it can be seen or shown that their professional life encourages vice in the community, by the constant shield which it offers against the consequences of vice, the defense amounts to nothing. If a debauchee or a sensualist of any sort finds impunity for his excesses in the professional skill of his physician, and relies upon that skill to shield him from the consequences of his sins, be they what they may, his physician becomes the partner of his guilt for gold, and a professional pander to his appetites. He may find professional brethren to defend him, but before the unsophisticated moral sense of the world he will be a degraded man, and stand condemned.

There are such men in the world as professional pardoners of sin. There are men in priestly robes who, on the confession of a penitent, or one who assumes the position of a penitent, release him professionally from the consequences of his misdeeds. Unless history has lied, there have been men among these to whom the vicious have gone for shrift and pardon for a consideration, and received what they went for, on every occasion of overt crime when the voice of conscience in their superstitious souls would not be still, and who have retired from the confessional ready for more crimes, from whose spiritual consequences they have intended and expected to find relief in the same way. It is not necessary to charge such desecration of the priestly office upon any one. We have no reason to believe that in this country such things are common; but we know that priests are human, and that there have been bad and mercenary men among them. It is only necessary to suppose cases like this, to see that a priest may, in the exercise of his professional functions, become the partner of the criminal in his crimes, a friend and protector of vice, and a foe to the purity and good order of society. He can set up his professional defense, and find professional defenders, perhaps; but any child, capable of comprehending the question, will decide that he is degraded and disgraced.

What is true, or may be true, of these professions, is true of any profession. Nothing is more notorious than that there are lawyers who are public nuisances—who encourage litigation, who are universally relied upon by criminals for the defense of crime, and whose reputation and money have indeed been won by their ability to clear the guilty from the consequences of their wrong-doing. Between these low extremes of professional prostitution and the high ground occupied by the great mass of legal men, there are many points where self-interest, united with incomplete knowledge, is powerful to lead the best minds into doubtful ways, and engage them in the support of doubtful causes or the defense of doubtful men. It is freely admitted that the best lawyer may find questions of personal morality and professional propriety in his practice that are hard to settle, and that may conscientiously be settled incorrectly; but no lawyer needs to question whether it is right for him to strengthen the position of a notorious scamp, especially if that scamp is known to be a corrupter of the law by all the means in his power, and a wholesale plunderer of the people.

Let Us Be Virtuous.

The devil is a sharp financier. He manages to make good people, or people who think they are good, pay the dividends on all the stock he issues, and cash all his premiums on rascality. Sometimes, however, the good people get tired, and, taking on a fit of severe virtue, protest. In the city of New York there was a Committee of Seventy operating against seventy rogues multiplied by seven, and all the city was in a state of fierce indignation. It was found that the public purse had been shamelessly robbed—that the work had been going on for years—and that the robbers were men of power, both in and out of office. We say this was found to be the case, but we do not mean to intimate that the finding was a new one. No one was any more certain then than he had been for years that the tax-payers of the city were systematically robbed. It was just as well known then as it is now, that men in public office were making fortunes illegitimately. The figures which *The Times* and its coadjutors published did not add to the popular conviction in this matter. They simply showed how much the public had been robbed; and it was the magnitude of the figures that roused the moral indignation. The people knew their rulers were doing wrong, but they were too busy with making money to interfere. They knew they were stealing something, but thought it best to permit the theft; and they only became overwhelmingly conscientious when they found that the rogues were determined to have their last dollar. Then they grew wide awake, grasped their pockets, cried "stop thief!" and became virtuous.

Shall we—must we—confess that such enormous frauds and robberies as these which we notice are only rendered possible by a low condition of the public morality? Must we confess that only in New York city such things have happened? Must we confess that this shocking and unparalleled malfeasance is only an outcropping of a universally underlying baseness, and that there are ten thousand men in New York city alone who would have been glad to do exactly what our rulers have done, and would have done it with the opportunity? Think ye that these rogues are sinners above all Galileans? Let us acknowlege the truth. They were proceeded against not because they offended the public conscience, not because they did wrong, not because they were the enemies of public virtue, not because their example demoralized and debauched our children, not because they shamed and disgraced us in the eyes of the world, not because they stole from us constantly, and not because they used us as clean means to dirty ends, for all these had they been doing for years, with our knowledge and consent; but because they had stolen so enormously that we were in danger of being ruined. This roused us, and we found that we had a conscience, carried for convenience in the bottom of our pockets, and only stirred by thieves who reached very far down.

It is time that a community in which such robberies are

possible were alarmed for itself. We are overrun by men of easy virtue. Picking and stealing are going on everywhere. The community is full of men who are anxious to make money without earning it. They fill the lobby at the capitol, they fasten in various capacities upon railroad corporations, they hang upon insurance companies, they seek for sinecures everywhere. Their influence is intolerable, yet they are everywhere tolerated. They regard it as no wrong by whatsoever and in what way soever they may be benefited by a corporation. All means are fair which take money from a corporation. Stockholders are systematically robbed, and have been for many years, yet there is not moral force and earnestness enough in the popular protest to gain the slightest attention, or arrest the passage of the plunder for a moment. There is moral rottenness in every quarter. The "dead-head" is everywhere, and the dead-heart invariably keeps it company.

But let us rejoice that we have at last a protest. Ay, let us rejoice that a few have had the opportunity to do what many would be glad to do if they had the opportunity, and thus learn what a wilderness of wolves our apathy and toleration have sheltered and permitted to multiply, until our lives and fortunes are in danger. The popular greed for money, coupled with low morality, runs just as directly into robbery as a river tends to the sea. Opportunity is all that is needed to prove how universal and powerful is the propensity to steal. What the better elements of society need is union and determination in the effort to shut from rogues this opportunity. No bad man is fit for any office, and the good men of a city who do not think it worth while to unite for the simple purpose of being ruled by good men, have none but themselves to blame if they are robbed. Indeed, by refusing to unite for this purpose, they become participators in the crimes which they condemn.

American Honesty.

Any man who has traveled in Europe knows what the temptation is to buy and bring home articles that can be procured more cheaply there than in America, under the expectation that the customs officers will let them in free of duty; and every observer knows that millions of dollars' worth of goods are imported annually in this way that pay no revenue to the Government. It is notorious, too, that many of our citizens go to Canada to buy clothing, and wear it home for the purpose of cheating the Government. Men of wealth and luxuriously living women, who would scorn to deal dishonorably by their neighbors, rejoice in the privilege of cheating their own Government, and boast of their success in doing so. They do not even suspect that they are doing wrong in this thing. They have no idea that they are acting meanly or dishonestly. They look upon this genteel kind of smuggling as a smart and harmless trick, and display to their friends the results of their shrewdness with pride and self-gratulation. We may find among these smugglers thousands who look upon the corruptions of politicians with indignation; yet not one of them could succeed in his smuggling enterprises save through the unfaithfulness of public officers, whom they reward for their treachery with a gift.

Would it not be well for us to remember, before we condemn the dishonesty which is so prevalent in the public service, that the politicians and office-holders are, on the whole, as honest as the people are? All that either of them seem to need is a temptation to dishonesty to make them dishonest. The office-holder takes advantage of his position to cheat his Government, and every genteel smuggler who lands from a European vessel, or crosses the Canada line, does the same thing from the same motive. The radical trouble, with people and politicians alike, is the entertainment of the idea that stealing from the Government is not stealing at all—that a man has a right to get out of his Government all that he can without detection. They have not only brought their consciences into harmony with this idea, but they willfully break the law of the land. In short, for the sake of a trifling advantage in the purchase of goods, they are willing to deceive, to tempt public officers to forswear themselves, to break the laws of their country, and to deprive the Government that protects them of a portion of the means by which it sustains itself in that service.

It is a startling fact that there is never a train wrecked without pickpockets on board, who immediately proceed to plunder the helpless passengers. These may not be professionals. They may never have picked a pocket in their lives before, but the temptation develops the thief. There is never a battle fought in any place where there are not men ready to plunder the slain. The devil, or the wild beast, has been there all the time, only waiting for an invitation to come out. Men look on and see a great city badly managed—see mayors and aldermen and politicians engaged in stealing and growing rich on corruption; but these men find thousands ready on all sides to engage in corrupt contracts, to render false bills of service, and to aid them in all rascally ways to fill their pockets with spoil. The men whom we send to our Legislatures to represent us seem quite willing to become the tools of corrupt men, and it is marvelous to see with what joy the residents of any locality receive the patronage of the Government, whether needed or not. That member of Congress who secures to his district the expenditure of Government money for the building of any "improvement," no matter how absurdly unnecessary, does much to secure his re-election. There is no denying the fact that the people are just as fond of spoil as the politicians are.

We find fault with the management of corporations, but all our corporations have virtuous stockholders. Did anybody ever hear of these stockholders relinquishing any advantage derived from dishonest management? Do they protest against receiving dividends of scrip coming from watered stock? Do they not shut their eyes to "irregularities," so long as they are profitable, and do not compromise their interests before the law? There is not a corporation of any importance in America which is not regarded as a fair subject for plunder by a large portion of the community. If a piece of land is wanted by a corporation, it is placed at once at the highest price. Any price that can be got out of a corporation for anything is considered a fair price. Corporations are the subjects of the pettiest and absurdest claims from all sorts of men. Men hang upon some of them like leeches, sucking their very life blood out of them.

And now, what do all these facts lead to? Simply to the conclusion that dishonesty in our Government and dishonesty in all our corporate concerns is based on the loose ideas of honesty entertained by our people. We have somehow learned to make a difference between those obligations which we owe to one another as men, and those which we owe to the Government and to corporations. These ideas are not a whit more prevalent among office-holders and directors than they are among voters and stockholders. Men are not materially changed by being clothed with office and power. The radically honest man is just as honest in office as he is out of it. Corrupt men are the offspring of a corrupt society. We all need straightening up. The lines of our morality all need to be drawn tighter. There is not a man who is willing to smuggle, and to see customs officers betray their trust while he does it; willing to receive the results of the sharp practice of directors of corporations in which he has an interest; willing to receive the patronage of the Government in the execution of schemes not based in absolute necessity; willing to take an exorbitant price for a piece of property sold to the Government or to a corporation, who is fit to be trusted with office. When we have said this, we have given the explanation of all our public and corporate corruption, and shown why it is so difficult to get any great trust managed honestly. All official corruption is based on popular corruption—loose ideas of honesty as they are held by the popular mind; and we can hope for no reform until we are better based as a people in the everlasting principles of equity and right-doing. If we would have the stream clear, we must cleanse the fountain.

WOMAN.

Ownership in Women.

A man was recently hanged in Massachusetts for taking vengeance on one who had practically disputed his property in a girl. The man was a brute, of course, but he had an opinion that a girl who had given herself to him, in the completest surrender that a woman can make, was in some sense his—that her giving herself to another involved his dishonor—and that his property in her was to be defended to the extremity of death. A prominent newspaper, while recording the facts of the case, takes the occasion to say that this idea of ownership in women is the same barbarism out of which grow the evils and wrongs that the "woman movement" is intended to remove. If we were to respond that ownership in women, only blindly apprehended as it was by our brutal gallows-bird, is the one thing that saves us from the wildest doctrines and practices of the free-lovers, and is one of the strongest conservative forces of society, it is quite likely that we should be misunderstood; but we shall run the risk, and make the assertion.

There is an instinct in the heart of every woman which tells her that she is his to whom she gives herself, and his alone,—an instinct which bids her cling to him while she lives or he lives—which identifies her life with his—which makes of him and her twain, one flesh. When this gift is once made to a true man, he recognizes its significance. He is to provide for her that which she cannot provide for herself; he is to protect her to the extent of his power; she is to share his home, and to be his closest companion. His ownership in her covers his most sacred possession, and devolves upon him the gravest duties. If it were otherwise, why is it that a woman who gives herself away unworthily feels, when she finds herself deceived, that she is lost?—that she has parted with herself to one who does not recognize the nature of the gift, and that she who ought to be owned, and, by being owned, honored, is disowned and dishonored? There is no true, pure woman living who, when she gives herself away, does not rejoice in the ownership which makes her forever the property of one man. She is not his slave to be tasked and abused, because she is the gift of love and not the purchase of money; but she is his, in a sense in which she cannot be another man's without dishonor to him and damnation to herself.

Our gallows-bird was, in his brutal way, right. If he had been living in savage society, without laws, and with the necessity of guarding his own treasures, his act would have been looked upon as one of heroism by all the beauties and braves of his tribe. The weak point in his case was, that his ownership in what he was pleased to call "his girl" was not established according to the laws under which he lived. He was not legally married, and had acquired no rights under the law to be defended. What he was pleased to consider his rights were established contrary to law, and he could not appeal to law for their defense. He took the woman to himself contrary to law, he defended his property in her by murder, and he was hanged. He was served right. Hemp would grow on a rock for such as he anywhere in the world. There is no cure for the man who seduces and slays, but a broken neck.

There is nothing more menacing in the aspect of social affairs in this country than the effort among a certain class of reformers to break up the identity of interest and feeling among men and women. Men are alluded to with sneers and blame, as being opposed to the interests of women, as using the power in their hands—a power usurped—to maintain their own predominance at the expense of woman's rights and woman's well-being. Marriage, under this kind of teaching, becomes a compact of convenience, into which men and women may enter, each party taking along the personal independence enjoyed in a single state, with separate business interests and separate pursuits. In other words, marriage is regarded simply as the legal companionship of two beings of opposite sexes, who have their own independent pursuits, with which the bond is not permitted to interfere. It contemplates no identification of life and destiny. The man holds no ownership in woman which gives him a right to a family of children and a life devoted to the sacred duties of motherhood. The man who expects such a sacrifice at the hands of his wife is regarded as a tyrant or a brute. Women are to vote, and trade, and practice law, and preach, and go to Congress, and do everything that a man does, irrespective of the marriage bonds. Women are to be just as free to do anything outside of their homes as men are. They are to choose their careers and pursue them with just as little reference to the internal administration of their families as their husbands exercise. This is the aim and logical end of all the modern doctrines concerning woman's rights. The identification of woman with man, as the basis of the institution of the family, is scoffed at. Any ownership in woman, that comes of the gift of herself to him, and the assumption of the possession by him, with its life-long train of obligations and duties, is contemned. It is assumed that interests which are, and must forever remain, identical, are opposed to each other. Men and women are pitted against each other in a struggle for power.

Well, let it be understood, then, that men are opposed to these latter-day doctrines, and that they will remain so. They are determined that the identity of interest between men and women shall never be destroyed; that the sacred ownership in women, bestowed in all true marriage, shall never be surrendered; that the family shall be maintained, and that the untold millions of true women in the world who sympathize with them shall be protected from the false philosophies and destructive policies of their few misguided sisters, who seek to turn the world upside down. Political conventions may throw their sops to clamoring reformers, but they mean nothing by it. They never have redeemed a pledge to these reformers, and we presume they have never intended to do so. They expect the matter to blow over, and, if we do not mistake the signs of the times, it is rapidly blowing over, with more or less thunder and with very little rain. In the meantime, if the discussions that have grown out of these questions have tended to open a broader field to woman's womanly industry, or obliterated unjust laws from the statute-book, let every man rejoice. No good can come to woman that does not benefit him, and no harm that does not hurt him. Humanity is one, and man and woman rise or fall together.

Three Pieces of the Woman Question.

FIRST PIECE.

A survey of the States of the Union, and of the Union under the general government, will show to any candid observer that the legislation of the country, in all its departments, is above, rather than below, the average moral sense of the nation. The fact is seen in the inadequate execution of the laws. There are many statutes relating to public morals and civil policy which appear to be the offspring of the highest and purest principles, that stand as dead letters in State and national law, simply because the average moral sense of the people does not demand and enforce their execution. They are enacted through the influence or by the power of men of exceptional virtue, who find, to their sorrow, that while it is easy to make good laws, it is difficult, and often impossible, to execute them. So far as we know, it has never occurred to them to call for the assistance of women in the execution of these laws, nor has it occurred to women to offer their assistance to them for this end. One or two questions, suggested by the discussions of the time, naturally grow out of this statement.

First:—Is it of any practical advantage to have better laws, until the average morality of the people is sufficient to execute those which we have?

Second:—Is it right that women should have an equal or a determining voice in the enactment of laws which they do not propose to execute, which they do not propose to assist in executing, which they could not execute if they would, and which they expect men to execute for them?

Third:—Supposing that women would give us better laws than we have (which is not evident), what would be the practical advantage to them or to us, so long as they must rely upon us to execute them—upon us, who find it impossible to enforce our own laws, some of the best of which are the outgrowth of the pure influence of women in home and social life?

SECOND PIECE.

In national and international life there are policies of action and attitude to be adopted and maintained. These policies sometimes cost a civil war for their establishment or defense, and, not unfrequently, a war with related nations. It so happens, in the nature of the case, that no single nation has it in its power to abolish war. The only way for a nation to live, when attacked by foes within or without, is to fight; and, in the present condition of the world, a national policy which has not behind it the power of physical defense is as weak and contemptible a thing as the world holds. Out of this statement, which we presume no one will dispute, there arise two questions.

First:—Would a lack of all personal risk and responsibility, on the part of those delegated to establish and pronounce the policy of a nation, tend to prudent counsels and careful decisions?

Second:—Is it right—is it kind and courteous to men—for women to demand an equal or a determining voice in the establishment of a national policy which they do not propose to defend, which they do not propose to assist in defending, which they could not defend if they would, and which they expect men to defend for them?

THIRD PIECE.

Mr. Gleason, the Tax Commissioner of Massachusetts, recently reported to the Legislature of that State that a tax of nearly two million dollars is paid annually by the women of the State on property amounting, at a low valuation, to one hundred and thirty-two million dollars. The fact is an interesting and gratifying one, in every point of view. Naturally it is seized upon by the advocates of woman-suffrage, and brought prominently forward to assist in establishing woman's claim to the ballot. The old cry of "no taxation without representation" is renewed, however much or little of essential justice may be involved in the phrase. Well, if women are, or ever have been, taxed as women (which they are not, and never have been); if they produced this wealth, or won it by legitimate trade (which they did not); if the men who produced it received their right to the ballot by or through it; if nine-tenths of the wealth of the State were not in the hands of business men whose pursuits have specially fitted them to be the guardians of the wealth of the State; if the counsels of these tax-paying women could add wisdom to the wisdom of these men; if the men who produced this wealth, and bestowed it upon these women, did it with distrust of the laws enacted by men for its protection, and with the desire for the social and political revolution which woman-suffrage would produce, in order that it might be better protected; if there were any complaint of inadequate protection to this property on account of its being in the hands of women—if all or any one of these suppositions were based in truth—then some sort of a plea could be set up on Mr. Gleason's exhibit by those who claim the ballot for woman. As the facts are, we confess our inability to find in it any comfort or support for those who seek for the revolution under consideration. On the contrary, we find that the ballot as it stands to-day, with its privileges, responsibilities, and limitations, secures to woman complete protection in the enjoyment of revenues which are proved to be immense, all drawn from land and sea by the hands of men whose largess testifies alike of their love and their munificence.

Women in the Colleges.

We are not among those who fancy that there are any remarkable social dangers connected with bringing the sexes together during the processes of their education. The question of admitting women to colleges hitherto devoted to young men has been, and still is, under serious consideration. It may be said that if it is really desirable that any considerable number of women should receive the same education that the young men of the colleges receive, they should have the opportunity to do so. It may be said, too, that this question of the education of women has only an indirect relation to the question of woman-suffrage, and should never be confounded with it. "The Woman Question" proper has no legitimate connection with the question of admitting women to the colleges where young men are educated. If the studies and the modes of study of the college are not to be modified in consequence of the admission of women, the men—teachers and students—need to make no objection, The society of women will do them good rather than harm. It is certainly one of the disadvantages of college and female boarding-school life that it is sexually isolated. There is no question that the daily association of the sexes when young, under judicious supervision and regulation, is much healthier than their separation. It is better that the sexes see each other daily than to dream of each other; and either the one or the other they always do. So, in our judgment, the question is not one mainly of social health and purity. If it is, then it is settled, and calls for no further discussion. It is the universal testimony of teachers, so far as we have learned, that morally the sexes do well together in school—do better, indeed, than when separated. The association of men and women in a school or college is just as safe and healthful as their association in all ordinary life. Men and women are never shut away from each other for long periods of time without damage and disaster. Imagination is unduly excited, feeling becomes morbid, and manners are degraded by such separations; and the earlier they can be dispensed with the better.

Can they be dispensed with altogether? We think not. We have never yet felt called upon to part with our old opinion that a man is not a woman, and that a woman is not a man; that, as a consequence, their spheres of labor and office differ, and that their educational training should have reference as well to their peculiarities of constitution as to the spheres of life they are to occupy. Now if any college is adapted just as well to the training of young women as of young men, it is well adapted to the training of neither. If at Vassar and Holyoke women do not have a better chance than at Amherst and Harvard, Vassar and Holyoke are grossly at fault, and Amherst and Harvard are anything but what they pretend to be—first-class institutions for the training of young men, to lead the lives and do the work of men. If any of these young men's colleges are particularly desirable institutions for the education of women, they need reforming, unless it is proposed to change them into female seminaries.

The claiming of places for women in young men's colleges as a right, and the denunciation of their exclusion as a wrong to woman, are the special functions of fanatics and fools. There are no rights and wrongs in the matter. It is entirely a matter of policy with regard to that which is best, on the whole, for both young men and young women. Granted that morally they would do good to each other in the college, as they undoubtedly do in the primary and preparatory schools; granted that they would purify each other socially, and stimulate each other intellectually; granted that such association would soften and simplify the manners of all concerned; the facts still remain, that men are not women, that women are not men, and that for their differing spheres of life and labor they need a widely different training. It certainly is not an object for society to make women more like men than they are, or in any way to divert them from a full and fine development of their womanhood.

It ought to be said, on behalf of the women of America, that they have not, in any considerable or influential numbers, demanded admission to the colleges which have been specially designed for the training of young men. The demand has been made by theorists and dreamers, among men mostly. The truth is that there is no call for these changes of policy which deserves attention. The schools provided for the education of women are growing better and better every year. Colleges for women are springing up all over the country, and Vassar is unquestionably a better place for young women—all sheltered by the single roof of the institution—than Amherst or Harvard or Yale or Union can be, adapted as they all are to the wants of young men, as well as to their lack of wants. There are no wise fathers and mothers who would not prefer Vassar or Holyoke to Harvard or Yale as a training-place for their daughters. They can reach any grade of learning and culture in these institutions which they desire, with special adaptations of institutional appointment and machinery to their wants as women, and special choice and arrangement of their studies to the womanly sphere of life they are to occupy. The managers of the colleges for men will do what they think best in regard to the proposed change, but we believe they will have the support of the best men and women in every part of the country if they decidedly and persistently refuse to make it.

The Moral Power of Women.

Nothing in American history has more nobly illustrated the moral power of women, than the notorious Western crusade against the vice of drinking, and the traffic upon which it feeds. The exhibition and demonstration of this power are so full of suggestion and instruction, both to men and women, that they demand more than a passing consideration, especially in their bearing upon some of the most stirring questions of the time.

Why was it in that crusade that the hardened rum-seller who, behind his bar, had dealt out the liquid death to his victims for years, quailed before a band of praying, beseeching women—women who, coming from their comfortable retirement, braved wind and storm and mud—braved obloquy and misrepresentation and curses, and all the harsh obstacles that brutality could throw in their path, to compass a reform that should keep their natural supporters and protectors pure and prosperous? Why was it that men looking on formed new resolutions of sobriety, and reformed the vicious habits of their lives? Why was it that changes which involved the destruction of a brutal business, and of habits to which hundreds of thousands were wedded with all the power of a burning appetite, awakened no more violence than they did? Why was it that so many good men, whose souls protested against the sacrifice of ease and privacy which these women made, bowed to the movement as something supremely Christian, and, therefore, veritably divine?

First, of course, because there was no man, however brutal, who did not know that the women were right—that whisky was a curse, not only to those who drank it, but to the unoffending who did not drink it. Every man felt that the action of the women was an embodiment and expression of the dictates of his own conscience. Approached in a way which disarmed all violent opposition, with an appeal to God and to all the manliness which he possessed, the vilest panderer to a debased appetite trembled not only before the pure embodied conscience without, but before the answering conscience within. He heard God's voice in the souls which approached him, and the same voice in his own soul. There was something terrible in this. A mob which would tear his house down, a descent of the officers of the law, the threats of outraged fathers and brothers, would only have stimulated his opposition, and given him an apology for continuing his crime; but this quiet appeal to his conscience, by those whose consciences he knew to be pure, was awful to him.

Second, the mind of man is so constituted as to feel most sensitively the praise and the blame of women. It is hard for any man to feel that he rests under the censure of all the good women by whom he is surrounded. The harshest words that were spoken against the crusaders were spoken by the women whom they found behind the bars they visited; and these poor creatures were speaking to win the approval of the brutal men they loved. A man who has not some woman, somewhere, who believes in him, trusts him and loves him, has reached a point where self-respect is gone. All men, who deserve the name of men, desire the respect of women; and when a man finds himself in a business which fixes upon him the disapproval of a whole community of women, a power is brought to bear upon him which he certainly cannot ignore, and which he finds it difficult to resist. The power of woman, simply as woman, has had too many illustrations in history to need further discussion here. A man's self-respect can only be nursed to its best estate in the approval of the finer sense and quicker conscience of the women who know him.

The third reason was that the end which these women sought was purely and beneficently a moral one. They were not after money, they did not pursue revenge, they did not seek political power or preferment, they worked in the interest of no party. All they desired, and all they labored for, was the reform and safety of their husbands, brothers, fathers and sons, and the extinction of those temptations and sources of temptation which endangered them. They bore no ill-will to the dram-seller, but the moment he relinquished his traffic, they covered him with their kindness and sympathy. They not only did not have the sympathy of party men, as such, but they were denied the sympathy of portions of the Christian Church. They pursued a much desired moral end by purely moral means. They sought nothing for themselves, but everything for the men they loved, and for the men that other women loved. The element of self-sacrifice was in it all. They went from peaceful home pursuits, from the retirement which was most congenial to them, from prayers where they begged for the blessing of heaven upon their enterprise, into the street, into foul dens of debauchery, into private expostulations with brutal men, into atmospheres reeking with ribaldry, and all to save others. No man with a spark of manliness in him—which, after all, is only godliness expressed in human character—could regard such a spectacle as that without being moved to admiration and reverence.

And now for the lesson which this crusade—now retired into history—teaches us. It will be a hard one for some women to learn, but a desire for the conservation of the best forces of society demands that it shall not only be stated, but heeded. The ballot, even when exercised in the right direction, has not yet, in any State, proved a cure for drunkenness. No law that has been enacted for the suppression of dram-selling, even in States where special constabulary machinery has been instituted for executing it, has done so much for the end sought as this crusade has done. In Massachusetts, the necessity of reform is as urgent as in New York. Does any one suppose that the moral power which the women wield to-day would be in their hands to wield if they held the ballot? Not a bit of it. They are strong because they are not political. They are strong because they have no party to serve, no personal ambitions to push, no selfish ends to seek. If the Western women had had the ballot, how long is it to be supposed that their crusade would have been without political leadership and political perversion? If these women had been the representatives of political power, how much toleration would they have received at the hands of those whose interests they imperiled or destroyed? What kind of treatment would an office-holder have had in their ranks? Would an office-holder have dared to be seen in their ranks at all? If woman had the ballot, such a crusade would simply have been impossible. To respond that it would have been unnecessary, is to trifle with the subject. Men would be obliged to execute whatever laws women might pass, under any circumstances, and they would execute the laws passed through the votes of women no better than they do their own.

Further, let it be witnessed, that the women who did the most of the work in that crusade never have asked for the ballot, and never will do so. They would regard the conferment of political suffrage upon them as a calamity, and it would undoubtedly be a calamity. It would rob them of their peculiar power—a power which all experience proves cannot be preserved too carefully. Woman cannot afford the ballot. It would tie her hands, weaken her influence, destroy her disinterestedness in the treatment of all public questions, and open into the beautiful realms of her moral power ten thousand streams of weakness and corruption. The woman who said that the crusade "meant the ballot," proved only by that speech how poorly qualified she was to use a ballot. She ought to have seen in the crusade something greater than the ballot—something almost infinitely above the poor machinery of politics—something by the side of which the ballot would be only a toy. The crusade did not mean the ballot; it meant that woman does not need the ballot, cannot afford to take the ballot, will not have the ballot; and on this conviction let all American society gratefully felicitate itself.

Provision for Wives and Children.

The disasters that have occurred in the business circles of New York during the last few months are full of practical suggestions, upon which the daily press has made abundant comment; but one of them has received but little notice—viz.: the effect of these disasters upon the families of the sufferers. These, with many dependents, were sharers in the prosperity of those who have gone down to poverty. They lived in fine houses, and had all the privileges which wealth bestowed. Many of these business men had wives, who had been helpers and household economists through all the years of early struggle, and who held a strong moral claim upon a portion of the wealth which they have seen swept away without the power to lift a finger or say a word in self-protection. In a day, they have seen the accumulations of years melt away, and themselves and their little ones made poor. The husband and father, with burdens too heavy to be borne in his office or his counting-room, goes to his home to be tortured with the spectacle of a straitened life, among those who are more precious to him than all his wealth had been. It is quite likely that he will find heroism and self-denial and cheerfulness there; but his pain will not be wholly cured by these, and he must always regret that when he had the power to secure a competence to his dependents he did not do it.

A large majority of the business men of New York carry a heavy life insurance; but this, at the very moment of the failure of any one of them, is not only no help to him, but, by its yearly demands upon his resources, a constant drag upon his efforts and prosperity. It may be, indeed, that he will be unable to keep up his yearly premiums, and so be obliged to sacrifice all that he has paid during the previous years. Life insurance makes a provision for his death, but none at all for a disaster that may destroy his power to provide for his family just as effectually as his removal from the world. His power even to keep his life insured goes with his power to make money, and thus his family is left helpless whether he live or die.

All men who deal in stocks, all who are in commercial or mercantile life, and all who are engaged in manufactures, have much at risk. Wars, revulsions, bad crops, capricious legislation, changes in the channels of trade, over-production—one or more of these, and other adverse causes, come in at unlooked-for seasons, and prove to them all that they hold their wealth by a very uncertain tenure. There is no man who does business at all who may not be ruined by a combination of circumstances that he can neither foresee nor control.

Now, we know of no way by which a man can protect his family but by taking a competent sum from his business and bestowing it upon them outright, and securing it to them, in the days of actual wealth and prosperity. A man who, by honest enterprise, has secured wealth, has the right to bestow it where he chooses. When such a man endows a seminary, or establishes a charity of any sort, we praise him. We acknowledge his right to do what he will with his own; and we ought not only to acknowledge his right to endow his family with the means of support, but insist that it is his duty to do so, even before he endows his seminary or establishes his charity.

There are two objections to this course, one of them coming from the man himself, and the other from the community. The man insists, either that he cannot spare the necessary sum from his business, or that he believes he can do better for his family by risking his all; while the community, trusting him, reckons among his means that which he seems to own, even when, in fact, it is owned by his wife, the transfer never having been publicly known. It is against the man's mistakes that we wish specially to protest. He has no moral right to risk his all, when its loss would make his family poor, provided he has more than enough to do a fair, safe business. This is the fatal blunder that nearly all men make. Their business grows, and its requirements grow, with their consent, or by their strenuous efforts. Large, superfluous wealth is their aim, and it is this inexcusable motive which prevents them from doing justice to their dependents. If they would abandon this aim, there would be nothing in the way of a wise and provident policy.

The objection on the part of the community is, under the present condition of affairs, a sound one; but a little legislation would set this aside. If the transfer of money or property to one's wife and family were legally required to be made as public as the gift of a considerable sum to a public institution is naturally made, there would be no difficulty in the matter. If, when a man endows his wife with property, the act could only be made legal by the publication of the fact, and by a public statement of the sum transferred, showing that his available capital had been reduced by that amount, the business community would be protected. We see no valid objection to this. There are many ways in which, for public reasons, the private affairs of a man are required to be made known, and there is nothing in this transaction which should exempt it from publicity. Rascality would avail itself of this privilege, without doubt, if it could; but the privilege may be protected by all the safeguards that legislation can throw around it. A man may be compelled to prove that he has the right to dispose of a portion of his estate in the way proposed, without prejudice to his creditors or the community. We write without any knowledge of what the laws are, but with a very distinct idea of what they may and ought to be. We are, at least, sure that there ought to be some way in which men of wealth may justly,—with every obligation to the community fairly considered,—protect their wives and little ones in the possession of a portion of their means honestly won; and we hope that those who are wise and powerful will see to it before new disasters come to plunge other families into ruin, and remind them of a duty too long neglected.

WOMAN AND HOME.

The New York Woman.

What kind of a being is the typical New York Woman? Our neighbors across the water evidently regard her as something very different from the typical Englishwoman; and they form their judgments not so much by what they know of the New York Woman at home, as by what they see of her abroad. They find her extravagant in her tastes, something more than self-assured in her bearing, "loud" in her dress, and superficial in her education and accomplishments—if she has any. Now we do not admit that a woman who can be thus characterized is the type of New York womanhood. The world does not hold better women, or better educated women, or better mannered women, than are to be found in great numbers in this much defamed city; but the Englishman does not see them, for they jealously guard their society when he comes here, and when they travel they are unobtrusive and do not attract his attention. The average traveling Englishman in New York knows just as little of the best society of New York as the average traveling American does of the best society of London.

Yet the Englishman has an apology in what he sees, and, perhaps, in all that he sees, for the severity of his judgment. There is a type of womanhood in New York—and it has, alas! far too many representatives—of which every American, everywhere, has reason to be ashamed. The same type can be found in all the large cities of the country, but it exists in its perfection here. It lives in hotels and boarding-houses; it travels, it haunts the fashionable watering-places; it is prominent at the opera and the ball; in short, it is wherever it can show itself and its clothes. It rejoices over a notice of itself in the *Evening Chatterbox*, or the *Weekly Milk and Water*, as among the proudest and most grateful of its social achievements. Its grand first question is: "Wherewithal shall I be clothed?" and when that is answered as well as it can be, the next is: "How and where can I show my clothes so as to attract the most men, distress the greatest number of women, and make the most stunning social sensation?" We have no fear of exaggerating in this characterization. We have seen these women at home and away; and their presumption, boldness, vanity, idleness, display, and lack of all noble and womanly aims are a disgrace to the city which produces them, and the country after whose name they call themselves.

Of course there is a sufficient cause for the production of this type of woman, and it is to be found in her circumstances and way of life. It is prevalent among the *nouveaux riches*—among those of humble beginnings and insufficient breeding and education. It is fostered in boarding-houses and hotels—those hot-beds of jealousy and personal and social rivalry and aimless idleness. The woman who finds herself housed and clothed and fed and petted and furnished with money for artificial as well as real wants, without the lifting of a finger, or the burden of a care, and without the culture of head or heart that leads her to seek for the higher satisfactions of womanhood, becomes in the most natural way precisely what we have described. It would be unnatural for her to become anything else. The simple truth is, that unless women have a routine of duty that diverts their thoughts from themselves, and gives them something to think of besides dress and the exhibition of it, they degenerate. The only cure for this that we know of is universal housekeeping. There is no man who can afford to pay a fair price for board, who cannot afford to keep house; and housekeeping, though it be never so humble, is the most natural and the healthiest office to which woman is ever called. There is no one thing that would do so much to elevate the type of New York womanhood as a universal secession from boarding-house and hotel life, and a universal entrance upon separate homes. Such a step would increase the stock of happiness, improve health of body and health of mind, and raise at once the standard of morals and manners.

The devil always finds work for idle hands to do, whether the hands belong to men or women; but American men are not apt to be idle. They are absorbed in work from early until late, and leave their idle wives, cooped up in rooms that cost them no care, to get rid of the lingering time as they can. Is it kind to do this, or is it cruel? If it is kind in its motives, it is cruel in its results. The whole system of boarding-house and hotel life is vicious. To live in public, to be on dress parade every day, to be always part and parcel of a gossiping multitude, to live aimlessly year after year, with thoughts concentrated upon one's person and one's selfish delights, to be perpetually without a routine of healthy duty, is to take the broadest and briefest road to the degradation of all that is admirable and lovable in womanhood. It is to make, by the most natural process, that gay, gaudy, loud, frivolous, pretentious, vain, intriguing, unsatisfied, and unhappy creature which the Englishman knows as "The New York Woman."

Dressing the Girls.

The complaint made by certain women, and by certain men on behalf of women, that the provisions for woman's education are not equal to those for the education of men, has about as much foundation as other complaints from the same sources, and has no more. If there are any institutions for educating young men that are better furnished and more efficient than Vassar and Mount Holyoke and Rutgers, and other colleges that could be mentioned, are for the education of young women, we do not know where they are located. The public school systems of every State of the Union open to both sexes every advanced department alike; and when we come to the highest class of private schools, the provisions made for girls are incomparably superior to those made for boys. We do not know of a single boys' school in the United States that is the equal in all respects of scores, if not hundreds, of schools devoted to the education and culture of young women. The model school for young women has become already the highest achievement of our civilization.

When we bring within four walls, beneath a single roof, from fifty to one hundred young women, who from year's end to year's end are in the constant society of the best teachers that money can procure; who are instructed in every branch of learning that they may desire, and are taught every fine art for which they have any aptitude; who are feasted with concerts and readings and social reunions, and are led into every walk of culture for which their richly-freighted time gives leisure; who move among tasteful appointments, and lodge in good rooms, and eat at bountiful tables, and are subjected to every purifying and refining influence that Christian love and thoughtfulness can bring to bear upon them, we are prepared to show about as strong a contrast to the average boy's school, academy, and college, as it is possible to imagine. Yet we paint no fancy picture. It is drawn from the literal reality. There are thousands of American young women in schools like this which we describe, supported there at an expense greater by from twenty-five to fifty per cent. than the average amount devoted to young men of corresponding ages in first-class institutions. It costs from one thousand to two thousand dollars a year to support a girl at these schools—including the expense of dress—and men all over the United States, who have the means to do it, are educating their daughters in this way and at this cost. The truth is, that there are no such provisions made for men as there are for women. They are obliged to get their education in cheaper schools and in a rougher way.

It is because the education of girls is so expensive and has become so much of a burden, that we write this article. To pay for a single girl's schooling and support at school a sum which is quite competent to support in comfort a small family —a sum greater than the average income of American families— is a severe tax on the best-filled purse. It can be readily seen, however, that the school itself neither receives nor makes too much money. The extraordinary expense for many girls is in the matter of dress. It is a shame to parents and daughters alike that there are a great many young women in American boarding-schools whose dress costs a thousand dollars a year, and even more than that sum. The effect of this over-dressing on the spirit and manners of those who indulge in it, as well as on those who are compelled to economical toilets, is readily apprehended by women, if not by men. This extravagant dressing is an evil which ought to be obviated in some way. How shall it be done? America is full of rich people—of people so freshly in the possession of money that they know of no way by which to express their wealth except through lavish display. They build fine houses, they buy showy equipages, and then burden themselves with dress and jewelry. Human nature in a young woman is, perhaps, as human as it is anywhere; and so there comes to be a certain degree of emulation or competition in dress among school-girls, and altogether too much thought is given to the subject,—to a subject which in school should absorb very little thought.

We know of but one remedy for this difficulty, and that is a simple uniform. We do not know why it is not just as well for girls to dress in uniform as for boys. There are many excellent schools in England where the girls dress in uniform throughout their entire education. We believe that a uniform dress is the general habit in Catholic schools everywhere. By dressing in uniform, the thoughts of all the pupils are released from the consideration of dress; there is no show of wealth, and no confession of poverty. Girls from widely-separated localities and classes come together, and stand or fall by scholarship, character, disposition, and manners. The term of study could be lengthened by the use of the money that would thus be saved; and while a thousand considerations favor such a change, we are unable to think of one that makes against it. There is no virtue and no amiable characteristic of young women that would not be relieved of a bane and nursed into healthy life by the abandonment of expensive dress at school. Who will lead the way in this most desirable reform?

Home and its Queen.

There are not many propositions, in this captious world and questioning age, that are permitted to pass unchallenged. It used to be supposed that Adam was the first man, but there are those who doubt it now. The solid democratic faith in universal suffrage is shaken in a multutide of minds by the facility with which the demagogue appropriates a popular privilege to his own corrupt purposes. Our good old Bible, out of which has come all that is worth anything in our civilization, and in which the most of us trust, has been the butt of the skeptic for centuries, and hears strange questions in these days from the lips of those who pretend to preach its truth. Still, two and two make four, the sun is larger than the earth, and we have yet to hear any man or woman deny that in the quality of the homes of the nation abides the nation's destiny. If these homes are nurseries of manly and womanly virtue, and schools of economy and prosperity, the natural outcome and expression of them will be a government of justice and freedom, and social institutions that shall be liberal and pure.

There is probably not an unperverted man or woman living who does not feel that the sweetest consolations and best rewards of life are found in the loves and delights of home. There are very few who do not feel themselves indebted to the influences that clustered around their cradles for whatever of good there may be in their characters and conditions. Home, based upon Christian marriage, is so evidently an institution of God, that a man must become profane before he can deny it. Wherever it is planted, there stands a bulwark of the State. Wherever it is pure, and true to the Christian idea, there lives an institution conservative of all the nobler interests of society. Of this realm woman is the queen. It takes its cue and its hue from her. If she is in the best sense womanly,—if she is true and tender, loving and heroic, patient and self-devoted,—she consciously or unconsciously organizes and puts in operation a set of influences that do more to mould the destiny of the nation than any man, uncrowned by power or eloquence, can possibly effect. The men of the nation are what their mothers make them, as a rule; and the voice which those men speak in the expression of their power is the voice of the women who bore and bred them. There can be no substitute for this. There is no other possible way in which the women of the nation can organize their influence and power that will tell so beneficently upon society and the State. Neither woman nor the nation can afford to have home demoralized, or in any way deteriorated by the loss of her presence, or the lessening of her influence there. As a nation we rise or fall as the character of our homes, presided over by woman, rises or falls; and the best gauge of our best prosperity is to be found in the measure by which these homes find multiplication in the land. In true marriage, and the struggle after the highest ideal of home life, is to be found the solution of more of the ugly problems that confront the present generation—moral, social, and political—than we have space to enumerate.

Thus far few will differ with us, we imagine; and further than this we do not care to go, except to say that whatever there may be in the schemes so industriously put forward for changing the position and sphere of woman which will tend to make home better, and its queen more modest and gentle and pure, shall have our earnest support. If an active competition with man in professional or mercantile life will fit woman for home life, and help to endow her with those virtues whose illustration is so essential to her best influence in the family, let her by all means engage in this competition. If the studies and apprenticeships necessary to make such a life as this successful are those which peculiarly fit women to be wives and mothers, and prepare them to preside over the homes of the people, let us change our educational institutions to meet the necessity, and do it at once. If woman's power over the ballot-box, now exercised by shaping the voter, and lifting the moral tone of the nation at home, will be made better and more unselfish by giving her a hand in political strife, and the chance for an office, let her vote by all means. If those virtues and traits of character which are universally recognized as womanly are nurtured by participation in public life—if woman grows more modest, sweet, truthful, and trustworthy by familiarity with political intrigues, or by engaging in public debates—if her home grows better and more influential for good in consequence of her absence from it, then we advocate without qualification her entrance upon public life at once, and demand that the broadest place shall be made for her. If the number of true marriages is to be increased by a policy that tends to make the sexes competitors with each other for the prizes of wealth and place, and secures to any marked degree their independence of each other, then let that policy be adopted.

This good, thus contingently specified, is the grand desideratum of our country and our time. Our suppositions involve questions of vital, paramount importance. They stand before and above all other questions connected with woman's work, woman's rights, and woman's future. They ought to be settled by a wise consideration and discussion; and we believe that when they shall be settled thus, all good men and women will find themselves upon a common platform, and the questions which agitate us now will have vanished.

AMUSEMENTS.

THEATRES AND THEATRE-GOING.

The recent discussion of the influence of theatres has brought up the old subject again, and called for a re-statement of what we regard as the true and rational position of the church upon the question. The radical mistake of the Protestant Church of this country is that lack of discrimination, in its condemnation of theatres, which has gone to the extreme of making that a sin in itself which is not a sin at all. To go to the theatre, for an evening's entertainment, is regarded by multitudes as a flagrant wrong. So wrong is it considered in itself, or so bad is it in example, that ministers are shut out of the theatre as a class, with sweeping completeness. For a clergyman to be seen in a theatre, is to compromise his position and influence. We know that many clergymen regard this as a hardship, for they have told us so; but their unwise predecessors have made the bed for them, and they are obliged to lie in it. The public opinion that has been generated in the church, by pulpit criticism and denunciation, has built a wall around the theatre so high that men holding responsible positions in the church cannot cross it.

For this position of the church, the stage itself is very largely responsible. The stage has always been under strong temptations to self-degradation. If it had always been pure;

if the amusements it has offered to the public had always been innocent; if it had not at one period of its history been a breeding place of vice; if it had not presented strong attractions to those who seek the society of lewd women; if profanity and poorly disguised obscenity had never had a place in the plays presented; if impure imaginations had not been cherished among the young by half nude dancing girls; in brief, if the animal nature—the lower nature—had not been addressed so persistently by those who have assumed the entertainment of the public, the church would never have taken the position that it has. It is not to be wondered at that the protest was strong, when the provocation was so shameless. The older men of the present day remember the horrible "Third Tier" of their youth. They remember, too, the *double entendre*, the polite profanity, the broad jest, that woke the disgusting cheers of "the pit." It is no justification of an institution that has arrogated to itself the title of "a school of morals," that it offered what was demanded, and what the public most willingly paid for. It was a part of the legitimate office of the stage to protect public morals and to educate the public into a pure taste. The enmity of the church toward the stage has not been without cause.

But the stage is better than it was, on the whole. We have vile theatres in New York, to-day—altogether too many of them—plays presented that degrade or vitiate the taste, and the morals of those who witness them—men and women on the boards who are base in character and life. On the other hand, we have theatres whose aims are high, and actors and actresses who have pride of personal character, and a desire and determination to hold their most interesting art to purity and respectability. These people—faithful husbands and wives, intellectual men and women, good fathers, mothers, maidens, friends and citizens—naturally chafe under the wholesale condemnation which the church visits upon them. We cannot blame them for this. We can only ask them to be patient with a state of things which a multitude of their predecessors and many of their contemporaries have helped to bring about. The church is gradually working toward their recognition, and they must give it time to move.

There was a time, and it was not long ago, when cards were banished from every Christian household. The older men and women of the church very well remember when a pack of cards found in a boy's trunk would be taken as proof that the devil had a very strong hold upon its owner. Millions of men and women have been bred to believe that card-playing was—with or without reason—a sin in itself. That time has passed away already, and the innocent little pasteboards have become a source of amusement in great multitudes of Christian families. Children never could see any reason in their exclusion, and the church is stronger in the child's mind for the change that has occurred. Billiards were once so associated with vicious resorts and vicious practices, that a man disgraced himself by appearing where they were. Now a billiard-table is in nearly every house that can afford one, and is purchased in many instances as a home-guardian of the morals of the boys. Novel-reading was once as thoroughly under ban as theatre-going. We remember the time when the novel-reader hid his books—read them when he ought to have been asleep—stole their charms on rainy days, in garrets or on hay-mows, and then passed them into the hands of some other sly thief of pleasure, who still passed them on, until they were worn out. Well, the first novels were poor. They gave false ideas of life, and were condemned *en masse* by the church; but the church found at an early day that it wanted novels for its own purposes. Now the great majority of Sunday-school books are novels of a religious sort, while every Christian library holds Scott and Dickens and Thackeray; and the public libraries and the reading-clubs, all over the land, find more readers for their novels than for any other class of books. They have become the sources of moral, political, and social instruction, as well as of general entertainment, within as well as without the church.

We allude to these sources of amusement and the great change that has occurred with regard to them, for the purpose of illustrating that which is certainly progressing in relation to the theatre. We have parlor theatricals, and they are recognized more and more as harmless and instructive amusements. We have dramatic exhibitions in our educational institutions. We go to the opera really for its music, but we are obliged to get this through the representation of the most vapid dramatic compositions that can be imagined. In short, we have acknowledged, in many ways, that the representation of a play is not wrong in itself, while our Christian travelers make their pilgrimages to Ober Ammergau to witness a play that degrades the great Christian tragedy to the commonplace of spectacular drama. The time is rapidly coming—provided, of course, that those who have the theatre in charge stand, as good men and women, by their obligations to the public, and uphold the dignity of their art—when Christians will seek amusement in their presence, from their performances; when they will discriminate between theatres as they do between novels, and when the premium of their presence and patronage will be offered to those who serve them conscientiously.

As a people, we have no such superfluity of amusements and recreations that we can afford to hold one under ban, that is in itself harmless and legitimate. We work under great pressure, and need much more recreation than we get. If a man thus pressed feels that a pure dramatic representation refreshes him, he ought to be at liberty to avail himself of it; and the time is certainly coming when he will do so. The histrionic art is as legitimate as any art, and any man or woman who practices it worthily and well, deserves our honor, —ay, our honor and our sympathy, for the art-life is a hard life to live under any circumstances. To be obliged to rely for a livelihood upon the plaudits of the multitude, and to be subject to the caprices of the press and the public, and the jealousies that are inseparable from all art-life, is a hardship from which the bravest man and woman may well shrink. If, among those who have so many temptations to strike a low key that they may at least please "the groundlings," there is a considerable number who appeal to the nobilities of human nature, let us give them our hands and help them to build up a pure taste in the public mind. We have only to remember that the theatre is with us, that it will stay, and that the church has a great responsibility concerning the stage of the future. If it supposes that condemning it at a street's length, and indiscriminately, will discharge its duty, it will find itself sadly mistaken.

The Struggle for Wealth.

No one can settle down in a European city or village for a month, and observe the laboring classes, without noticing a great difference between their aspirations, ambitions and habits, and those of corresponding classes in this country. He may see great poverty in a continental town, and men and women laboring severely and faring meanly, and a hopeless gap existing between classes; he may see the poor virtually the slaves of the rich; but he will witness a measure of contentment and a daily participation in humble pleasures to which his eyes have been strangers at home. There is a sad side to this pleasant picture. Much of this apparent contentment and enjoyment undoubtedly comes from the hopelessness of the struggle for anything better. An impassable gulf exists between them and the educated and aristocratic classes—a gulf which they have recognized from their birth; and, having recognized this, they have recognized their own limitations, and adapted themselves to them. Seeing just what they can do and cannot do, they very rationally undertake to get out of life just what their condition renders attainable. There is no far-off, crowning good for them to aim at; so they try to get what they can on the way. They make much of fête-days, and social gatherings, and music, and do what they can to sweeten their daily toil, which they know must be continued while the power to labor lasts.

In America it is very different. A humble backwoodsman sits in the presidential chair, or did sit there but recently; a tailor takes the highest honors of the nation; a canal-driver becomes a powerful millionaire; a humble school-teacher grows into a merchant prince, absorbing the labor and supplying the wants of tens of thousands. In city, state and national politics, hundreds and thousands may be counted of those who, by enterprise, and self-culture, and self-assertion, have raised themselves from the humblest positions to influence and place. There is no impassable gulf between the low and the high. Every man holds the ballot, and, therefore, every man is a person of political power and importance. The ways of business enterprise are many, and the rewards of success are munificent. Not a year, nor, indeed, a month, passes by, that does not illustrate the comparative ease with which poor men win wealth or acquire power.

The consequence is that all but the wholly brutal are after some great good that lies beyond their years of toil. The European expects always to be a tenant; the American intends before he dies to own the house he lives in. If city prices forbid this, he goes to the suburbs for his home. The European knows that life and labor are cheap, and that he cannot hope to win by them the wealth which will realize for him the dream of future ease; the American finds his labor dear, and its rewards comparatively bountiful, so that his dream of wealth is a rational one. He, therefore, denies himself, works early and late, and bends his energies, and directs those of his family into profitable channels, all for the great good that beckons him on from the far-off, golden future.

The typical American never lives in the present. If he indulges in a recreation, it is purely for health's sake, and at long intervals, or in great emergencies. He does not waste money on pleasure, and does not approve of those who do so. He lives in a constant fever of hope and expectation, or grows sour with hope deferred or blank disappointment. Out of it all grows the worship of wealth and that demoralization which results in unscrupulousness concerning the methods of its acquirement. So America presents the anomaly of a laboring class with unprecedented prosperity and privileges, and unexampled discontent and discomfort.

There is surely something better than this. There is something better than a life-long sacrifice of content and enjoyment for a possible wealth, which, however, may never be acquired, and which has not the power, when won, to yield its holder the boon which he expects it to purchase. To withhold from the frugal wife the gown she desires, to deny her the journey which would do so much to break up the monotony of her home-life, to rear children in mean ways, to shut away from the family life a thousand social pleasures, to relinquish all amusements that have a cost attached to them, for wealth which may or may not come when the family life is broken up forever—surely this is neither sound enterprise nor wise economy. We would not have the American laborer, farmer and mechanic become improvident, but we would very much like to see them happier than they are, by resort to the daily social enjoyments which are always ready to their hand. Nature is strong in the young, and they will have society and play of some sort. It should remain strong in the old, and does remain strong in them, until it is expelled by the absorbing and subordinating passion for gain. Something of the Old World fondness for play, and daily or weekly indulgence in it, should become habitual among our workers. Toil would be sweeter if there were a reward at the end of it; work would be gentler when used as a means for securing a pleasure which stands closer than an old age of ease; character would be softer and richer and more childlike, when acquired among genial, every-day delights. The all-subordinating strife for wealth, carried on with fearful struggles and constant self-denials, makes us petty, irritable and hard. When the whole American people have learned that a dollar's worth of pure pleasure is worth more than a dollar's worth of anything else under the sun; that working is not living, but only the means by which we win a living; that money is good for nothing except for what it brings of comfort and culture; and that we live not in the future, but the present, they will be a happy people—happier and better than they have been. "The morrow shall take thought for the things of itself," may not be an accepted maxim in political economy, but it was uttered by the wisest being that ever lived in the world, whose mission it was to make men both good and happy.

SUMMER PLAY.

There are few sadder things in life than the dying out of the impulse and disposition to play. A man begins life with an overflow of vitality and animal spirits which makes him bright, genial and playful. He sympathizes with children, and even with the brutes, in their playful moods, enjoys society, and engages on all favorable occasions in recreative exercise of the body and amusements of the mind. Then comes the struggle for competency or wealth, and for twenty years, while his children are young, he works, settling more and more hopelessly into routine, until his competency or wealth is won, when he wakes to the fact that his impulse to play and his power to enjoy it are gone. He finds that he has lost his sympathy with youth, that he regards their pursuits as frivolous and tiresome, and that there is no interest in life to him except in daily toil, and in the quiet fireside rest which follows it, uninterrupted by social intrusions from without, or social duties that call him forth from his retirement.

What New York would become without its summer recreations we cannot imagine. The heat of the summer months, which not only dries up trade, but drives every man, woman and child beyond its limits who has the means to leave them, is the one saving power of city life. It is the play of the summer, the enforced idleness, the necessity of filling with amusement the lingering days, which keep the whole city from going on to perfect wreck. The steady strain of nine months' business, the feverish anxieties of trade, the overtaxation of mind and body, the wearying round of social assemblies, if kept up through the whole year, would drive men mad or crush them into the grave. We have no doubt that people in the country wonder why New Yorkers are willing to leave their splendid and commodious houses, and submit to the numberless inconveniences and inferior fare of way-side places. They would have but to spend one active winter in the city to understand it all. They would then know how precious the privilege would be to flee from hot sidewalks and burning walls, and the ceaseless din of wheels, and lie down, care-free, in the country silence, beneath an apple-tree, or a maple, with the fresh green earth around and the wide blue heaven above them.

It is of the greatest importance to those who have the privilege of leaving the city in the summer that they go where they may be free, and where real play may be unrestricted by any of the conventionalities of society. There is no objection to the filling up of the fashionable watering-places by fashionable people who have nothing to do the whole year round but to play. There are enough of these to populate Newport and Saratoga and Long Branch, and there will be enough of those who are amused for a little time by looking at them to keep the hotels full; but the well-to-do working men and women can do infinitely better for themselves and their children than to seek dwellings in such places for the summer. What they want is liberty, away from the centres of observation, where they can dress as they choose and do what they like. The very soul of play is liberty, and there can be no true recreation without it.

Nothing can be more cruel and nothing more foolish than to place children where they must be dressed every day in fresh and fashionable clothes, and their freedom to play curtailed for the sake of appearances. What childhood needs is perfect freedom among the things of nature—freedom to romp, to make mud-pies, to leap fences, to row, to fish, to climb trees, to chase butterflies, to gather wild-flowers, to live out of doors from morning until night, and to do all those things that innocent and healthy childhood delights in, in cheap, strong clothes provided for the purpose. Exactly that which childhood needs, manhood and womanhood needs—perfect liberty and perfect carelessness. So, whether the dweller by the sea go inland for his summer play, or the resident of the inland city go to the sea, he should seek some spot unvisited by those devoted to fashionable display, and pass his time in unrestricted communion with nature, and in those pursuits and amusements which, without let or hinderance, perform the office of recreation.

It is pleasant to think of these hundreds of thousands who scatter out into the country like spray beaten off from the city walls by the waves of summer. The weary men of study or of business, the tired women, the pale children—how they will dream and wander and rest! Thousands of greedy eyes will drink in the freshness and beauty of the sea by day, and sleep through its nightly lullaby. They will bathe in its waters, and sail upon its bosom, and live and grow strong upon its treasured life. Other thousands will take themselves to some quiet country village, with pleasant social surroundings, and with village bells to make Sunday-morning music for them. Still other thousands will climb the hills, or roam through the woods. There will be fishing by day and floating for deer at night among the Adirondacks, or among the forests of Maine. Every inland and ocean steamer will bear some of them. Every railroad train will be used in their service. It is the great play-time of city life. The farmer has his rest and recreation in winter; the citizen, only in the summer.

While it is pleasant to think of all this play—it is sad to think of those who are by necessity kept at home. For those there is the park, the most beautiful pleasure-ground in the world—if they will but use it—and the bay, over which the boats are pushing all the time. An excursion is an every-day affair, and the country and the sea are at the very doors of us all. And for the poor children—we have seen what a single newspaper has done and can do for them. The provision for them made once should be made again and again on an enlarged scale, so that no poor, tired dweller on Manhattan Island may be compelled to pass the summer without one day of freedom and privilege on the fresh sea or the green and odor-breathing shore.

Novel-Reading.

The novel has become, for good or for evil, the daily food of the civilized world. It is given to youngest childhood in Mother Goose and other extravagant and grotesque inventions, it is placed in the hands of older childhood and youth through the distributing agencies of a hundred thousand publishing houses and Sunday-school libraries, and prepared for the eyes of the adult world by every magazine and weekly newspaper that finds its way into Christian homes. Among all peoples and all sorts of people, of every age and of every religious and social school, it is the only universally accepted form of literature. History, poetry, philosophy, science, social ethics and religion are accepted respectively by classes of readers, larger or smaller; but the novel is read by multitudes among all these classes, and by the great multitudes outside of them, who rarely look into anything else. The serial novel is now an invariable component of the magazine in America and England; the French *feuilleton* has been so long established as to be regarded as a necessary element in the newspaper; while in Germany, the land of scholars and philosophers and scientific explorers, the story-tellers are among the most ingenious and prolific in the world.

It all comes of the interest which the human mind takes in human life. If history and biography are less read than the novel, it is because the life found in them is less interesting or in a less interesting form. The details of individual experience and of social life are far more engaging to ordinary minds than the proceedings of parliaments and the intercourse of nations. From these latter the life of the great masses is far removed. The men and women whom one meets at a social gathering, and the dramatic by-play and personal experience of such an occasion, will absorb a multitude of minds far beyond the proceedings of a Board of Arbitration that holds in its hands the relations of two great nations, and possibly the peace of the world.

The daily life of the people is not in politics, or philosophy, or religious discussion. They eat and drink, they buy and sell, they lose and gain, they love and hate, they plot and counterplot; their lives are filled with doubts and fears and hopes, and realizations or disappointments of hope; and when they read, they choose to read of these. It is in these experiences that all classes meet on common ground, and this is the ground of the novel. In truth, the novel is social history, personal biography, religion, morals, and philosophy, realized or idealized, all in one. Nay, more: it is the only social history we have. If the social history of the last hundred years in England and America has not been written in the novels of the last fifty, it has not been written at all. In the proportion that these novels have been accepted and successful have their plots, characters, spirit, properties and belongings been taken from real life. There is no form of literature in which the people have been more inexorably determined to have truthfulness than in that of fiction. History, under the foul influence of partisanship, has often won success by lying, but fiction never. Under the inspirations of ideality, it has presented to us some of the very purest forms of truth which we possess.

So universally accepted is the novel that it has become one of the favorite instruments of reform. If a great wrong is to be righted, the sentiments, convictions and efforts of the people are directed against it through the means of a novel. It is mightier to this end than conventions, speeches, editorials and popular rebellions. If a social iniquity is to be uncovered that it may be cured, the pen of the novelist is the power employed. The adventurer, the drunkard, the libertine, the devotee of fashion and folly, are all punctured and impaled by the same instrument, and held up to the condemnation or contempt of the world. At the same time, we are compelled to look to our novels rather than to our histories and biographies for our finest and purest idealizations of human character and human society. There is nothing more real and nothing more inspiring in all history and cognate literature, than the characters which fiction, by the hands of its masters, has presented to the world.

There was a time when the church was afraid of the novel; and it is not to be denied that there are bad novels—novels which ought not to be read, and which are read simply because there are people as bad as the novels are; but the church itself is now the most industrious producer of the novel. It is found next to impossible to induce a child to read anything but stories; and therefore the shelves of our Sunday-school libraries are full of them. These stories might be better, yet they undoubtedly contain the best presentation of religious truth that has been made to the infantile mind. The pictures of character and life that are to be found in a multitude of these books cannot fail of giving direction and inspiration to those for whom they are painted. Among much that is silly and preposterous and dissipating, there is an abundance that is wholesome and supremely valuable. Religious novels, too, have become a large and tolerably distinct class of books, of very wide acceptance and usefulness in the hands of men and women. The church, least of all estates, perhaps, could now afford to dispense with the novel, because it is found that the novel will be produced and universally consumed.

The trash that is poured out by certain portions of the press will continue to be produced, we suppose, while it finds a market. The regret is that such stuff can find a market, but tastes will be crude and morals low in this imperfect world for some time to come. Let us be comforted in the fact that sensuality tires, that there is education indirect if not direct in coarse art, and that there will naturally come out of this large eating of trash a desire for more solid food. A long look at the yellow wearies, and then the eye asks for blue. If we look back upon our own experience, we shall doubtless find that we demand a very different novel now from that which formerly satisfied or fascinated us, and that we ourselves have passed through a process of development which helps us to pronounce as trash much that formerly pleased us. Let us hope for the world that which we have realized for ourselves.

Winter Amusements.

One of the most puzzling questions which parents have to deal with is that which relates to the amusements of their children, and especially of those among them who have reached young manhood and young womanhood. The most of us are too apt to forget that we have once been young, and that, while we are tired enough with our daily work to enjoy our evenings in quiet by our firesides, the young are overflowing with vitality, which must have vent somewhere. The girls and young women particularly, who cannot join in the rough sports of the boys, have, as a rule, a pretty slow time of it. They go to parties when invited; but parties are all alike, and soon become a bore. A healthy social life does not consist in packing five hundred people in a box, feeding them with ices, and sending them home with aching limbs, aching eyes, and a first-class chance for diphtheria. But the young must have social life. They must have it regularly; and how to have it satisfactorily—with freedom, without danger to health of body and soul, with intellectual stimulus and growth—is really one of the most important of social questions.

It is not generally the boy and the girl who spend their days in school who need outside amusement or society. They get it, in large measure, among their companions, during the day; and, as their evenings are short, they get along very comfortably with their little games and their recreative reading. It is the young woman who has left school and the young man who is preparing for life, in office or counting-room, in the shop or on the farm, who need social recreation which will give significance to their lives, and, at the same time, culture to their minds. If they fail to unite culture with their recreations, they never get it. It is not harsh to say that nine young men in every ten go into life without any culture. The girls do better, because, first, they take to it more naturally, and, second, because, in the absence of other worthy objects of life, this is always before them and always attainable. The great point, then, is to unite culture with amusement and social enjoyment. Dancing and kindred amusements are well enough in their time and way, but they are childish. There must be something better; there is something better.

It is an easy thing to establish, either in country or city

neighborhoods, the reading-club. Twenty-five young men and women of congenial tastes, habits, and social belongings can easily meet in one another's houses, once during every week, through five or six months of the year. With a small fund they can buy good books, and, over these, read aloud by one and another of their number, they can spend an hour and a half most pleasantly and profitably. They will find in these books topics of conversation for the remainder of the time they spend together. If they can illuminate the evening with music, all the better. Whatever accomplishments may be in the possession of different members of the club may be drawn upon to give variety to the interest of the occasion. This is entirely practicable, everywhere. It is more profitable than amateur theatricals, and less exhaustive of time and energy. It can be united with almost any literary object. The "Shakspere-Club" is nothing but a reading-club, devoted to the study of a single author; and Shakspere may well engage a club for a single winter. Such a club would cultivate the art of good reading, which is one of the best and most useful of all accomplishments. It would cultivate thought, imagination, taste. In brief, the whole tendency of the reading-club is toward culture—the one thing, notwithstanding all our educational advantages, the most deplorably lacking in the average American man and woman.

There was a time when the popular lecture was a source not only of amusement but of culture—when it stimulated thought, developed healthy opinion, conveyed instruction, and elevated the taste. The golden days when Sumner, Everett and Holmes, Starr King and Professor Mitchell, Bishop Huntington and Bishop Clark, Beecher and Chapin, Emerson, Curtis, Taylor and Phillips, were all actively in the field, were days of genuine progress. Few better things could happen to the

American people than the return of such days as those were; and the "lecture system," as it has been called, is declining in its usefulness and interest, simply because it has not men like these to give it tone and value. A few of the old set linger in the field, but death, old age, and absorbing pursuits have withdrawn the most of them. The platform is not what it was. The literary trifler, the theatrical reader, the second or third rate concert, have dislodged the reliable lecture-goers; and the popular lecture will certainly be killed if bad management can kill it. The standard has not been raised or even maintained; it has been lowered—lowered specially, and with direct purpose, to meet the tastes of the vulgar crowd.

Well, the young people, in whose hands the "lecture system" has always been, can mend all this, if they consider it worth the pains. Certainly, the coming into contact with a thoroughly vitalized man of brains is a very stimulating experience. The privilege of doing so should not be lightly relinquished; and, whenever a course of lectures is well conducted, it ought to meet with a generous patronage from all who have young people on their hands to be entertained and improved.

But even the lecture, desirable as it is, is not necessary. In a city like New York, there ought to be five hundred clubs of young people, established for the purposes of social and intellectual amusement, with culture in view as the great ultimate end. The exercises may take a great many forms which it is not necessary for us even to suggest. Books may be read, original papers may be presented, musical rehearsals may form a part of the entertainment, products of art may be exhibited, there may be dramatic and conversational practice, and practice in French and German. There is no limit to the variety of exercises that may be profitably entered upon. And what is good for the young people of the great cities will be just as good for young people everywhere.

A Word for Our Wanderers.

There is a great deal of private, and a measure of public, fault-finding with the fact that multitudes of our American people go abroad to spend their time and money. We have forgotten the number of millions which it is calculated are spent in going up and down, and walking to and fro, in Europe—frittered away on gewgaws, invested in silks which neither pay a revenue to the Government nor a profit to the American shop-keepers, expended on foreign steamers in the outward and homeward passages, etc., etc. It never occurs to the growlers, we presume, that we are getting from the other side, all the time, more than we send over there. In the first place, there are always here, with annually increasing numbers, a considerable throng of tourists who spend liberally. They are nearly all of the richer class; for America is not a country in which a foreigner can live more cheaply than he can at home. Of course this class cannot offset the throng we annually send to Europe and steadily support there, but every incoming vessel brings its tribute of immigrants, who come here to remain. We have no statistics, but it must be true that these, who bring all their worldly possessions, import, in the aggregate, an amount far surpassing what we export among our travelers. We send by fifties, they come by thousands. They come with their little hoards accumulated through frugal generations, and these little hoards amount, in a single year, to a very large sum. But they bring something better than money—life and industry. Every man and woman, as a rule, is an addition to the productive capital of the country. How incalculably large have been the contributions of the immigrant to the wealth, the greatness, and the comfort of America! The immigrant has dug all our canals, built all our railroads, and been the burden-bearer in all enterprises requiring brawn and bone.

There are nine chances in ten that the person who cooks what we eat, waits upon us at table, milks the cow, hoes the corn, drives the coach, grooms the horse, mows the hay, mans the vessel, digs the ditch, spins the cotton, washes the clothes and makes the bed, is a foreigner. Indeed, it is more than probable that a full moiety of all the money which Americans spend abroad is won from the profits on foreign labor. It is well enough to remember this, and not to grudge the money which buys abroad so much pleasure, instruction, and health for our weary and over-worked people.

There is another class of fault-finders who have their little fling at the wanderers—a fling somewhat worn by long use, but still quite effective when employed against, or among, the thoughtless. The stay-at-homes need something, of course, to console them, and to keep themselves in countenance; and we hear from their wise lips such utterances as these: "They had much better stay at home and travel in their own country than to go to Europe." "I should be ashamed to go to Europe until I had seen something of America." "If I hadn't seen Niagara, or the Mammoth Cave, or the Mississippi River, I should be ashamed to travel abroad." Any one of these wise statements, flung at a man's head, is regarded as sufficient to settle him if he is a wanderer abroad, and happens not to have been a great traveler at home. It is supposed, indeed, to decide the whole matter—to condemn the man who travels into foreign lands, and justify the man who sticks to his own door-yard and does not travel anywhere.

Well, travel in one's own country is very desirable, if a man has the time and can afford the expense and the hardship; but for a New Yorker to go to Niagara involves the travel of nine hundred miles out and back by rail. To see Chicago or any of the Western cities costs two thousand miles of travel. To see the Yosemite involves six thousand miles of travel. There is not a great object of natural interest in the country a sight of which does not cost a great deal of money and a great deal of fatigue. To go to the Far West, to climb the Colorado Mountains, or to visit any of the great objects of natural curiosity in that region, involves hardship that ladies particularly, unless exceptionally rugged, cannot endure at all. And when we have seen all, what have we seen? Grand things, to be sure--wonderful works of nature—and nothing else. Our cities are new, and with a brief history, confined almost entirely to the details of their quick material development. We see everywhere the beginnings of the life of a great nation, and they bear a striking resemblance to each other.

Now, when a man finds himself with money to spend, he likes to go where he can get the most for it. He takes himself and his family to Europe, and finds himself everywhere on historic ground. He can hardly travel twenty-five miles without meeting with something—some majestic river, some castle, some old cathedral, some gallery of art, some palace, some ancient battle-ground—which charms his attention. To the traveler, London is a vast store-house of historic associations. Cheapside, the Strand, Piccadilly, Threadneedle street —all these are names just as familiar to him as Broadway; and a hundred names of literary men, statesmen, poets, philosophers, are associated with them. Westminster Abbey is a place to meditate and weep in. To sit down in this stately and hallowed pile is to sit down with the worthiest of fifty generations. The Tower, the great Museum, the picture galleries, the ten thousand other objects of interest, compel the traveler to feel that he is in another world, to whose wealth almost countless generations have contributed. Scotland is like fairy-land to him. He walks over the territory where Sir Walter walked. His lungs inhale the same air, his eyes look upon the same hills, and valleys, and streams that inspired the Wizard. He crosses the Channel into sunny France, the land of the vine. He finds a new people, with another language, other traditions, another civilization. He reaches its beautiful capital, visits its wonderful churches, traverses the Louvre day after day until his mind is surfeited with beauty, mingles with the gay life upon the Champs Elysées and the Boulevards, rides in the Bois, goes to Fontainebleau and Versailles and all the beautiful environs, no one of which is without its special historic interest, or its treasury of art or architecture.

From France he goes to Switzerland, a country containing the most interesting natural scenery, perhaps, in the world, and all fitted up for exhibition. The smoothest roads sweep over the highest mountain-passes. There are guides ready and competent for every possible expedition; mules saddled and bridled, and ready to bear the traveler anywhere. The hotels are perfection, and every provision is made for comfort. There are thousands of travelers, representing all nationalities, who are never-failing subjects of interest and amusement. And there are the Matterhorn, and the Jungfrau, and Mont Blanc! There is but one Switzerland in the world. One can stand in its sunny vineyards and gaze upon fields of everlasting snow. One can sit in the comfort or luxury of his hotel, and watch the mountains as they change at sunset from jagged brown and shining white to purple cloud, and from purple cloud to some celestial semblance of a cloud, until he feels that he has reached the spiritual meaning of it all, and has learned something of the secrets of the other world.

From Switzerland he goes to Italy. He lingers among the lakes, he pauses in Genoa, climbs the tower at Pisa, sails some bright morning into the Bay of Naples, with Vesuvius smoking on his right, and the beautiful city fronting him like a vision of heaven, after the long tossing on the bosom of a bluer Mediterranean than he ever before dreamed of. He visits Pompeii asleep on one side of the bay, and Baiæ, the old watering-place of the Romans, quite as soundly asleep on the other. He eats oranges in Sorrento, and wishes he could stay there forever; and then he goes to Rome—to St. Peter's, to the galleries, to the Coliseum, to the marvelous churches, to the Catacombs, and finds that it would take years to exhaust what it holds for him of interest and instruction. He glides in the moonlight over the grand canal in Venice, wanders through the Doge's palace, mounts the Campanile, and thinks by day and dreams by night of the old life, the old commerce, the old and dying civilization. He visits the marble-flowering garden at Milan, passing beautiful old cities, always leaving behind unseen more than he sees, and still he has all Germany, Russia, Norway, Sweden, Austria, and Spain left.

But he has spent a year, and got more pleasure for his money, more priceless memories, more useful knowledge, more culture in language, and manners, and art than it would be possible for him to get at home in fifty years. This may be "treason;" and, if it is, we hope it will be "made the most of." The truth is, our country is young. Our architecture is new and raw, our galleries of art are yet to be created, and nothing among us has retired so far into the past that a halo of romance has gathered over it. To stand in a foreign church or cathedral, and remember that it was old when our country was discovered, is to realize how young our nation is. It is not natural scenery that our wanderers go to see, though that is not lacking. It is the objects of human interest that they seek—the records of old civilization with which every city is crowded, and which look down from pathetic ruins or time-defying towers, from every hill-top and mountain. The tide of foreign travel cannot be diverted from these by all the croaking in the world, and ought not to be.

THE TEMPERANCE QUESTION.

THE LIQUOR INTEREST.

Tramp, tramp, tramp, the boys are marching: how many of them? Sixty thousand! Sixty full regiments, every man of which will, before twelve months shall have completed their course, lie down in the grave of a drunkard! Every year during the past decade has witnessed the same sacrifice; and sixty regiments stand behind this army ready to take its place. It is to be recruited from our children and our children's children. "Tramp, tramp, tramp"—the sounds come to us in the echoes of the footsteps of the army just expired; tramp, tramp, tramp—the earth shakes with the tread of the host now passing: tramp, tramp, tramp, comes to us from the camp of the recruits. A great tide of life flows resistlessly to its death. What in God's name are they fighting for? The privilege of pleasing an appetite, of conforming to a social usage, of filling sixty thousand homes with shame and sorrow, of loading the public with the burden of pauperism, of crowding our prison-houses with felons, of detracting from the productive industries of the country, of ruining fortunes and breaking hopes, of breeding disease and wretchedness, of destroying both body and soul in hell before their time.

The prosperity of the liquor interest, covering every department of it, depends entirely on the maintenance of this army. It cannot live without it. It never did live without it. So long as the liquor interest maintains its present prosperous condition, it will cost America the sacrifice of sixty thousand men every year. The effect is inseparable from the cause. The cost to the country of the liquor traffic is a sum so stupendous that any figures which we should dare to give would convict us of trifling. The amount of life absolutely destroyed, the amount of industry sacrificed, the amount of bread transformed into poison, the shame, the unavailing sorrow, the crime, the poverty, the pauperism, the brutality, the wild waste of vital and financial resources, make an aggregate so vast—so incalculably vast—that the only wonder is that the American people do not rise as one man and declare that this great curse shall exist no longer. Dilettante conventions are held on the subject of peace, by men and women who find it necessary to fiddle to keep themselves awake. A hue-and-cry is raised about woman-suffrage, as if any wrong which may be involved in woman's lack of the suffrage could be compared to the wrongs attached to the liquor interest!

Does any sane woman doubt that women are suffering a thousand times more from rum than from any political disability?

The truth is that there is no question before the American people to-day that begins to match in importance the temperance question. The question of American slavery was never anything but a baby by the side of this; and we prophesy that within ten years, if not within five, the whole country will be awake to it, and divided upon it. The organizations of the liquor interest, the vast funds at its command, the universal feeling among those whose business is pitted against the national prosperity and the public morals—these are enough to show that, upon one side of this matter, at least, the present condition of things and the social and political questions that lie in the immediate future are apprehended. The liquor interest knows there is to be a great struggle, and is preparing to meet it. People both in this country and in Great Britain are beginning to see the enormity of this business—are beginning to realize that Christian civilization is actually poisoned at its fountain, and that there can be no purification of it until the source of the poison is dried up.

The country is to be sincerely congratulated on the fact that the wine interest of the United States does not promise much. Little native wine, after all our painstaking, finds its way to a gentleman's table. The California wines are a disappointment and a failure, and the Western wines are the same. Neither the dry nor the sparkling Catawba takes the place of anything imported. They are not popular wines, and we congratulate the country that they never can be. The lager beer interest is endeavoring, in convention, to separate itself from the whisky interest, claiming to be holier and more respectable than that. They are all to be lumped together. They are all opposed to sobriety, and, in the end, we shall find them all fighting side by side for existence against the determined indignation of a long-suffering people.

A respectable English magazine reports, as a fact of encouraging moment, that of the fifty thousand clergymen of the Church of England as many as four thousand actually abstain from the use of spirits! So, eleven-twelfths of the clergymen of the English Church consent to be dumb dogs on the temperance question! How large the proportion of wine-drinking clergymen may be in this country we do not know, but we do know that a wine-glass stops the mouth on the subject of temperance, whoever may hold it. A wine-drinking clergyman is a soldier disarmed. He is not only not worth a straw in the fight; he is a part of the *impedimenta* of the temperance army. We have a good many such to carry, who ought to be ashamed of themselves, and who very soon will be. Temperance laws are being passed by the various Legislatures, which they must sustain, or go over, soul and body, to the liquor interest and influence. Steps are being taken on behalf of the public health, morals, and prosperity, which they must approve by voice and act, or they must consent to be left behind and left out. There can be no concession and no compromise on the part of temperance men, and no quarter to the foe. The great curse of our country and our race must be destroyed.

Meantime, the tramp, tramp, tramp sounds on,—the tramp of sixty thousand yearly victims. Some are besotted and stupid, some are wild with hilarity and dance along the dusty way, some reel along in pitiful weakness, some wreak their mad and murderous impulses on one another, or on the helpless women and children whose destinies are united to theirs, some stop in wayside debaucheries and infamies for a moment, some go bound in chains from which they seek in vain to wrench their bleeding wrists, and all are poisoned in body and soul, and all are doomed to death. Wherever they move, crime, poverty, shame, wretchedness and despair hover in awful shadows. There is no bright side to the picture. We forget: there is just one. The men who make this army get rich. Their children are robed in purple and fine linen, and live upon dainties. Some of them are regarded as respectable members of society, and they hold conventions to protect their interests! Still the tramp, tramp, tramp goes on, and before this article can see the light, five thousand more of our poisoned army will have hidden their shame and disgrace in the grave.

The Delusions of Drink.

King Solomon has the credit of being the wisest man that ever lived: and he declared that he who is deceived by wine, the mocker, and strong drink, the raging, is *not* wise. The delusions of drink are as old as drink itself, and are as prevalent now as in Solomon's time. There are men who honestly believe that alcoholic drink is good for them; yet there is not one of them who would touch it except as a prescribed medicine if it were not for its pleasant taste. The delusion touching its healthfulness grows out of the desire to justify an appetite which may either be natural or acquired. If a man likes whisky or wine, he likes to think that it is good for him, and he will take some pains to prove that it is so, both to himself and others.

Now, alcohol is a pure stimulant. There is not so much nutriment in it as there is in a chip. It never added anything to the permanent forces of life, and never can add anything. Its momentary intensification of force is a permanent abstraction of force from the drinker's capital stock. All artificial excitants bring exhaustion. The physicians know this, and the simplest man's reason is quite capable of comprehending it. If any man supposes that daily drink, even in small quantities, is conducive to his health, he is deluded. If he possesses a sluggish temperament, he may be able to carry his burden without much apparent harm, but burden it is, and burden it will always be.

After a man has continued moderate drinking long enough, then comes a change—a demand for more drink. The old quantity does not suffice. The powers which have been insensibly undermined, clamor, under the pressure of business, for increased stimulation. It is applied, and the machine starts off grandly; the man feels strong, his form grows portly, and he works under constant pressure. Now he is in a condition of great danger, but the delusion is upon him that he is in no danger at all. At last, however, drink begins to take the place of food. His appetite grows feeble and fitful. He lives on his drink, and, of course, there is but one end to this —viz.: death! It may come suddenly, through the collapse of all his powers, or through paralysis, or it may come slowly through atrophy and emaciation. His friends see that he is killing himself, but he cannot see it at all. He walks in a delusion from his early manhood to his death.

A few weeks ago one of our city physicians publicly read a paper on the drinking habits of women. It was a thoughtful paper, based on a competent knowledge of facts. It ought to have been of great use to those women of the city who are exposed to the dangers it portrayed, and especially to those who have acquired the habits it condemned. Soon afterward there appeared in the columns of a daily paper a protest from a writer who ought to be a good deal more intelligent than he is, against the doctor's conclusions. The health and physique of the beer-drinking Englishwoman were placed over against the health and physique of the water-drinking American women, to the disadvantage of the latter. The man is deluded. It is not a year since Sir Henry Thompson, one of the most eminent medical men in England,—a man notoriously beyond the reach of any purely Christian considerations,—declared against the beer-drinking of England on strictly sanitary grounds. Our littérateur declares that the Englishwoman can outwalk her American sister. That depends entirely upon the period of life when the task is undertaken. The typical Englishwoman who has stood by the beer diet until she is more than forty years old, is too fat to walk anywhere easily out of doors, or gracefully within.

During our late civil war this matter of drinking for health's sake was thoroughly tried. A stock of experience and observation was acquired that ought to have lasted for a century. Again and again, thousands and thousands of times, was it proved that the man who drank nothing was the better man. He endured more, he fought better, he came out of the war healthier than the man who drank. Nothing is more easily demonstrable than that the liquor used by the two armies, among officers and men alike, was an unmitigated curse to them. It disturbed the brains and vitiated the councils of the officers, and debilitated and demoralized the men. Yet all the time the delusion among officers and men was, that there were both comfort and help in whisky.

The delusions of drink are numberless, but there is one of them which stands in the way of reform so decidedly that it calls for decided treatment. We allude to the notion that it is a nice thing to drink nice liquors or wines at one's home, to offer them to one's friends, and to make them minister to good fellowship at every social gathering, while it is a very different thing to drink bad liquor, in bad places, and in large quantities. A man full of good wine feels that he has a right to look with contempt upon the Irishman who is full of bad whisky. It is not a long time since the election of a professor in a British university was opposed solely on the ground that he neither drank wine nor offered it to his friends; and when, by a small majority, his election was effected, the other professors decided not to recognize him socially. There are thus two men whom these sticklers for wine despise—viz.: the man who gets drunk on bad liquor, and the man who drinks no liquor at all. Indeed, they regard the latter with a hatred or contempt which they do not feel for the poor drunkard. The absolute animosity with which many men in society regard one who is conscientiously opposed to wine-drinking, could only spring from a delusion in regard to the real nature of their own habits. The sensitiveness of these people on this subject, however, shows that they suspect the delusion of which they are the victims. They claim to be on the side of temperance. They deprecate drunkenness, and really don't see what is to be done about it. They wish that men would be more rational in their enjoyment of the good things of the world, etc., etc.; but their eyes seem blinded to the fact that they stand in the way of all reform. The horrible drunkenness of the larger cities of Great Britain, with which no hell that America holds can compare for a moment, can never be reformed until the drinking habits of the English clergy and the English gentry are reformed. With eleven-twelfths of the British clergy wine-drinkers, and water-drinkers tabooed in society, and social drinking the fashion in all the high life of the realm, the workman will stand by his gin, brutality will reign in its own chosen centres undisturbed, and those centres will increasingly become what, to a frightful extent, they already are—festering sores upon the body social, and stenches in the nostrils of the world.

The habits, neither of Great Britain nor America, will be improved until men of influence in every walk of life are willing to dispense with their drinking customs. Hundreds of thousands of English-speaking men go to a drunkard's grave every year. There is nothing in sanitary considerations as they relate to the moderate drinker, and surely nothing in the pleasures of the moderate drinker, to mitigate this curse. It is all a delusion. The water-drinker is the healthy man, and the happy man. Spirits, wine, beer, alcoholic beverages of all sorts, are a burden and a bane, and there is no place where a good man can stand unshadowed by a fatal delusion, except upon the safe ground of total abstinence. Until that ground is taken, and held, by good men everywhere, there can be no temperance reform. The wine-drinkers of England and America have the whisky-drinkers in their keeping. What do they propose to do with them?

THE WINE QUESTION IN SOCIETY.

It is universally admitted among sensible and candid people that drunkenness is the great curse of our social and national life. It is not characteristically American, for the same may be said with greater emphasis of the social and national life of Great Britain; but it is one of those things about which there is no doubt. Cholera and small-pox bring smaller fatality, and almost infinitely smaller sorrow. There are fathers and mothers, and sisters and wives, and innocent and wondering children, within every circle that embraces a hundred lives, who grieve to-day over some hopeless victim of the seductive destroyer. In the city and in the country—North, East, South and West—there are men and women who cannot be trusted with wine in their hands—men and women who are conscious, too, that they are going to destruction, and who have ceased to fight an appetite that has the power to transform every soul and every home it occupies into a hell. Oh, the wild prayers for help that go up from a hundred thousand despairing slaves of strong drink to-day! Oh, the shame, the disappointment, the fear, the disgust, the awful pity, the mad protests that rise from a hundred thousand homes! And still the smoke of the everlasting torment rises, and still we discuss the "wine question," and the "grape culture," and live on as if we had no share in the responsibility for so much sin and shame and suffering.

Society bids us furnish wine at our feasts, and we furnish it just as generously as if we did not know that a certain percentage of all the men who drink it will die miserable drunkards, and inflict lives of pitiful suffering upon those who are closely associated with them. There are literally hundreds of thousands of people in polite life in America who would not dare to give a dinner, or a party, without wine, notwithstanding the fact that in many instances they can select the very guests who will drink too much on every occasion that gives them an opportunity. There are old men and women who invite young men to their feasts, whom they know cannot drink the wine they propose to furnish without danger to themselves and disgrace to their companions and friends. They do this sadly, often, but under the compulsions of social usage. Now we understand the power of this influence; and every sensitive man must feel it keenly. Wine has stood so long as an emblem and representative of good cheer and generous hospitality, that it seems stingy to shut it away from our festivities, and deny it to our guests. Then again it is so generally offered at the tables of our friends, and it is so difficult, apparently, for those who are accustomed to it to make a dinner without it, that we hesitate to offer water to them. It has a niggardly—almost an unfriendly—seeming; yet what shall a man do who wishes to throw what influence he has on the side of temperance?

The question is not new. It has been up for an answer every year and every moment since men thought or talked about temperance at all. We know of but one answer to make to it. A man cannot, without stultifying and morally debasing himself, fight in public that which he tolerates in private. We have heard of such things as writing temperance addresses with a demijohn under the table; and society has learned by heart the old talk against drinking too much—"the excess of the thing, you know"—by those who have the power of drinking a little, but who would sooner part with their right eye than with that little. A man who talks temperance with a wine-glass in his hand is simply trying to brace himself so that he can hold it without shame. We do not deny that many men have self-control, or that they can drink wine through life without suffering, to themselves or others. It may seem hard that they should be deprived of a comfort or a pleasure because others are less fortunate in their temperament or their power of will. But the question is whether a man is willing to sell his power to do good to a great multitude for a glass of wine at dinner. That is the question in its plainest terms. If he is, then he has very little benevolence, or a very inadequate apprehension of the evils of intemperance.

What we need in our metropolitan society is a declaration of independence. There are a great many good men and women in New York who lament the drinking habits of society most sincerely. Let these all declare that they will minister no longer at the social altars of the great destroyer. Let them declare that the indiscriminate offer of wine at dinners and social assemblies is not only criminal but vulgar, as it undoubtedly is. Let them declare that for the sake of the young, the weak, the vicious—for the sake of personal character, and family peace, and social purity, and national strength—they will discard wine from their feasts from this time forth and forever, and the work will be done. Let them declare that it shall be vulgar—as it undeniably is—for a man to quarrel with his dinner because his host fails to furnish wine. This can be done now, and it needs to be done now, for it is becoming every day more difficult to do it. The habit of wine-drinking at dinner is quite prevalent already. European travel is doing much to make it universal; and if we go on extending it at the present rate, we shall soon arrive at the European indifference to the whole subject. There are many clergymen in New York who have wine upon their tables and who furnish it to their guests. We keep no man's conscience, but we are compelled to say that they sell influence at a shamefully cheap rate. What can they do in the great fight with this tremendous evil? They can do nothing, and are counted upon to do nothing.

If the men and women of good society wish to have less drinking to excess, let them stop drinking moderately. If they are not willing to break off the indulgence of a feeble appetite for the sake of doing a great good to a great many people, how can they expect a poor, broken-down wretch to deny an appetite that is stronger than the love of wife and children, and even life itself? The punishment for the failure to do duty in this business is sickening to contemplate. The sacrifice of life and peace and wealth will go on. Every year young men will rush wildly to the devil, middle-aged men will booze away into apoplexy, and old men will swell up with the sweet poison and become disgusting idiots. What will become of the women? We should think that they had suffered enough from this evil to hold it under everlasting ban, yet there are drunken women as well as drinking clergymen. Society, however, has a great advantage in the fact that it is vulgar for a woman to drink. There are some things that a woman may not do, and maintain her social standing. Let her not quarrel with the fact that society demands more of her than it does of men. It is her safeguard in many ways.

The Way we Waste.

One of the facts brought prominently before the world during the last few years is, that France is rich. The ease with which she has recovered from the disastrous war with Prussia, and the promptness with which she has met, not only her own, but Prussia's enormous expenses in that war, have surprised all her sister nations. Every poor man had his hoard of ready money, which he was anxious to lend to the State. How did he get it? How did he save it? Why is it that, in a country like ours, where wages are high and the opportunities for making money exceptionally good, such wealth and prosperity do not exist? These are important questions at this time with all of us. Business is low, industry is paralyzed, and the question of bread stares multitudes in the face.

Well, France is an industrious nation, it is said. But is not ours an industrious nation too? Is it not, indeed, one of the most hard-working and energetic nations in the world? We believe it to be a harder-working nation than the French, with not only fewer holidays, but no holidays at all, and with not only less play, but almost no play at all. It is said, too, that France is a frugal nation. They probably have the advantage of us in this, yet to feed a laboring man and to clothe a laboring man and his family there must be a definite, necessary expenditure in both countries. The difference in wages ought to cover the difference in expenses, and probably does. If the American laborer spends twice as much, or three times as much, as the French, he earns twice or three times as much; yet the American laborer lays up nothing, while the French laborer and small farmer have money to lend to their Government. Their old stockings are long and are full. The wine and the silk which the French raise for other countries must be more than counterbalanced by our exported gold, cotton, and breadstuffs, so that they do not have any advantage over us, as a nation, in what they sell to other nations? We shall have to look further than this for the secret we are after.

There lies a book before us written by Dr. William Hargreaves, entitled, "Our Wasted Resources." We wish that the politicians and political economists of this country could read this book, and ponder well its shocking revelations. They are revelations of criminal waste—the expenditure of almost incalculable resources for that which brings nothing, worse than nothing, in return. There are multitudes of people who regard the temperance question as one of morals alone. The men who drink say simply, "We will drink what we please, and it's nobody's business. You temperance men are pestilent fellows, meddlesome fellows, who obtrude your tuppenny standard of morality upon us, and we do not want it, and will not accept it. Because you are virtuous, shall there be no more cakes and ale?" Very well, let us drop it as a question of morality. You will surely look at it with us as a question of national economy and prosperity; else, you can hardly regard yourselves as patriots. We have a common interest in the national prosperity, and we can discuss amicably any subject on this common ground.

France produces its own wine, and drinks mainly cheap wine. It is a drink which, while it does them no good, according to the showing of their own physicians, does not do them harm enough to interfere with their industry. Their drinking wastes neither life nor money as ours does, and they sell in value to other countries more than they drink themselves. During the year 1870, in our own State of New York, there were expended by consumers, for liquor, more than one hundred and six millions of dollars, a sum which amounted to nearly two-thirds of all the wages paid to laborers in agriculture and manufactures, and to nearly twice as much as the receipts of all the railroads in the State, the sum of the latter being between sixty-eight and sixty-nine millions.

The money of our people goes across the bar all the time faster than it is crowded into the wickets of all the railroad stations of the State; and where does it go? What is the return for it? Diseased stomachs, aching heads, discouraged and slatternly homes, idleness, gout, crime, degradation, death. These, in various measures, are exactly what we get for it. We gain of that which is good, nothing—no uplift in morality, no increase of industry, no accession to health, no growth of prosperity. Our State is full of tramps, and every one is a drunkard. There is demoralization everywhere, in consequence of this wasteful stream of fiery fluid that constantly flows down the open gullet of the State.

But our State is not alone. The liquor bill of Pennsylvania during 1870 was more than sixty-five millions of dollars, a sum equal to one-third of the entire agricultural product of the State. Illinois paid more than forty-two millions, and Ohio more than fifty-eight millions. Massachusetts paid more than twenty-five millions, a sum equal to five-sixths of her agricultural products, while the liquor bill of Maine was only about four millions and a quarter. Mr. Hargreaves takes the figures of Massachusetts and Maine to show how a prohibitory law does, after all, reduce the drinking; but it is not our purpose to argue this question.

What we desire to show is, that, with an annual expenditure of $600,000,000 for liquors in the United States—and all the figures we give are based upon official statistics—it is not to be wondered at that the times are hard and people poor. Not only this vast sum is wasted; not only the capital invested is diverted from good uses, and all the industry involved in production taken from beneficent pursuits, but health, morality, respectability, industry, and life are destroyed. Sixty thousand Americans annually lie down in a drunkard's grave. It were better to bring into the field and shoot down sixty thousand of our young men every year, than to have them go through all the processes of disease, degradation, crime, and despair through which they inevitably pass.

With six hundred millions of dollars saved to the country annually, how long would it take to make these United States rich not only, but able to meet, without disturbance and distress, the revulsions in business to which all nations are liable? Here is a question for the statesman and the politician. Twenty-five years of absolute abstinence from the consumption of useless, and worse than useless, liquors, would save to the country fifteen billions of dollars, and make us the richest nation on the face of the globe. Not only this sum—beyond the imagination to comprehend—would be saved, but all the abominable consequences of misery, disease, disgrace, crime, and death, that would flow from the consumption of such an enormous amount of poisonous fluids, would be saved. And yet temperance men are looked upon as disturbers and fanatics! And we are adjured not to bring temperance into politics! And this great, transcendent question of economy gets the go-by, while we hug our little issues for the sake of party and of office! Do we not deserve adversity?

The Temperance Question and the Press.

A very significant movement relating to the temperance question has been inaugurated in Massachusetts. Its special suggestiveness resides in the fact that it originates with the friends of the Maine law, and is a tacit acknowledgment of the incompetency of that law to fulfill the purpose for which it was designed. It is now determined to bring to the aid of that law the old temperance machinery, so long thrown into disuse by the expectation that the law would take its place, and perfect the reform it had begun. We greet the restoration of this machinery as a good movement; but, while we give it our hearty approval, we cannot fail to remember that it was found incompetent of itself to achieve the result at which it aimed. Whether it will succeed better as an auxiliary to the law, remains to be seen. That it will help somewhat, we cannot doubt; but the truth is that all these spasmodic and semi-professional efforts at reform—these bands, and brotherhoods, and pledges, and organizations, and appeals—have proved themselves to be of very little permanent usefulness. After the people had been educated by them, or had been under their influence for many years, they relapsed fearfully the moment these means were dropped, and it was undertaken to enforce a law whose efficiency would depend upon the public sentiment which they had developed. After those who had taken the reform into their hands had conscientiously and thoroughly worked their scheme for many years, they found, to their dismay, that not enough of temperance sentiment had been developed to sustain for a day, in efficient practical operation, the law which was to render all further moral efforts unnecessary.

In our judgment, we must have in this country something more and better than Maine laws, and something more and better than temperance organizations and the stereotyped machinery of temperance movements. Neither this law nor this machinery, separately or in combination, has proved itself sufficient to effect the desired reform. We believe, however, that the reform is possible, that the agent to effect it exists, and that that agent has already a foothold in every intelligent house in the land. We have no question that the press of America, fully discharging its duty as a censor, enlightener, and educator of the people, can do more to make the nation temperate in five years than all the temperance laws, lectures, and organizations have been able to effect in twenty-five years. Is it not true, to-day, that not one newspaper in twenty-five, the country through, manifests a positive interest in the temperance question and persistently casts its influence against the use of intoxicating drinks? Is it not true that there is no question of public morals toward which the general American press is so uniformly indifferent, and in regard to which it assumes so little responsibility as this?

There is a good reason for this fact somewhere—a sufficient one, at least, or it would not exist. It is not because the editorial fraternity are without convictions on the subject, that they say nothing about it. It is not because they are tipplers themselves, or because they lack opportunity of acquaintance with the sad results of intemperance. It is mainly because they have consented to regard the question as practically taken out of their hands. Unless they have manifested entire willingness to become the organs and tools of the temperance organizations of the country,—to say their words, push their schemes, and advocate their measures,—without question or discrimination—those organizations have chosen to regard them as enemies of the temperance cause. It would be impossible for any set of men to manifest greater bigotry and intolerance towards all who have seen fit to differ with them on moral and legal measures than have characterized those zealous and thoroughly well-meaning reformers who, through various organizations, have assumed the custody and management of this question. Editors who have undertaken to discuss the question independently—as they are in the habit of discussing all public questions—have been snubbed and maligned until they have dropped it in disgust, and turned the whole matter over to those who have doubted or denounced them. Editors have not been alone in this surrender. It is notorious that more than one legislature, in more than one State, has passed laws for the suppression of intemperance that it had no faith in whatever, because the self-appointed champions of the temperance reform demanded them, and would have nothing else. It has not been safe for legislators to oppose the schemes of these men—safe for their reputation for sobriety. It has been assumed and declared that all men who were not with them, in whatever movement they chose to institute, were friends of free rum and the upholders of vice and crime. So legislators have given them their own imperious way, and washed their hands of responsibility by the consideration that temperance men had "got what they wanted."

The time for a new departure is come. It is punctuated by the shifting and uncertain movements of those who have "had their own way" for many years, and who find themselves as far from the goal at which they aimed as they were when they started. The press, independently, must take this question in hand, and educate the people to temperance. The truth is that there is not a country on the face of the earth where stimulants are needed so little, and where they are capable of producing so much mischief, as in our own. Our sparkling, sunny atmosphere, and the myriad incentives to hope and enterprise in our circumstances, are stimulants of God's own appointment for the American people. This pouring down of intoxicating liquors is ten thousand times worse than waste—it is essential sacrilege. This straining of the nerves, this heating of the blood, this stimulation or stupefaction of the mind, this imposition of cruel burdens upon the digestive organs, is a foul wrong upon Nature. Tens of thousands of valuable lives are sacrificed every year to this Moloch of strong drink. The crime, the beggary, the disgrace, the sorrow, the disappointment, the disaster, the sickness, the death that have flowed in one uninterrupted stream from the bottle and the barrel, throughout the length of the land, are enough to make all thinking and manly men curse their source and swear eternal enmity to it. The American people need to have it proved to them that under no circumstances are the various forms of intoxicating drink good for them. They are not yet convinced of this, although they know, of course, that the abuse of drink brings all the evils that can be imagined. Every juvenile periodical, every newspaper, every magazine, every review, owes it to the country to teach this fact persistently. There has been something in the way in which the temperance reform has been pursued which has brought upon it the stigma of fanaticism. That stigma ought to be obliterated—so thoroughly obliterated, that the man who weakly yields to a degrading appetite, or wantonly courts such an appetite, and the danger and disgrace it brings, shall feel that he bears a stigma which marks his degradation among a generation of clean and healthy men. In short, temperance must be made not only respectable, but fashionable. The wine-bibber and the beer-drinker, as well as those of stronger stomachs and coarser tastes, must be made to feel that they are socially disgraced by their habits. In the family, in the school, everywhere, by all the ordinary means of approach to young and plastic minds, the virtue of temperance should be inculcated. It is fashionable for the young to drink wine to-day. It must not be to-morrow; and in order that it may not be, the accepted leaders of public opinion must tell the people the truth, and enforce upon the people the obligations of duty. That world of high life which sends down its powerful influence upon all the life beneath it never was influenced by professional temperance reformers, or by temperance organizations, and is not likely to be. The clergymen it listens to, the papers, and magazines, and books it reads, and the social authorities it respects, must inculcate temperance until it shall be a shame to place a wine-bottle before a friend.

O Heaven! for one generation of clean and unpolluted men!—men whose veins are not fed with fire; men fit to be the companions of pure women; men worthy to be the fathers of children; men who do not stumble upon the rock of apoplexy at mid-age, or go blindly groping and staggering down into a drunkard's grave, but who can sit and look upon the faces of their grandchildren with eyes undimmed, and hearts uncankered. Such a generation as this is possible in America; and to produce such a generation as this, the persistent, conscientious work of the public press is entirely competent, as an instrumentality. *The press can do what it will;* and if it will faithfully do its duty, Maine laws will come to be things unthought of, and temperance reformers and temperance organizations will become extinct.

Rum and Railroads.

We hear a great deal in these days of the influence of railroad corporations in public affairs,—of their power to control large bodies of men and shape the policy of States. That danger lies in this power, there is no question. In many States it has been the agent of enormous corruption, and in some it has lorded it over legislature, judiciary, and executive alike. With abounding means at its disposal, it has done more to corrupt the fountains of legislation than any other interest; and more than any other interest does it need the restraining and guiding hand of the law, on behalf of the popular service and the popular virtue.

There is one influence of railroads, however, that has not been publicly noticed, so far as we know, and to this we call attention.

There is an influence proceeding from the highest managing man in a railroad corporation which reaches further, for good or evil, than that of almost any other man in any community. If the president or the superintendent of a railroad is a man of free and easy social habits; if he is in the habit of taking his stimulating glass, and it is known that he does so, his railroad becomes a canal through which a stream of liquor flows from end to end. A rum-drinking head-man, on any railroad, reproduces himself at every post on his line, as a rule. Grog-shops grow up around every station, and for twenty miles on both sides of the iron track, and often for a wider distance, the people are corrupted in their habits and morals. The farmers who transport their produce to the points of shipment on the line, and bring from the depots their supplies, suffer as deeply as the servants of the corporations themselves.

This is no imaginary evil. Every careful observer must have noticed how invariably the whole line of a railroad takes its moral hue from the leading man of the corporation. Wherever such a man is a free drinker, his men are free drinkers; and it is not in such men persistently to discountenance a vice that they persistently uphold by the practices of their daily life. A thorough temperance man at the head of a railroad corporation is a great purifier; and his road becomes the distributor of pure influences with every load of merchandise it bears through the country. There is just as wide a difference in the moral influence of railroads on the belts of country through which they pass as there is among men, and that influence is determined almost entirely by the managing man. There are roads that pass through none but clean, well-ordered, and thrifty villages; and there are roads that, from one end to the other, give evidence, in every town upon them, that the devil of strong drink rules and ruins. The character of ten thousand towns and villages in the United States is determined, in a greater or less degree, by the character of the men who control the railroads which pass through them. These men have so much influence, and, when they are bad men, are such a shield and cover for vice, which always keeps for them its best bed and its best bottle, that nothing seems competent to neutralize their power.

The least that these corporations—to which the people have given such great privileges—can do, is to see that such men are placed in charge as will protect the people on their lines of road from degeneracy and ruin. To elect one man to a controlling place in a railway corporation whose social habits are bad, is deliberately, in the light of experience and of well-established facts, to place in every ticket-office and freight-office, and every position of service and trust on the line, a man who drinks; to establish grog-shops near every station; and to carry a moral and industrial blight along the whole line of road whose affairs he administers. "Like master like man;" and like man his companion and friend, wherever he finds him in social communion.

Women and Wine.

Woman has never been associated with wine without disgrace and disaster. The toast and the bacchanal that, with musical alliteration, couple these two words, spring from the hot lips of sensuality, and are burdened with shame. A man who can sing of wine and women in the same breath, is one whose presence is disgrace, and whose touch is pollution. A man who can forget mother and sister, or wife and daughter, and wantonly engage in a revel in which the name of woman is invoked to heighten the pleasures of the intoxicating cup, is, beyond controversy and without mitigation, a beast. Let not the name by which we call the pure and precious ones at home be brought in to illuminate a degrading feast.

Of the worst foes that woman has ever had to encounter, wine stands at the head. The appetite for strong drink in man has spoiled the lives of more women—ruined more hopes for them, scattered more fortunes for them, brought to them more shame, sorrow, and hardship—than any other evil that lives. The country numbers tens of thousands—nay, hundreds of thousands—of women who are widows to-day, and sit in hopeless weeds, because their husbands have been slain by strong drink. There are hundreds of thousands of homes, scattered all over the land, in which women live lives of torture, going through all the changes of suffering that lie between the extremes of fear and despair, because those whom they love, love wine better than they do the women whom they have sworn to love. There are women by thousands who dread to hear at the door the step that once thrilled them with pleasure, because that step has learned to reel under the influence of the seductive poison. There are women groaning with pain, while we write these words, from bruises and brutalities inflicted by husbands made mad by drink. There can be no exaggeration in any statement made in regard to this matter, because no human imagination can create anything worse than the truth, and no pen is capable of portraying the truth. The sorrows and the horrors of a wife with a drunken husband, or a mother with a drunken son, are as near the realization of hell as can be reached in this world, at least. The shame, the indignation, the sorrow, the sense of disgrace for herself and her children, the poverty,—and not unfrequently the beggary,—the fear and the fact of violence, the lingering, life-long struggle and despair of countless women with drunken husbands, are enough to make all women curse wine, and engage unitedly to oppose it everywhere as the worst enemy of their sex.

And now what do we see on every New-Year's Day? Women all over the city of New York—women here and there all over the country, where like social customs prevail—setting out upon their tables the well-filled decanters which, before night shall close down, will be emptied into the brains of young men and old men, who will go reeling to darker orgies, or to homes that will feel ashamed of them. Woman's lips will give the invitation, woman's hand will fill and present the glass, woman's careless voice will laugh at the effects of the mischievous draught upon their friends, and, having done all this, woman will retire to balmy rest, previously having reckoned the number of those to whom she has, during the day, presented a dangerous temptation, and rejoiced over it in the degree of its magnitude.

O woman! woman! Is it not about time that this thing were stopped? Have you a husband, a brother, a son? Are they stronger than their neighbors who have, one after another, dropped into the graves of drunkards? Look around you, and see the desolations that drink has wrought among your acquaintances, and then decide whether you have a right to place temptation in any man's way, or do aught to make a social custom respectable which leads hundreds of thousands of men into bondage and death. Why must the bottle come out everywhere? Why can there not be a festal occasion without this vulgar guzzling of strong drink?

Woman, there are some things that you can do, and this is one: you can make drinking unpopular and disgraceful among the young. You can utterly discountenance all drinking in your own house, and you can hold in suspicion every young man who touches the cup. You know that no young man who drinks can safely be trusted with the happiness of any woman, and that he is as unfit as a man can be for woman's society. Have this understood: that every young man who drinks is socially proscribed. Bring up your children to regard drinking as not only dangerous but disgraceful. Place temptation in no man's way. If men will make beasts of themselves, let them do it in other society than yours. If your mercenary husbands treat their customers from private stores kept in their counting-rooms, shame them into decency by your regard for the honor of your home. Recognize the living, terrible fact that wine has always been, and is to-day, the curse of your sex; that it steals the hearts of men away from you, that it dries up your prosperity, that it endangers your safety, that it can only bring you evil. If social custom compels you to present wine at your feasts, rebel against it, and make a social custom in the interests of virtue and purity. The matter is very much in your own hands. The women of the country, in what is called polite society, can do more to make the nation temperate than all the legislators and tumultuous reformers that are struggling and blundering in their efforts to this end.

Mitigating Circumstances.

Among the various reasons assigned by those interested in procuring the commutation of the sentence pronounced upon a convicted murderer in this city, for demanding the executive clemency, we did not see one which was really stronger than any other. It is strange that this was overlooked by both the parties opposing each other in this movement. In a reverend gentleman's letter to the Governor, we find the statement that the murderer was drunk when he inflicted the fatal blow upon his victim. Granting that this was the case—for there is no doubt of it—the question arises as to the responsibility for this man's drunkenness. To a great and criminal extent the responsibility undoubtedly rested upon him: but has it occurred to this community, which so loudly calls for protection against murderous ruffianism, that it has consented to the existence of those conditions which all history has proved make murderous ruffianism certain? There is no reasonable doubt that every murderer now confined in the Tombs committed his crime under the direct or indirect influence of alcoholic drinks. Either under the immediate spur of the maddening poison, or through the brutality engendered by its habitual use, the murderous impulse was born. It is reasonably doubtful whether one of these criminals would have become a criminal if whisky had been beyond his reach. Does any one doubt this? Let him go to the cells and inquire. If the answer he gets is different from what we suggest, then the cases he finds will be strangely exceptional.

Now, who is to blame for establishing and maintaining all the conditions of danger to human life through murder? Why, the very community that complains of the danger, and calls for the execution of the murderers. So long as rum is sold at every street corner, with the license of the popular vote, men will drink themselves into brutality, and a percentage of those thus debasing themselves will commit murder. The sun is not more certain to rise in the morning than this event is to take place under these conditions. Fatal appetites are bred under this license. Diseased stomachs and brains are produced under it by the thousand. Wills are broken down, and become useless for all purposes of self-restraint. And all this is done, let it be remembered, with the consent of the community, for a certain price in money, which the community appropriates as a revenue. Then, when this enced by Mr. Squeers at finding himself so respectable would be more than matched by the surprise of a national metropolis at finding itself redeemed to virtue and personal safety.

And now what will the community do about it? Nothing. The wine-bibbers among our first families will sip at the delicious beverage among themselves, feed it to their young men, and nurse them into murderers and debauchees, and vote for the license of a traffic on which they depend for their choicest luxuries. Goodish men will partake of it, for their stomach's sake and for their often infirmities. The Frenchman will destroy his bottle of Bordeaux every day; the German will guzzle the lager that swells him into a tight-skinned, disgusting barrel; and the whisky-drinker, under the license that all these men claim for themselves, will poison himself, body and soul, and descend into a grave that kindly covers his shame, or into crime and pauperism that endanger the property and life of the city, or sap its prosperity. In the mean time the ruffian or the murderer, acting under the influence of his maddening draughts, will maim and kill, and the very men who helped him to the conditions sure to develop the devil in him will clamor for his life.

Double Crimes and One-sided Laws.

A little four-page pamphlet has recently fallen into our hands, entitled "Crimes of Legislation." Who wrote it, or where it came from, we do not know; but it reveals a principle so important that it deserves more elaborate treatment and fuller illustration. These we propose to give it, premising, simply, that the word "crimes" is a misnomer, as it involves a malicious design which does not exist. "Mistakes in Legislation" would be a better title.

There are two classes of crimes. The first needs but one

actor. When a sneak-thief enters a hall and steals and carries off an overcoat, or a man sits in his counting-room and commits a forgery, or a ruffian knocks a passenger down and robs him, he is guilty of a crime which does not necessarily need a confederate of any sort. The crime is complete in itself, and the single perpetrator alone responsible. The second class of crimes can only be committed by the consent or active aid of a confederate. When a man demands, in contravention of the usury laws, an exorbitant price for the use of money, his crime cannot be complete without the aid of the man to whom he lends his money. When a man sells liquor contrary to law, it involves the consent and active co-operation of the party to whom he makes the sale. He could not possibly break the law without aid. The same fact exists in regard to a large number of crimes. They are two-sided crimes, and necessarily involve two sets of criminals.

In the face of these facts, which absolutely dictate discriminative legislation that shall cover all the guilty parties, our laws have, with great uniformity, been one-sided for the double crime as well as for the single. The man who lends money at usurious rates is accounted the only guilty party in the transaction. The borrower may have come to him with a bribe in his hand to induce him to break the law—may have been an active partner in the crime—and still the lender is the only one accounted guilty and amenable to punishment. The man who sells intoxicating liquors contrary to law could never sell a glass, and would never buy one to sell, but for the bribe outheld in the palm of his customer; yet the law lays its hand only upon the seller.

Now, if we look into the history of these one-sided laws for double crimes, we shall learn that they are precisely those which we find it almost, or quite, impossible to enforce; and double crime by its nature; yet, how one-sided are the laws which forbid it! Is a poor girl, who has not loved wisely, and has been forsaken, the only one to blame when beastly men press round her with their hands full of bribes enticing her into a life of infamy? Yet she alone is punished, while they go scot free. And yet we wonder why prostitution is so prevalent, and why our laws make no impression upon it! Some ladies of our commonwealth have protested against a proposed law for some sort of regulation of prostitution—putting it under medical surveillance. And they are right. If men who frequent houses of prostitution are permitted to go forth from them to scatter their disease and their moral uncleanness throughout a pure community, then let the women alone. In a case like this, a mistake of legislation may amount to a crime. We do not object to medical surveillance, but it should touch both parties to the social sin. No law that does not do this will ever accomplish anything toward the cure of prostitution. We have some respect for Justice when she is represented blindfold, but when she has one eye open—and that one winking—she is a monster.

Our whole system of treating double crimes with one-sided laws, our whole silly policy of treating one party to a double crime as a fiend, and the other party as an angel or a baby, has been not only inefficient for the end sought to be obtained, but disastrous. The man who offers a bribe to another for any purpose which involves the infraction of a law of the State or nation is, and must be, an equal partner in the guilt; and any law which leaves him out of the transaction is utterly unjust on the face of it. If it is wrong to sell liquor, it is wrong to buy it, and wrong to sell because, and only because, it is wrong to buy. If prostitution is wrong, it is wrong on both sides, and he who offers a bribe to a weak woman, with-

SOCIAL INTERCOURSE.

Good Manners.

Mr. James Jackson Jarves, in a late number of *The Independent*, has an exceedingly interesting and well-written paper on "Fine Manners as a fine Art." It is written from the standpoint of an artist, and relates mainly to the æsthetic element in manners. We do not propose to criticise it, and we allude to it only to point out and emphasize the distinction between good manners and fine manners. A manner may be fine without being good, and good without being fine. It may also be good and fine at the same time. The manner of an aristocrat, who looks down upon nine persons in ten whom he may happen to meet, may be fine, but it is not good. The manner of a Frenchman—a member of the Latin race, which Mr. Jarves praises—may be fine, but it is not good, because it is not based in that profound respect for woman without which all fine manners exhibited in his intercourse with her are no better than an insult.

And this brings us to the only point we choose to make in this article. A catholic love of humanity, and a genuine respect for its rights, is the only sound basis for good manners. A tender and pure regard for woman, added to this among men, furnishes all the spring and impulse necessary for the best and finest forms of politeness. It is not necessary to go underneath a fine exterior and a show of self-depreciation and outgoing deference and respect, there lives and dominates a selfishness that is hideous and hateful.

As we are in the habit of praising the Frenchman's politeness, so are we in the habit of speaking very contemptuously of the manners of the characteristic American. That in the lower forms of American social life there is much that is rude and uncouth is admitted; but it is also claimed that, in some respects, the American is the best-mannered man living. He is never quarrelsome, his whole education has made him careful to respect the rights of those around him, and he entertains a regard for woman which the characteristic representative of no other nation shares with him. The theory on which the institutions of his country are founded, and the influence of those institutions upon him since the day of his birth, are favorable to the development in him of that respect for the rights of all men which is essential as the basis of good manners. In no country but America can a woman, unattended, travel wheresoever she will without insult, or the danger of insult. There are no countries in the world in which a woman traveling alone would travel in so much danger as in those most noted for fine manners.

American society is comparatively new. We have very little among us that is traditional. The national style of manners is in a formative state; but we certainly possess the basis for good manners in a pre-eminent degree. We are a good-natured, facile people, not ungraceful, and certainly not lacking in self-possession. We have need only to respect ourselves a little more, cease looking across the water for models, and give as graceful an expression as we can to our sentiments toward universal man and woman, to become the acknowledged possessors of good manners.

Fine manners will not become universal and characteristic of American life for many years. The absorption of the American mind in the development of the material resources of the country, in the prosecution of its industrial interests, and in the pursuit of wealth, forbids that æsthetic culture whose natural outgrowth is fine manners. Good manners, which we already possess, and for which we hold the only legitimate and reliable basis, need simply to be refined. The refinement of good manners will not come to us through the pursuit of "fine manners as a fine art," but they will come as a natural outgrowth of general æsthetic culture. As the nation becomes more refined, manners will be only one of the forms and modes through which the growing idea of that which is graceful and beautiful will express itself. The man who feels finely will act finely, provided he mingle sufficiently in society to act freely. There is no value in any form of fine art without fine feeling, and there must be something better than the character of the typical Latin on which to base a style of manners worth possession or emulation. Manners pursued as an art, for their own sake, will become artificial, and thus react upon character in a very disagreeable and dangerous way.

Social Usages.

There are some details of social usage that are so childish, and, withal, so inconvenient and burdensome, as to demand a public denunciation. Nobody likes them, everybody desires to be relieved of them, and all seem to be powerless to reform them. Their burdensomeness forms a serious bar to social intercourse, and their only tendency is to drive some men and women out of society altogether, and to worry and weary those who remain subject to them.

A person is invited to an "informal" reception. Special pains may be, and often are, taken to impress him with the idea that such a reception is, indeed, "informal." The idea is very good. The proposition is to bring together a circle of friends in a familiar way, without expensive dress on the part of the guests, or an expensive entertainment on the part of the hostess. It is an attractive sort of invitation, but woe to the man or woman who accepts it according to its terms. The man and the woman who attend in anything but full evening dress will find themselves singular, and most uncomfortable. They have taken their hostess at her word, and find, instead of a party of familiar friends, who can sit down and enjoy an hour of social intercourse, a highly dressed "jam," which comes late and departs late, and is treated to an elaborate supper. People have, at last, learned that if there is anything that must be dressed for elaborately, it is an "informal reception," and that there is really no greater cheat than the invitation which calls them together. The consequence is that we have no really informal gatherings of men and women in what we call "society."

Again, when we invite a guest to dinner at six, we expect him to come at, or before, that hour. It is counted the height of impoliteness for a guest to keep a dinner waiting a moment. This is just as it should be; but when we invite a guest at eight o'clock, to a reception or a party, what then? Why, we do not expect him until nine, we do not ordinarily get him until half-past nine, and are not surprised at his entrance at any subsequent hour before the company breaks up. Why the rule should be good for the dinner that is not good for the assembly does not appear, except that in the case of the dinner it is a question of hot or cold soup that is to be decided. At eight the host and hostess are in their vacant rooms, be-gloved and waiting. They are there for an hour, wishing their guests would come. At last one makes his appearance, and, with a guilty look, whips up-stairs. Then he waits until another joins him, and another, and another, and so at last he descends. All have lost the only opportunity they will have for a pleasant chat with those who have invited them—lost, indeed, the only chance they will have of a look at the flowers, at the pictures, and the enjoyment of an undisturbed chat, with comfortable seats and surroundings. All dread to be first, and so all wait, and thus thrust far into the night their hour of departure. The company that should be at home at eleven, and in bed at half-past eleven, do not find their beds until one the next morning.

To the man of business such hours as mingling in social life imposes are simply killing. They are the same to women who have family duties to perform. They wipe the bloom of youth from the cheeks of girls in from one to three seasons; and thus social life in the great cities, instead of being a blessing and a delight, as it should be, becomes a burden and a bore. Many are driven by considerations of health and comfort out of social life altogether, and those who remain rely upon the rest of summer to restore them sufficiently to stand another campaign. We submit that this is an unexaggerated representation of the present state of things, and protest that it demands reform.

Every hour that a man spends out of his bed after half-past ten at night is a violence to nature. They have learned this in Germany, where, in many towns, their public amusements terminate at half-past nine, and, in some cases, even earlier than this. It is in this direction that a reform should be effected in America, so far as every variety of public and social assembly is concerned. An invitation at eight should mean what it says, and be honored in its terms. In this way social life would be possible to many to whom it is now practically denied, and become a blessing to all.

It is not hard to institute a reform of this kind. All it wants is a leading; and half a dozen of our social queens could do the work in a single season. It used to be deemed essential to a social assembly that a huge, expensive supper be served at its close, and this at an hour when no man or woman could afford to eat a hearty meal. We have measurably outlived this in New York. It is "quite the thing" now to serve light and inexpensive refreshments. The man who dines at six needs no heavy supper before he goes to bed. He not only does not need it, but he cannot eat it without harm. Its expensiveness is a constant bar to social life; and let us be thankful that this abuse, at least, is pretty well reformed already. Other abuses and bad habits can be reformed just as easily as this, because reform is in the line of the common sense and the common desire. The leading, as we have said, is all that is wanted, and when we commence another season such leading ought to be volunteered. Something surely ought to be done to make social life a recreative pleasure, and not a severe tax upon the vital forces as it is at present.

Social Taxes.

The typical American is not an unsocial person. Indeed, he is very far from being anything of the kind. Foreigners regard the American as one who has a particular fondness for living with his windows up and his doors open. Yet it is doubtless true that there is a notable lack of freedom and ease in the intercourse of American society, and that the coming together of men and women for the interchange of thought and feeling is attended with difficulties that only the rich may successfully encounter. If half a dozen friends are invited to dinner it is deemed necessary to crowd the table with superfluous viands and dainty and costly dishes. If the same number are invited to tea, there is hardly less expense and trouble incurred. Instead of the simple tea, and the light food that appropriately accompanies it, in the ordinary life of the family, there is a supper, in which salads and solid dishes, cold and hot, and all expensive, are crowded upon the jaded appetite. Even this is not enough. Before the guests depart, they are often beset again with dainty offerings of ice and fruit and coffee.

When we come to more ambitious gatherings we encounter more preposterous folly. An ordinary social party is a huge feast, which begins at the time when people ought to be going to bed, ends when they ought to be getting up, and crowds the stomach with luxurious and burdensome food and drinks at the time when it ought to be in its profoundest rest. One such party exhausts the resources of the family which gives it for a year or two, unless they are people of abounding wealth, turns their house upside down, and breaks up their whole family life for a fortnight. The payment for entertainment, in music and dainties and flowers, makes the purse-carrier groan, and wrings from him the glad declaration that his duty is done for a twelve-month, at least! One party is just like every other party, except that one is more or less expensive than another. There is rivalry of dress among the women, to be sure, and such new toilets as they can afford to make from time to time, and often such as they cannot afford to make; but there are the same old fiddles, playing the same old quadrilles and waltzes; there is the same caterer and the familiar ices and salads; the same "How do you *do?*" and the same "Good-Night," and "We have had such a splendid time!"

Now we protest that there must be some better way than this. The great multitude are those who, in some calling or profession, work for their bread. To furnish a dinner and tea such as we have described, would be felt by them as a severe tax. No matter how intellectual and socially valuable these people may be, they shrink from entering society that imposes such burdens. As they feel it to be impossible for them to return in kind the expensive civilities which a wealthy neighbor extends to them, they shrink back into their own houses and go nowhere. Everywhere, and all the time, these costly entertainments, at dinner and tea and social assembly, operate as a bar to social intercourse. Indeed, they have become, in the full, legitimate meaning of the word, a nuisance. To those who give them they are not pleasant in any respect. They are provided with no expectation of a compensating pleasure; and few besides the young—to whom any opportunity for dancing and frolicking is agreeable—take the slightest satisfaction in them. They are glad when their toilet is made, glad when the refreshments are offered, glad when the show is over and they can go home, glad when they get safely to bed, and particularly glad the following morning if they can look over their coats and dresses and find that they are not ruined.

Have we exaggerated in the least in these representations? Nay, have we not told the exact, notorious truth? We protest again, then, that there must be some better way. Here is another opportunity for woman to do good; for it is woman, in her social pride and in her pride of housekeeping, who has more to do with this thing than man. The woman who can make her drawing-room attractive by informal gatherings of men and women, who shall not be put through the tortures of the toilet, nor burdened with a sense of obligation by the luxuries prepared for their entertainment, is the real social queen. The essential vulgarity of the phase of social life which we are considering is decided by the simple fact that the great question of the hostess concerns the stomachs of her guests, and the great question of her guests relates to the decoration of their own backs. It elevates nobody, it refines nobody, it inspires and instructs nobody, and it satisfies nobody. Yet we go on, year after year, upholding these social usages which we despise. Let us find the better way, and follow it!

The Tortures of the Dinner-Table.

In the space of twenty-five years we have heard twenty-five men, more or less, make successful dinner-table speeches. Of these, ten were sensible men who entertained their companions by trying to talk like fools; ten were fools who were equally entertaining in their endeavor to talk like sensible men; and five—the only persons of the number who enjoyed the eminence and the exercise—were drunk, and neither knew nor cared whether they talked sense or nonsense. As a rule, the successful dinner-table orator is a shallow man—one whose thoughts are on the surface, whose vocabulary is small and at quick command, and whose lack of any earnest purpose in life leaves him free to talk upon trifles. We all remember what earnest, strong, logical speeches Abraham Lincoln used to make, when he stood before the people in the advocacy of great principles and a great cause; and we remember, too, with pain, how tame and childish and awkward he was when he appeared before them to acknowledge a compliment, or to say something which should be nothing. Inspired by a great purpose, he could do anything; with nothing to say, he could say nothing. It is thus with the great majority of our best men. There is nothing in which they succeed so poorly as in a dinner-table speech, and there is nothing which they dread so much. The anticipation of it is torture to them; the performance is usually a failure. At last, they learn to shun dinner-tables, and to tell weak lies in apology for their non-attendance.

There is something very absurd in the submission of so many men to this custom of speech-making. There is never a public dinner, or a dinner which may possibly merge into formality of toast and talk, without its overhanging cloud of dread. There is probably not one man present, from him who expects to be called upon for a speech to him who is afraid that the demand will at last reach him, who would not pay a handsome price to be out of the room and its dangers. To multitudes of men, the viands of a feast are gall and bitterness, through this haunting dread of the moment when, with bellies full and brains empty, they shall find themselves on their feet, making a frantic endeavor to say something that shall bring down the fork-handles, and give them leave to subside.

Why a dinner-table should be chosen as an oratorical theatre, we cannot imagine. There could not be selected a moment more inauspicious for happy speech than that in which all the nervous energy centres itself upon digestion. A man cannot have even a happy dream under such circumstances. Dancing the sailor's hornpipe with dumb-bells in one's coat pockets is not advisable, and it is possible that it is not advisable under any circumstances. It is very rare that a dinner party prefers to sit and listen to interminable speeches, for it is almost as hard to listen as to talk when the stomach is full of the heavy food of a feast. Nothing but stimulating drink loosens the tongue under such circumstances, or puts a company into that sensitively appreciative mood which responds to buncombe and bathos. The drinking which is resorted to for making these occasions endurable, is often shameful, and always demoralizing. Not a good thing ever comes of it all, nobody enjoys it, speakers and hearers dislike it, and still the custom is continued. It is like the grand dress parties, which nobody likes, yet which all attend and all give, to the infinite boring of themselves and their friends.

The discourtesies often visited upon gentlemen at public dinner-parties deserve an earnest protest. Men are called to their feet not only against their known wishes, but against pledges, and compelled to speech that is absolute torture to them. The boobies who thus distress modest and sensitive men ought to be kicked out of society. No one has a right to give an innocent man pain by compelling him to make of himself a public spectacle, or summoning him to a task that is unspeakably distasteful to him. No man ought ever to be called upon at such a place, except with his full consent previously obtained; and he who forces a modest man to a task like this in the presence of society, fails in the courtesy of a gentleman. The truth is that no dinner is pleasant unless it be entirely informal. The moment it takes on a formal character its life as a social occasion is departed; and those who foster the custom of speech-making drive from their society multitudes of men who would be glad to meet them—whose presence would give them pleasure and do them good. Let us have done with this foolishness.

TOWN AND COUNTRY.

The Loneliness of Farming-life in America.

An American traveler in the Old World notices, among the multitude of things that are new to his eye, the gathering of agricultural populations into villages. He has been accustomed in his own country to see them distributed upon the farms they cultivate. The isolated farm-life, so universal here, either does not exist at all in the greater part of continental Europe, or it exists as a comparatively modern institution. The old populations, of all callings and professions, clustered together for self-defense, and built walls around themselves. Out from these walls, for miles around, went the tillers of the soil in the morning, and back into the gates they thronged at night. Cottages were clustered around feudal castles, and grew into towns; and so Europe for many centuries was cultivated mainly by people who lived in villages and cities, many of which were walled, and all of which possessed apppointments of defense. The early settlers in our own country took the same means to defend themselves from the treacherous Indian. The towns of Hadley, Hatfield, Northfield, and Deerfield, on the Connecticut River, are notable examples of this kind of building; and to this day they remain villages of agriculturists. That this is the way in which farmers ought to live we have no question, and we wish to say a few words about it.

There is some reason for the general disposition of American men and women to shun agricultural pursuits which the observers and philosophers have been slow to find. We see young men pushing everywhere into trade, into mechanical pursuits, into the learned professions, into insignificant clerkships, into salaried positions of every sort that will take them into towns and support and hold them there. We find it impossible to drive poor people from the cities with the threat of starvation, or to coax them with the promise of better pay and cheaper fare. There they stay, and starve, and sicken, and sink. Young women resort to the shops and the factories rather than take service in farmers' houses, where they are received as members of the family; and when they marry, they seek an alliance, when practicable, with mechanics and tradesmen who live in villages and large towns. The daughters of the farmer fly the farm at the first opportunity. The towns grow larger all the time, and, in New England, at least, the farms are becoming wider and longer, and the farming population are diminished in numbers, and, in some localities, degraded in quality and character.

It all comes to this, that isolated life has very little significance to a social being. The social life of the village and the city has intense fascination to the lonely dwellers on the farm, or to a great multitude of them. Especially is this the case with the young. The youth of both sexes who have seen nothing of the world have an overwhelming desire to meet life and to be among the multitude. They feel their life to be narrow in its opportunities and its rewards, and the pulsation of the great social heart that comes to them in rushing trains and passing steamers and daily newspapers, damp with the dews of a hundred brows, thrill them with longings for the places where the rhythmic throb is felt and heard. They are not to be blamed for this. It is the most natural thing in the world. If all of life were labor,—if the great object of life were the scraping together of a few dollars, more or less,—why, isolation without diversion would be economy and profit; but so long as the object of life is life, and the best and purest and happiest that can come of it, all needless isolation is a crime against the soul, in that it is a surrender and sacrifice of noble opportunities.

We are, therefore, not sorry to see farms growing larger, provided those who work them will get nearer together; and that is what they ought to do. Any farmer who plants himself and his family alone—far from possible neighbors—takes upon himself a terrible responsibility. It is impossible that he and his should be well developed and thoroughly happy there. He will be forsaken in his old age by the very children for whom he has made his great sacrifice. They will fly to the towns for the social food and stimulus for which they have starved. We never hear of a colony settling on a western prairie without a thrill of pleasure. It is in colonies that all ought to settle, and in villages rather than on separated farms. The meeting, the lecture, the public amusement, the social assembly, should be things easily reached. There is no such damper upon free social life as distance. A long road is the surest bar to neighborly intercourse. If the social life of the farmer were richer, his life would by that measure be the more attractive.

After all, there are farmers who will read this article with a sense of affront or injury, as if by doubting or disputing the sufficiency of their social opportunities we insult them with a sort of contempt. We assure them that they cannot afford to treat thoroughly sympathetic counsel in this way. We know that their wives and daughters and sons are on our side, quarrel with us as they may; and the women and children are right. "The old man," who rides to market and the post-office, and mingles more or less in business with the world, gets along tolerably well; but it is the stayers at home who suffer. Instead of growing wiser and better as they grow old, they lose all the graces of life in unmeaning drudgery, and instead of ripening in mind and heart, they simply dry up or decay. We are entirely satisfied that the great curse of farming life in America is its isolation. It is useless to say that men shun the farm because they are lazy. The American is not a lazy man anywhere; but he is social, and he will fly from a life that is not social to one that is. If we are to have a larger and better population devoted to agriculture, isolation must be shunned, and the whole policy of settlement hereafter must be controlled or greatly modified by social considerations.

The Overcrowded Cities.

There is hardly a city in the United States which does not contain more people than can get a fair, honest living, by labor or trade, in the best times. When times of business depression come, like those through which we have passed, and are passing, there is a large class that must be helped, to keep them from cruel suffering. Still the cities grow, while whole regions of the country,—especially its older portions,—are depopulated year by year. Yet the fact is patent to-day that the only prosperous class is the agricultural. We often witness the anomaly of thrifty farmers and starving tradesmen. The country must be fed, and the farmers feed it. The city family may do without new clothes, and a thousand luxurious appliances, but it must have bread and meat. There is nothing that can prevent the steady prosperity of the American farmer but the combinations and "corners" of middle-men, that force unnatural conditions upon the finances and markets of the country.

This is not the first occasion we have had for allusion to this subject, and it is not likely to be the last. The forsaking of the farm for city life is one of the great evils of the time, and, so far, it has received no appreciable check. Every young man, apparently, who thinks he can get a living in the city, or at the minor centres of population, quits his lonely home upon the farm and joins the multitude. Once in the city, he never returns. Notwithstanding the confinement and the straitened conditions of his new life, he clings to it until he dies, adding his family to the permanent population of his new home. Mr. Greeley, in his days of active philanthropy, used to urge men to leave the city—to go West—to join the agricultural population, and thus make themselves sure of a competent livelihood. He might as well have talked to the wind. A city population can neither be coaxed nor driven into agricultural pursuits. It is not that they are afraid of work. The average worker of the city toils more hours than the average farmer in any quarter of the country. He is neither fed nor lodged as well as the farmer. He is less independent than the farmer. He is a bond-slave to his employers and his conditions; yet the agricultural life has no charms for him.

Whatever the reason for this may be, it is not based in the nature of the work, or in its material rewards. The farmer is demonstrably better off than the worker of the city. He is more independent, has more command of his own time, fares better at table, lodges better, and gets a better return for his labor. What is the reason, then, that the farmer's boy runs to the city the first chance he can get, and remains, if he can possibly find there the means of life?

It can only be found, we believe, in the social leanness, or social starvation, of American agricultural life. The American farmer, in all his planning, and all his building, has never made provision for life. He has only considered the means of getting a living. Everything outside of this—everything relating to society and culture—has been steadily ignored. He gives his children the advantages of schools, not recognizing the fact that these very advantages call into life a new set of social wants. A bright, well-educated family, in a lonely farm-house, is very different material from a family brought up in ignorance. An American farmer's children, who have had a few terms at a neighboring academy, resemble in no degree the children of the European peasant. They come home with new ideas and new wants; and if there is no provision made for these new wants, and they find no opportunities for their satisfaction, they will be ready, on reaching their majority, to fly the farm and seek the city.

If the American farmer wishes to keep his children near him, he must learn the difference between living and getting a living; and we mistake him and his grade of culture altogether if he does not stop over this statement and wonder what we mean by it. To get a living, to make money, to become "forehanded"—this is the whole of life to agricultural multitudes, discouraging in their numbers to contemplate. To them there is no difference between living and getting a living. Their whole life consists in getting a living; and when their families come back to them from their schooling, and find that, really, this is the only pursuit that has any recognition under the paternal roof, they must go away. The boys push to the centres or the cities, and the girls follow them if they can. A young man or a young woman, raised to the point where they apprehend the difference between living and getting a living, can never be satisfied with the latter alone. Either the farmer's children must be kept ignorant, or provision must be made for their social wants. Brains and hearts need food and clothing as well as bodies; and those who have learned to recognize brains and hearts as the best and most important part of their personal possessions, will go where they can find the ministry they need.

What is the remedy? How shall farmers manage to keep their children near them? How can we discourage the influx of unnecessary—nay, burdensome—populations into the cities? We answer: By making agricultural society attractive. Fill the farm-houses with periodicals and books. Establish central reading-rooms, or neighorhood clubs. Encourage the social meetings of the young. Have concerts, lectures, amateur dramatic associations. Establish a bright, active, social life, that shall give some significance to labor. Above all, build, as far as possible, in villages. It is better to go a mile to one's daily labor than to place one's self a mile away from a neighbor. The isolation of American farm-life is the great curse of that life, and it falls upon the women with a hardship that the men cannot appreciate, and drives the educated young away.

THE RICH AND THE POOR.

EMPLOYERS AND EMPLOYED.

The relations of employer and employed have existed since civilization began. Nothing has been done without capital: nothing has been done without labor. To realize what is regarded as the ideal condition, associations of laborers with capital have been organized,—co-proprietary and co-operative,—with varying results. After all attempts of this kind, the fact seems well established that industrial unions and partnerships will never become the rule, and that labor and capital will respectively be at the disposal of different men. Those who have labor to sell, without money to invest in the materials and products of their own industry, will always be a large proportion of the community. If the capital of the world were to be equally divided to-day, it would not take a month to re-establish the old division of capitalists and laborers. There are organizing, directing, controlling minds, which would manage at once to win capital, and employ the industry of others; and even the accidents of life would make many poor men rich. There is no possibility of maintaining equality of condition among men. The capitalist, with money to be employed in commerce, agriculture and manufactures, and the laborer, with various industry and skill to sell, will live side by side while the world stands. The natural wish of the first will always be to get the best profit he can on his money, and of the other to get the best price he can for his labor.

The great, practical question with both classes concerns the relations that exist between them. Shall those relations be friendly and harmonious, or discordant and inimical? Is there any real ground for opposition and jealousy? The strikes of laborers, the formation of trades-unions, the speeches uttered and the editorials published on the tyranny of capital, show that at least a portion of the laboring community consider themselves aggrieved by those who employ them. To some extent this is undoubtedly true. There are men who would make their laborers their slaves, and who would gladly obtain their labor at the lowest price compatible with the maintenance of their laboring power. There are corporations without souls, which have no more consideration for the muscles and the skill that they employ in their mills and shops, than they have for the horses employed outside. It is entirely natural for labor to organize against such men and such corporations, and to look upon them as enemies. Where personal rights are unrecognized, where capital refuses to see in the laborer anything but its dependent and servant, where oppressions are practiced, there will and must be rebellion. The man or the corporation whose supreme object is to get the most out of the laborer for the least consideration in money, will be sure to have laborers who will aim to get the most money possible for the smallest consideration in labor. Laborers will do this independently or in combination, and their action will be entirely justifiable, though it may not always be wise.

The iniquity of trades-unions is that they make no distinction between good and bad employers, and breed universal discontent and demoralization. Even in this day of wide and deep distress among capitalists,—this day of shrunken values and business stagnation,—when, but for the sake of the poor, capital would greatly prefer to lie idle, there are bands of men who quarrel with their wages, and feel that they are badly used.

Now we believe that the majority of employers intend to do full justice to those whom they employ. We believe that in this day of trial and loss, there are men who are doing more than they can afford to do, in order to keep their laborers from distress. At this time, as at all times, they are the subjects of the inexorable law of demand and supply, and so, with a great supply and no demand, they stagger feebly along with their business, that those dependent on them may be fed. They are men who recognize the inter-dependence of labor and capital, and are willing to share the trials of the time with those who minister to their prosperity in better days.

Now labor stultifies itself and makes itself an object of contempt when it fails to recognize and reward a just and generous disposition on the part of capital. A laborer who will join a band of fellow-craftsmen in the attempt to extort an increase of wages from an employer who uses him well in adversity and fairly in prosperity, surrenders his manhood, either to his own selfishness, or to the despotism of his fellows. We hope strikes have done good. It would be a pity that the amount of suffering they have caused should have been of no avail. If they have checked any tendency to oppression on the part of capital; if they have taught the holder of money not to claim too much of the profits of industry, we are glad. But we are sure there is a better way, and that now is a good time to enter upon it. It is a good time for capitalists to ask themselves the question whether they have always recognized the rights of labor, and given it an appropriate reward—whether they have ever tried to win the heart of labor—whether they have given it brotherhood and endeavored to minister to its comfort, happiness and elevation. It is a good time, too, for the laborer to ask himself the question whether he has always sufficiently considered the fact that capital runs all the risk, while he runs none; that it is liable to be destroyed by flame, or dissipated in financial disaster; and that his ability to feed and clothe his wife and little ones depends upon the prosperity of capital. It is a good time, too, for him to remember that capital bears the great burdens of society, that it pays the enormous taxes of the time, that it supports all the charities, and that, whether there is labor for the laborer or not, the laborer is fed. It is a good time for him to remember that in the last resort of necessity, capital does not permit him or his children to go houseless and without bread.

In short, it is a good time, in their common trouble, for the capitalist and the laborer to learn that they are brethren, and dependent in many ways upon one another. When this period of depression passes away, as it must soon,—for the world moves on,—it is quite possible that work will be recommenced upon a more modest basis of wages on one side and profits on the other. We hope, then, that employers and employed will lay aside all the old jealousies and resentments, and learn to be not only just but generous towards each other. There are communities in America, blessed by capitalists who share in many ways with their laborers the fruit of their prosperity. Public halls, reading-rooms, libraries, comfortable houses and the best schools, bestowed by employers, have made some manufacturing villages a collection of intelligent and happy homes, and even labor itself a choice privilege. There is nothing that the laborer wants so much as recognition as a man, and a chance for his family. When the employer has the power to give both and gives both, he ought not to be troubled with strikes or jealousies, or the inefficiency of those who do his work.

The Neglect of the Rich.

If any of the millionaires of the City of New York have felt grieved because we have not called upon them, or because we do not even know their faces when we happen to meet them, we beg their pardon. We have had no intention to slight them, or to count them out of the circle of humanity by reason of their comparative independence of it. We do not blame them for being rich, unless they have procured their wealth by oppression of the poor. Some of them have become rich because they were brighter and more industrious than the rest of us, and recognized quicker than we the elusive faces of golden opportunites. We can find no fault with them for this, but rather with ourselves. Some of them inherited wealth, and have no responsibilities concerning it save those connected with the spending of it. Some of them acquired it by accident—by the rise of real estate that they had held, perhaps, unwillingly, or by an unlooked-for appreciation of the value of stocks. However their wealth may have been acquired—always excepting that which has been won by immoral practices—we wish to have them understand that we think none the worse of them for their pleasant fortune. We regard them still as men and brothers, who delight in the sympathy of their fellows, and whose hearts are warmed by the popular confidence and good-will.

We confess that we have never been quite able to understand why it is that those who have been fortunate in life should be compelled, in consequence, to sacrifice their early friendships and their old friends. Two boys begin life together.

They may, or may not, be relatives; but they are bosom friends. They confide to one another their plans and ambitions, and start out on the race for fortune, neck-and-neck. One outstrips the other, and reaches his goal gladly and gratefully. He has thrown no hinderances in the path of his friend. He has, on the contrary, encouraged him; and, so far as it was proper for him to do so, given him assistance. Finding at last that he is hopelessly floundering in the way, or that he has tripped and fallen, he goes back to him to exchange a friendly word, but he is met by cold looks and averted eyes. The successful man has committed no sin except that of becoming successful. He has lost none of his affection for his friend, but he has lost his friend. Thenceforward there is between the two a great gulf fixed, and that gulf is fixed by the unsuccessful man. He has taken to himself the fancy that the successful man must hold the unsuccessful man in dishonor, and that he cannot possibly meet him again on the even terms which existed when their lives were untried plans.

There are few successful men, we imagine, who have not been vexed and wounded by the persistent misapprehensions and distrust of those whom they loved when they were young, and whom they would still gladly love if they could be permitted to do so. There is not an hour, on any day, in this city, in which thriving men do not cross the street to meet old friends who, because they are not thriving, strive to avoid them —not an hour in which they do not try by acts of courtesy and hearty good-will to hold the friendship of those whom they have left behind in the strife for fortune. Excepting a few churls and coxcombs, they all do this until they get thoroughly tired of it, and finally give it up as a bad job. They know that they have done their duty. They know that they have not entertained a thought or performed an act of wrong toward those who shun them. Their consciences are clear, and, at last—half in sorrow, half in anger—they consent that the knot that once united two harmonious lives shall be severed forever.

There are many men who cannot bear prosperity when it comes to them, but their number is small compared to those who cannot bear the prosperity of others. There is no finer test of true nobility of character than that furnished by the effect of the good fortune of friends. The poor man who rejoices in the prosperity of his neighbor, and meets him always without distrust and with unshaken self-respect, betrays unconsciously a nature and character which a king might envy. To such a man every rich man bows with cordial recognition, while he cannot fail to regard with contempt the insolent churl who meets him with bravado and the offensive assertion of an equality which he does not feel, as well as the cowardly sneak who avoids and distrusts him.

A great deal is said about the insolence of riches and the neglect or disregard of the poor on the part of those who possess them, but, in sober truth, there is a neglect of the rich on the part of the poor that is quite as unjust and quite as hard to bear. If there is a gulf between the rich man and the poor man, the latter does quite as much to dig it and keep it open as the former. There are multitudes of rich men whose wealth has the tendency to enlarge their sympathies, and to fill them with good-will, particularly toward all those whom they have known in their less prosperous years. To these men of generous natures the loss of sympathy and friendship is a grievous deprivation.

Money does not make the man. The poor man will tell us this as if he believed it, but either he does not believe it, or he believes that the rich man does not believe it; certainly, in his intercourse with the rich man, he does not manifest his faith in this universally accepted maxim. He merely accepts the rich man's courtesies as condescension and patronage, and is offended by them. No; let no poor man talk of the pride and superciliousness of riches until his self-respectful poverty is ready to meet those riches half way, and to have faith in the good-will and common human sympathy of those who bear them.

Strike, but Hear.

We suppose that there is nothing simpler than simple addition, excepting, perhaps, those people who have no talent for it, of whom, unfortunately, there is a considerable number, especially among the striking craftsmen. If it were to be announced to-day that ten dollars will hereafter be the average price of a day's labor, among all the trades, we do not doubt that it would be regarded by the toiling multitudes as the gladdest and grandest event that had ever occurred in the history of the national industry. Let us see, then, if we can, what the effect of such an advance in the price of labor would be. This is a rich country; and every rich country has a multitude of artificial wants. To supply these wants, there have been organized a large number of productive industries; and hundreds of thousands of laborers are fed by them. The first effect of a doubling of the price of labor would be to destroy all those industries which are engaged in producing things that men and women can do without. When the price of the necessaries of life is raised, the use of luxuries is reduced in a corresponding degree. This law is just as unvarying in its operation as the law of gravitation. A man who spends $10,000 a year, giving $2,000 of it to luxuries, drops his luxuries, and spends his

$10,000 on a smaller number of people. He dismisses a servant, and gives up his carriage. He stops buying flowers and giving entertainments. Every man and woman who had anything to do in feeding his artificial wants loses his patronage; and thus whole classes of people would, by such an advance in the price of labor, be thrown out of employment and into distress. This, however, would be only an indirect or incidental damage to the laboring interest, though it would be a damage to that interest alone. The rich would really suffer very little by it.

There are certain things that we must all have—the rich and the poor alike—houses to live in, clothes to wear, and bread and meat to eat. What effect would such a change have upon these? A house that cost $3,000 to build yesterday, will cost $6,000 to-morrow. The brickmaker, the stone-cutter, the mason, the carpenter, all working at double wages, would, by that very fact, advance the price of their own rent in a corresponding degree. The tenement that rents for $250 to-day will rent for $500 to-morrow, and if it cannot be rented for that sum, it will not be built at all. The same thing will be true concerning what are called the necessaries of life. If it costs twice as much money to produce a barrel of flour to-day as it did yesterday, it will double in price. Every article of produce, every garment that we buy for ourselves or our children, will have added to its price exactly what has been added to the cost of its production or manufacture; and when this excess has been added to the excess of rent, the laborer will find himself at the end of his first year no whit benefited by what seemed to hold the promise of a fortune. We cannot imagine a man with common sense enough to labor intelligently who will be unable to see at a glance that our conclusions on this point are inevitable.

Now there is beyond this direct result of a doubling of the price of labor an indirect effect upon the price of real estate, which greatly enhances the trouble of the laborer. The destruction of various branches of industry, and the rendering of other branches either precarious or insufficient in their profits, would inevitably concentrate capital, so far as possible, upon real estate. Idle or poorly-employed capital is always seeking for an investment; and if banking and manufacturing and trade become unprofitable, through a disturbance of just relations between labor and capital, the man who has money puts it into real estate. Under this stimulus real estate rises at once. If the price of labor were doubled, the advance in rents from this cause alone would not only be appreciable but decidedly onerous. The inevitable tendency of every strike is to drive capital out of manufacturing into real estate, to raise the price of real estate, and to raise the laborer's rent.

We have supposed this extreme case in order to show the laborer, as we could do in no other way, the tendency of his measures to secure large wages by arbitrary means. That there is a point beyond which it is not safe for him to go, is just as demonstrable as any problem in mathematics. There is a point beyond which it is not safe for him to push his demand for increased wages, or for fewer hours of labor, which is the same thing. Our impression is that he has reached that point, and we are speaking in his interest entirely. The labor market should always be in that condition which tends to draw capital away from real estate. Then rents will be low, provisions will stand at a reasonable price, every hand will find sufficient employment with sufficient pay, and labor and capital be mutually dependent friends. We sympathize with every effort of the laborer to better his condition, and our simple wish is to warn him against supposing that increased wages beyond a certain point, which he seems already to have reached, will be of the slightest use to him. There is an average price for a day's labor which capital can afford to pay, and which alone labor can afford to receive. Beyond this all is disorder, injustice, and pecuniary adversity and loss to every class. The extorted dollar which capital cannot afford to give to labor is a curse to the hand that receives it.

Something that Wealth can do for Labor.

However much of perplexity may surround the questions arising from the relations of wealth to labor, there are some aspects of these questions about which we are sure there ought not to be a very great difference of opinion. A man has a right to get rich. There is not a laborer in the country who is not personally interested in the universal recognition of this right. The desire for wealth is a legitimate spur to endeavor, a good motive to the exercise of wholesome economy, and a worthy incentive to honest and honorable work. It is not the highest motive of life, but there is nothing wrong or unworthy in it, so long as it is held in subordination to personal integrity and neighborly good-will. There always will be rich men and there always ought to be rich men. There must be accumulations and combinations of capital, else there will be no fields of labor and enterprise into which, for the winning of livelihood and wealth, the new generations may enter. We may go further and say that there always will be, and always ought to be, laborers. Men are born into the world who are better adapted to labor with the hands than with the head,—better adapted to production than trade; better adapted to execution than invention. Nobody is to blame for this. It is the order of nature, and, being the order of nature, it is wise. The world could not move were the facts different. By the capital and the business capacity of one man, whole neighborhoods and towns made up of laborers thrive and rear their families; and the relations between the head and the hands of such towns and neighborhoods seem, and doubtless are, perfectly natural and perfectly healthful.

It is not with the fact that a man is rich that the representatives of labor quarrel, for the representatives of labor would all like to become rich themselves. What they particularly desire is to become richer than they are. What they supremely desire is to share in the wealth which they see others accumulating. This, of course, can never be done, except by a natural business process. Practical co-operation and the assumption of the same business risks to which capitalists expose themselves, and the exercise of the same business capacity, can alone give to labor all the wealth which it produces. All the friends of labor—and there are multitudes of them among the rich—will rejoice in any success which co-operation and a combination of small savings will give to it. There is no other mode of procedure that is healthy or even legitimate. Strikes and trades-unions and all organized efforts for forcing up wages are just as unnatural and outrageous and tyrannical as combinations of capital are for the reduction of wages or—what is practically and morally the same—for raising the cost of the means of living. Capital has something to complain of as well as labor in the matter of service and wages. It is undoubtedly and undeniably as difficult to get a day's work done by skillful and conscientious hands as it is to get a fair reward for such work; and so long as this shall remain true it becomes labor to be modest and somewhat careful in its demands.

After the Chicago fire, three friends met, two of whom had been burned out of house and home and the immense accumulations of successful lives. One of the unfortunates said to the other two: "Well, thank God, there was some of my money placed where it couldn't burn!"—saying which he turned upon his heel cheerfully, and went to work at his new life. His brother in misfortune turned to his companion and said: "That man gave away last year nearly a million of dollars, and if I had not been a fool I should have done the same thing." This brings us to what we wish to say in this article, viz.: that it is not wealth that is objectionable,—all the wealth that a man can use for his own benefit and the benefit of his family and heirs—but the superfluous wealth, that is both a care and a curse—superfluous wealth that goes on piling up by thousands and millions while great public charities go begging, while institutions of learning languish, while thousands are living from hand to mouth, while the sittings of churches are so costly that the poor cannot take them, while halls and libraries and reading-rooms are not established in communities in which they are needed to keep whole generations of young men from going to perdition, and while a thousand good things are not done which only that superfluous wealth can possibly do.

What, in fact, does the laborer want? He would like wealth, but will be entirely content (if demagogues will let him alone), if he can have some of those civilizing and elevating privileges which only wealth can purchase. If the laborer, at the close of his day or week of toil, can walk into a nice reading-room and library, in which he has the fullest right and privilege; if, on Sunday, he can enter a church which superfluous wealth has made his own; if he can send his ambitious and talented boy to college, and so give to him the same chance to rise in the world as that enjoyed by the son of his employer; if he can feel that if great disaster should come upon him there are funds which wealth has provided to save him from want—funds which he knows were dug by labor out of the earth, and are thus returned to labor by those who have accumulated more than they need, he will be content and happy, and he ought to be. Now let us go still further, and declare that, as a rule, he ought to have all these possessions and privileges. It is reasonable for him to ask for and expect them. For this country to go on as it is going now, is to bring upon it even a worse state of things than at present exists in England, if such a consummation be possible. There are, literally, millions of men in England who labor in utter hopelessness. Every one of them knows that he must work for bread while he can get work, and while he can stand, and that then there is nothing before him but death or the work-house. Think of an alternative like this standing in the near or distant future before millions of workers! It is enough to make a mountain shudder. Yet there are thousands of men in England who keep lands for game, and can only spend their incomes by squandering them on vice and fashionable ostentation. In this country the process is begun. Gigantic fortunes are growing up on every hand. There are already many men who are worth many millions of dollars. The men of superfluous wealth in all parts of the country, have it in their power to settle some of the most important questions that are now up, and are likely to arise, between capital and labor. They also have it in their power to make their names immortal as benefactors of their country, and of that great interest out of whose productive energy every dollar they hold has been drawn.

The superfluous wealth held in this country would found ten thousand scholarships in the various colleges of the United States for the poor, furnish every town with a respectable library and reading-room, give sittings in churches to ten millions of people who have none, and found hospitals and funds of relief for labor to meet all emergencies. Nay, what is more, and in some respects better, it could lend in many instances to labor the capital necessary to secure the profits upon its own expenditures. Superfluous wealth can certainly do all this. Is there any man who holds it, and who, placing his hand upon his heart and lifting his face, dares to say that he has no duties that lie in these directions?

Let us take a very simple case for the illustration of our point. In a certain Western State there is a firm engaged in the manufacture and sale of lumber. They own immense tracts of pine lands, employ twelve hundred laborers, turn out seventy-five million feet of lumber annually, and make half a million of dollars every year, more or less. Now, one hundred thousand dollars will pay them royally for their time, an equal sum will give a large percentage on their capital invested, and yet not one-half of their income is exhausted. Here are three hundred thousand dollars left which go to the accumulations of superfluous wealth. Now, for these employers to imagine that their duties to these twelve hundred laborers are all done when they have paid them their wages, is shamefully to fail to find the divine significance of opportunities. To educate, to christianize, to develop, to make happy and self-respectful, to found homes for and protect and prosper these people, is the office of the superfluous wealth won from the profits of their work. We venture to say that in no community in which the superfluous wealth is used in this way will there ever be any questions between wealth and labor that are hard to settle. The holders of such wealth, wherever they may be, bear mainly in their hands the responsibility of whatever difficulties may hereafter arise between wealth and labor in the United States. Let them look to it and be wise.

POLITICS AND POLITICAL MEN.

THE GENTLEMAN IN POLITICS.

We do not doubt that many thousands have shared with us the pleasure of reading Mr. Whitelaw Reid's Dartmouth address, on "The Scholar in Politics." The programme of active influence which he spreads before the American scholar is sufficiently extensive, and the arguments by which he commends it for adoption sufficiently strong and sound. Yet the question has occurred to us whether, after all, Mr. Carlyle's "Able Man," and Mr. Herbert Spencer's "Thinker," and Mr. Reid's "Scholar," who are one and the same person, are quite sufficient for the just and satisfactory handling of the matters which this address spreads before us in detail. "How are you going to punish crime?" We do not quite see what scholarship has to do with the settlement of that question, or what the scholar has to do with it, specially, beyond other men. "How are you going to stop official stealing?" The question may interest the scholar, and he ought, indeed, to assist in settling it aright; but as a scholar, specially, we do not see what he can do, or may be expected to do, beyond other men. "How are you going to control your corporations?" Here cultivated brains may help us to do something—to contrive something; yet, after all, what we want is not the way to control corporations, but corporations that do not need to be controlled.

"What shall be the relations between capital and labor?" The scholar ought to be able to help us here. "What shall be done with our Indians?" "How may we best appoint our civil officers?" These questions, with others relating to universal suffrage and the unlimited annexation of inferior races, make up Mr. Reid's very solid and serious catalogue.

There is work enough, legitimate work, for the American scholar, in the study and intelligent handling of these questions; but the fact that there is a considerable number of American scholars mixed up with every scheme of iniquity in the country leads us to suspect that the country is not to be saved by scholarship alone. There are two sides to the matter, as there are to most matters. In our late civil war, it was West Point pitted against West Point, each side being actuated by its own independent ideas of duty and patriotism. Military scholarship had a very important office to perform in settling the question between the two sections of the country, but it had to struggle with military scholarship in order to do it. We do not know why we are not quite as likely to find the scholar on the wrong side as on the right side of politics. Mr. Bancroft and Mr. Everett were neighbors once. They represented the height of scholarly culture, and the two extremes of political opinion. They certainly assisted in making respectable whatever was bad in the party to which they respectively belonged, whatever else they did or failed to do. All that we wish to say, in dissent from Mr. Reid, or rather, in addition to him, is that scholarship does not necessarily lead to any common good conclusion in politics, and that it may be, or may become, as base as any other element.

What we really want is gentlemen in politics. If our political men were only gentlemen, even if they were no more than ordinarily intelligent, we should find our political affairs in a good condition, and the great questions that stand before us in a fair way of being properly adjusted. A gentleman is a person who knows something of the world, who possesses dignity and self-respect, who recognizes the rights of others and the duties he owes to society in all his relations, who would as soon commit suicide as stain his palm with a bribe, who would not degrade himself by intrigues. There are various types of gentlemen, too, and the higher the type the better the politician. If his character and conduct are based on sound moral principle—if he is governed by the rule of right—that is better than mere pride of character or gentlemanly instinct. If, beyond all, he is a man of faith and religion—a Christian gentleman—he is the highest type of a gentleman; and in his hands the questions which Mr. Reid has proposed to the scholar would have the fairest handling that men are capable of giving them. The more the Christian gentleman knows, the better politician he will make, and in him, and in him only, will scholarship come to its finest issues in politics. We do not think that the worst feature of our politics is lack of intelligence in our politicians. There is a great deal of cultivated brain in Congress. Public questions are understood and intelligently discussed there. Even there, it is not always that scholarship shows superior ability. Men who show their capacity to manage affairs are quite as apt to come from the plainly educated as from the ranks of scholarship. Congress does not suffer from lack of knowledge and culture half as much as it does from lack of principle. It is the men who push personal and party purposes that poison legislation. If Congress were composed of gentlemen, we could even dispense with what scholars we have, and be better off than we are to-day.

In the government of our cities, we could very well afford to get along without scholars, if we could have only modestly educated gentlemen. If the heavy-jawed, florid-faced, full-bellied, diamond-brooched bully who now typifies the city politician were put to his appropriate work of railroad-building, or superintending gangs of ignorant workmen, and there could be put in his place good, quiet business men, of gentlemanly instincts and of sound moral principle, we could get along very comfortably without the scholar, though there would not be the slightest objection to him. In brief, we want better men than we have, a great deal more than we want brighter or better educated men. Scholarship is a secondary, rather than a primary consideration: the gentleman first, the scholar, if he is a gentleman, and not otherwise. If Christian gentlemen were in power, many of the questions that appeal to us for settlement would settle themselves. We should not be called up on, for instance, to stop official stealing. Instead of trying to ascertain how we shall punish murder, we should dry up the fountains of murder. Instead of seeking a mode of controlling corporations, we should only need to find some mode of putting only gentlemen into corporations. Our laws are good enough in the main: we want them executed, and in order that they may be executed, we need a judiciary of Christian gentlemen, with executive officers, loyal to the law. As long as notorious scamps, scholarly or otherwise, are in power, not much headway can be made in politics. Until we demand something more and something better in our politicians than knowledge or scholarship, until we demand that they shall be gentlemen, we shall take no step forward. George Washington got along very well as a politician on a limited capital of culture, and a very large one of patriotism and personal dignity. Aaron Burr was a scholar, whose lack of principle spoiled him for any good end in politics, and made his name a stench in the nostrils of his country.

THE BANE OF THE REPUBLIC.

There can be no doubt that the prolific source of all our notable political corruption is office-seeking. Almost never does a political office come to a man in this country unsought; and the exceptions are very rarely creditable to political purity. When men are sought for, and adopted as candidates for office, it is, ninety-nine times in every hundred, because they are available for the objects of a party. Thus it is that selfish or party interest, and not the public good, becomes the ruling motive in all political preferment: and the results are the legitimate fruit of the motive. Out of this motive spring all the intrigues, bargains, sales of influence and patronage, briberies, corruptions and crookednesses that make our politics a reproach and our institutions a by-word among the nations. We are in the habit of calling our government popular, and of fancying that we have a good deal to do in the management of our own affairs; but we would like to ask those who may chance to read this paper how much, beyond the casting of their votes, they have ever had to do with the government of the nation. Have they ever done more than to vote for those who have managed to get themselves selected as candidates for office, or those who, for party reasons, determined exclusively by party leaders—themselves seekers for power or plunder—have been selected by others? It is all a "Ring," and has been for years; and we, the people, are called upon to indorse and sustain it.

To indorse and sustain the various political rings is the whole extent, practically, of the political privileges of the people of the United States. The fact is abominable and shameful, but it is a fact "which nobody can deny." It humiliates one to make the confession, but it is true that very rarely is any man nominated for a high office who is so much above reproach and so manifestly the choice of the people that his sworn supporters do not feel compelled to sustain him by lies and romances and all sorts of humbuggery. The people are treated like children. Songs are made for them to sing. Their eyes are dazzled with banners and processions, and every possible effort is made to induce them to believe that the candidate is precisely what he is not and never was—the candidate of the people. Our candidates are all the candidates of the politicians, and never those of the people. Our choice is a choice between evils, and to this we are forced. Second and third-rate men, dangerous men, men devoured by the greed for power and place, men without experience in statesmanship, men who have made their private pledges of consideration for services promised, men who have selected themselves, or who have been selected entirely because they can be used, are placed before us for our suffrages, and we are compelled to a choice between them. Thus, year after year, doing the best we seem to be able to do, we are used in the interest of men and cliques who have no interest to serve but their own.

And all this in the face of the patent truth that an office-seeker is, by the very vice of his nature, character, and position, the man who ought to be avoided and never indorsed or favored. There is something in the greed itself, and more in the immodesty of its declaration in any form, which make him the legitimate object of distrust and popular contempt. Office-seeking is not the calling of a gentleman. No man with self-respect and the modesty that accompanies real excellence of character and genuine sensibility can possibly place himself in the position of an office-seeker, and enter upon the intrigues with low-minded and mercenary men, which are necessary to the securing of his object. It is a debasing, belittling, ungentlemanly business. It takes from him any claim to popular respect which a life of worthy labor may have won, and brands him as a man of vulgar instincts and weak character. We marvel at the corruptions of politics, but why should we marvel? It is the office-seekers who are in office. It is the men who have sold their manhood for power that we have assisted to place there, obeying the commands or yielding to the wishes of our political leaders. It is notorious that our best men are not in politics, and cannot be induced to enter the field, and that our political rewards and honors are bestowed upon those who are base enough to ask for them.

A few of the great men of the nation have, during the last thirty years, yielded to that which was meanest in them, and become seekers for the august office of the presidency. Now to wish for a high place of power and usefulness is a worthy ambition, especially when it is associated with those gifts and that culture which accord with its dignities and render one fit for its duties; but to ask for it, and intrigue for it, and shape the policy of a life for it, is the lowest depth to which voluntary degradation can go. These men, every one of them, have come out from the fruitless chase with garments draggled, and reputation damaged, and the lesson of a great life—lived faithfully out upon its own plane—forever spoiled. How much more purely would the names of Webster, and Clay, and Cass shine to-day had they never sought for the highest place of power; and how insane are those great men now living who insist on repeating their mistakes! It would be ungracious to write the names of these, and it is a sad reflection that it is not necessary. They rise as quickly to him who reads as to him who writes. The great, proud names are dragged from their heights, and made the foot-balls of the political arena. The lofty heads are bowed, and the pure vestments are stained. Never again, while time lasts, can they stand where they have stood. They have made voluntary exposure of their weakness, and dropped into fatal depths of popular contempt. Now, when we remember that we are ruled mainly by men who differ from these only in the fact that they are smaller, and have not fallen so far because they had not so far to fall, we can realize something of the degradation which we have ourselves received in placing them in power.

What is our remedy? We confess that we are well-nigh hopeless in the matter. Bread and butter are vigilant. Politics to the politician is bread and butter, and we are all so busy in winning our own that we do not take the time to watch and thwart his intrigues. The only remedy thus far resorted to—and that has always been temporary—is a great uprising against corruption and wrong. We have seen something of it in the popular protest against the thieves of the New York Ring. What we need more than anything else, perhaps, is a thoroughly virtuous and independent press. We believe it impossible to work effectually except through party organizations, but such should be the intelligence, virtue, and vigilance of the press and the people that party leaders shall be careful to execute the party will. We need nothing to make our government the best of all governments except to take it out of the hands of self-seeking and office-seeking politicians, and to place in power those whom the people regard as their best men. Until this can be done, place will bring personal honor to no man, and our republicanism will be as contemptible among the nations as it is unworthy in itself.

Our President.

In the good time coming—the golden age—the blessed thousand years—which all Christian people pray for and expect, we are to have, among the multitude of excellent things, our particular President. When will it be? And what will be his name? The time when can hardly be foretold; and it matters very little by what name we may call him; but we can tell even now what sort of a person he will be, and it is a comfort to think of the dignities and gracious amenities that will accompany his manly sway.

In the first place, he will be a gentleman, and will have the manners of a gentleman. No vulgar peculiarities will commend him to vulgar people. He will humiliate himself by no appeals to low taste for securing the popular approval and support. The dirty brood of office-seekers and contractors and jobbing mercenaries will stand abashed in his pure presence. Nay, he will be hedged about by a dignity that will protect him from the approach of those upon whom he can only look with loathing and contempt. Petty politicians will find in him no congenial society, and his councils will be those of statesmanship. The representatives of foreign governments will come with all the high and gentle courtesies of which they may be masters, to pay him court, as the first gentlemen in a nation of many millions. The people who have placed him in power will look up to him with affectionate pride as their model man; and as the highest product of American civilization.

Again, he will be a wise man, and wise particularly in statecraft, through a life of conscientious study and careful and familiar practice in positions that have naturally led to his final elevation. He will live in an age when the present low ideas of availability will have passed away, and when personal fitness will be the essential qualification for place. He will have been brought into competition with none but those of his own kind. No warrior burdened with laurels for great achievements in his awful profession, no literary chieftain though crowned King in his own peculiar realm, no demagogue fingering the strings of a thousand intrigues, no boor dazzling the populace with the shows of wealth and polluting the ballot-box with its gifts, will have degraded the contest which resulted in his election. He will have reached his seat because a wise nation believed him to be its wisest man.

He will be a man of honor too, a man who will sooner die than permit any good reason to exist for the suspicion that he will use the privileges of his place for the perpetuation of his power. He will be a "one term" man, who will never for an instant permit his personal prospects to influence him in the performance of public duty; and when that term shall expire, he will retire to a still higher elevation in the popular esteem and reverence, and will not sink into the humble and almost disgraceful obscurity to which so many of his unworthy predecessors have been condemned. He will represent in his faith and practice the religion on which his country's purity and prosperity rest; for in that grand day the cavils and questions and infidelities that disgrace our shallow age will have passed away, and the brain and heart of Christendom will be christianized. There will be reverence for worth in the popular heart, and a Christian nation will have none but a Christian ruler.

After St. Paul returned from his vision of those heavenly things which it was not lawful for him to speak about, the small affairs of the men around him, and the mean and vulgar ways of those with whom he associated and to whom he preached, must have been somewhat disgusting. So, after looking at the ideal president in "the good time coming," we confess to a spasm of pain as we contemplate the political conflict that begins the moment a President is elected, with relation to his successor. Is it to be a conflict of great principles of government, earnestly held by men equally wise? Is it to be a conflict between men equally pure and equally patriotic? Is it to be a conflict between statesmen who are brought forward because of wisdom acquired by long service of the State in other capacities? Is it to be a conflict between gentlemen mutually respecting one another? Is it to be a conflict in which the dominant desire shall be that the best man, the most honorable man, the truest Christian, the wisest man, the purest and highest statesman, may win? Or, are considerations of personal and party advantage to be dominant? Is slander to be let loose? Is dirt to be thrown? Are the proprieties of society to be so outraged by personalities, that all decent men will learn to shun politics as they would shun exposure to a foul disease? There certainly is a better way than the one we walk in, and there are some at least who would be glad to find it. Let us try to find it.

AMERICAN LIFE AND MANNERS.

The Old Types.

The country-bred men and women who have reached the age of fifty years are all able to recall a picture—lying now far back in the mellow atmosphere of the past—of a band of children, standing hand-in-hand by the side of the dusty highway, and greeting with smile and bow and "courtesy" every adult passenger whom they met on their walks to and from school. They were instructed in this polite obeisance by their teachers. It was a part of the old New England drill, which, so far as we know, has been entirely discontinued. We do not remember to have seen such a sight as this for twenty-five years. It would be such an old-fashioned affair to witness now, that multitudes would only reward it with a smile of amusement; yet with all our boasted progress can we show anything that is better or more suggestive of downright, healthy good-breeding? Are the typical boy and girl of the period better mannered, more reverent, more respectful toward manhood and womanhood, more deferential to age? Do they grow up with more regard for morality, religion, law, than they did then? Alas! with all our books, and our new processes of education, and the universal sharpness of the juvenile intellect of the day, we miss something that was very precious among the children of the old time—reverence for men and women, systematic courtesy in simple forms, and respect for the wisdom of the pulpit, the school-room and the fireside. If we were called upon to describe the model boy or girl, we should be obliged to call up the old type—the rude, healthy lads and lasses who snow-balled each other, battled with each other in spelling-bouts, and imbibed the spirit of reverence for their elders with every influence of church and school and home. We have made progress in some directions, but in some we have sadly retrograded. Our boys are all young men, and our girls are fearfully old. Our typical child has no longer the spirit of a child.

Occasionally, we meet what are popularly denominated "gentlemen of the old school." We have only enough of them among us to make us wish that we had many more,—men of courtly dignity, of unobtrusive dress, of manners that seem a little formal but which are, nevertheless, the manners of gentlemen. They remind us of the worthies of the old colonial time, and of the later time of the Revolution—of Washington and Madison and Franklin—of men whom all revered, and to whom all gave obeisance. Into what has this style of men grown, or into what have they been degraded? Looking where they would be pretty certain to congregate if they were in existence, we see them not. Has any one seen them at Newport during the past season? Have they abounded at Saratoga? Have they been found in dignified and graceful association with the President of the United States at Long Branch? Are they presiding over municipal affairs in our great cities? Do they enter largely into the composition of Congress, even after we have subtracted the gamblers and carpet-baggers? If we have them in considerable numbers, where are they? Certainly they have either ceased to be reproduced in our generation, or they are so much disgusted with the type of men met in public life and fashionable society that they studiously hide themselves from sight. There is little comfort in either alternative, but we must accept one or the other.

Progress has doubtless been made in many things. We are richer, better clothed, better housed, better fed and better educated than we used to be. Our railroads run everywhere; our well-nigh exhaustless resources have been broached in a thousand directions; we count the increase of our population by millions; the emigrations of the world all move toward us; colleges, churches and school-houses have gone up with the building of the States, and the States themselves have multiplied so rapidly that not one American in ten knows exactly how many are in the Union. All this is true; but during the past twenty-five years we judge that we have made no improvement in the typical American gentleman. The old type of merchants—the old type of statesmen—the old type of gentlemen—surely we have not improved upon these. The restless, greedy, grasping, time-serving spirit of our generation has vitiated and degraded this type, and in our efforts at improvement we may well go back to the past for our models.

What shall we say about the old type of women as compared with the present representatives of the best of the sex? The saintly, heroic, frugal, industrious wives and mothers of the earlier days of the Republic—have we improved upon them? Have the latter-day doctrines of woman's rights made them more modest, more self-denying, more virtuous, better wives and mothers, purer and more active Christians, better heads of the institution of home, more lovely companions for men? We are aware that the answer to those questions involves the approval or the condemnation of the doctrines themselves, and it is well that the men and women of America be called upon to see and decide upon those doctrines from this point of view. Is the type of American woman improved? Has it been improved in the last twenty years, especially inside the circles that have taken the improvement of the position of woman upon their hands? America is full of good women. As a rule they are undoubtedly better than the men, but certainly the men whose instincts are true are attracted most to those women who approach nearest to the ancient type.

The final result of our civilization is to be reckoned in character. If this is not satisfactory, nothing is satisfactory. If we are not rearing better children and ripening better men and women than we were a century ago, then something is radically wrong, and the quicker we retrace our steps to see where we have diverged from the right track the better. The typical American—man, woman and child—is the representative product of all the institutions and influences of our civilization. As the type improves or degenerates, do these institutions and influences stand approved or condemned before the world. Progress cannot be reckoned in railroads and steamboats, or counted in money, or decided in any way by the census tables. Are we producing better children and better men and women? That is the question which decides everything; and we have called attention to the old types in order that we may arrive at an intelligent conclusion.

The Sins of American Good-nature.

An intelligent foreigner, traveling in America, was asked what he regarded as the most prominent characteristic of the people of the country. He replied: "The Americans are the best-natured people on the face of the earth." His judgment was entirely just. There is no other people, of anything like equal intelligence, that so absolutely refuses to be irritated by the impositions and annoyances of life. If an American is cheated in a shop, he simply refrains from entering the shop again. Instead of returning and demanding his rights, he pockets his bad bargain, because he does not like a quarrel, and cannot afford to take the trouble of it. After paying for a seat in a horse-car, the American holds himself ready to yield his right to any lady who enters, and to continue yielding his right until he is packed, standing like a bullock in a cattle-train, with fifty others, one-half of whom, in England or France, never would have been permitted to step foot upon the platform. The American consents that there shall be no such word as "*complet*" attached to any public conveyance. If a railway conductor, or a hotel clerk, or a shopkeeper's clerk, or any other person whose business it is to be courteous to the public, puts on airs and snubs the American customer, it is the ordinary habit of that customer to "stand it" rather than protest and insist on the treatment which he ought to receive. Rogues get into office, and, with big hands in the public purse, help themselves to its contents, and continue to do this year after year, the owners of the purse all the time knowing the fact, yet being too easy and good-natured to make even an outcry. Everybody is busy, and so the evils that would stir the blood of an Englishman to boiling, and arouse all his combativeness, are quietly ignored or carefully shunned.

It is not a pleasant thing to say, or to reflect upon, but the plain truth is that there is something cowardly and unmanly in all this. We have no special admiration of the touchiness of an Englishman regarding the sacred rights of his personality. The hedgehog is not an agreeable bird, and we have no wish to see it substituted for the American eagle; but a bundle of quills is better calculated to command respect than a ball of putty. The man who stands stiffly in his tracks and says, "Touch me not!" presents a very much more respectable appearance than the man who dodges him and every other obstacle which he encounters in his way. We are all very much afraid of hurting the feelings of somebody, when we know, or ought to know, that somebody's feelings ought to be hurt, and that nothing would do somebody so much good as to have his feelings hurt. We forget that there are things of infinitely greater importance than bad people's feelings—things to which we owe infinitely higher duty. A man has no moral right to permit himself to be robbed or cheated. If he tamely submits to such a crime he becomes accessory to it, and encourages the rascal at whose hand he has suffered to make a victim of the next unsuspecting customer.

The characteristic American good-nature not only encourages and confers impunity upon all sorts of wrong, but it seriously reacts upon American character. It begets a toleration of every kind of moral evil that brings at last insensibility to it. There cannot be a very wide moral difference between the man who commits crime and the man who weakly tolerates it. The active sinner is, if anything, the braver and the nobler of the two. He at least manifests a courage which the other does not. There is nothing that America needs more than the bold and persistent assertion, in every practical way, of its sense of what is fair and honest, and right and proper and courteous, between man and man. If every good man would stand squarely by this, even at the sacrifice of his reputation for good-nature, he would find himself growing better day by day; he would find that the good elements of society were rapidly gaining influence, and that rogues were growing careful and getting scarce.

Corporations like those which manage our railroads will impose upon the public just as long as the popular good-nature will permit them to do so. Their primary object is to make money. They will furnish to the public just such accommodations as the public will be content with, and those accommodations will be insufficient and mean unless the public demand more and better.

There are more evils than we can count that grow directly or indirectly out of our national good-nature. Our hearts need hardening, and our backs need stiffening. We ought to possess more manliness, and we ought to exercise it. To insist upon our rights in a manly and temperate way, is to give a lesson in Christian civilization. It makes us stronger and more self-respectful, and restrains the spirit of lawlessness around us. One prominent reason why crime thrives and the public morals go from bad to worse, is that they meet with no rebuke. The good people bemoan the facts in a weak way among themselves, but they refuse to meet the evils they bewail, front to front, with open challenge and bold conflict. Crime is a coward in the presence of courageous virtue, and shrinks and crawls whenever it boldly asserts itself. Now, virtue shrinks and crawls, while crime struts the streets and deals out such privileges to retiring decency and cowardly good-nature as it can afford. It even imitates our good-nature, and smiles upon us from the high places of its power and privilege, and laughs over its profits—and its joke.

Æsthetics at a Premium.

Our good Americans who flock to Europe every year usually return prepared to talk about the absorption of the new world in practical affairs, and the lack of the æsthetic element in American life. It is not to be expected, they say, in a tone which carries any amount of patronage and pardon with it, that a people who have forests to fell, and railroads to build, and prairies to plant, and cities to rear, and mines to uncover, and a great experiment to make in democratic government, should have time to devote to matters of taste. These latter things come with accumulated wealth and centuries of culture. We are necessarily in the raw now. The material overlies the spiritual. The whole nation, under the stimulus of a greed for wealth and the wide facilities for procuring it, is base. The almighty dollar is the national god; but it is confidently expected and predicted that we shall do better by-and-by. Let us see if there are not a few evidences that the better day is dawning.

New York has her Central Park, in which may be seen more genuine art and taste than have been devoted to any other park in the world. The Champs Elysées of Paris, the Thiergarten of Berlin, and Hyde Park in London, are all inferior to the Central Park in every respect. Now, to show how the element of taste in our life is surpassing the element of use—how the spiritual predominates over the material and practical—we have only to refer to our docks. It must be a matter of the serenest satisfaction and the most complacent pride that we, who have the reputation of being a city of money-getters and worshipers of the useful and the material, can point to our docks as the dirtiest, the most insufficient, and the least substantial of any possessed by any first-class city on the face of the globe. To the strangers who visit us from abroad we can proudly say: You have accused us of supreme devotion to the material grandeur of our city and our land. Look at our rotten and reeking docks, and see how little we care for even the decencies of commercial equipment, and then, if you can get safely on shore, come up to our Central Park, and forget all the coarser elements of life in the appointments and atmosphere of taste which will there surround you!

Have we not just founded a Metropolitan Museum of Art? Have we not established the nucleus of a collection which is to go on gathering to itself the contributions of the world and the ages? Are not our capitalists hoarding money for it? Do not our merchant princes go on piling up their millions with the proud design of remembering it in their wills? Nay, is not America the great art market of the world? Do we not run Rome as we would run a mill? Have we not transformed Munich, with her thousand artists, into a manufactory? Is not all Paris under tribute to us? Is it not our gold that makes yellower than sunshine the air in the studios of Florence? Yet we are accused of supreme devotion to the material, and this, too, in face of the fact that our city markets would be accounted a disgrace to any city in Christendom! We do not even undertake to have markets that are decently clean. The costliest viands that crown our feasts come from realms foul with impure odors, and from stalls past which a clean skirt never sweeps without disaster. To the caitiff who should accuse us of a gross and sensual life, and of devotion to the matters of eating and drinking, we would say: look at Fulton Market,—the meanest shed that ever covered a city's food—and then, when you have seen how little we care for even the appearance of cleanliness, go with us to the Metropolitan Museum of Art, to a hundred private galleries on Fifth and Madison Avenues, and to the walls of drawing-rooms that are covered with millions of dollars worth of pictures, and acknowledge that the æsthetic holds us in absolute thrall, while we take no care for what we eat and what we drink!

New York a city devoted to the material! Why, it has not a single well-kept street! There is not one street in the whole city that is as clean any day as every principal street of Paris is every day. There are scores of streets that are piled with garbage from one end to the other. There are scores of streets so rough with worn-out pavements that no ordinary carriage can be driven through them at a rapid rate without the danger of breaking it. There are streets by the hundred that hold people so thoughtless of even the common decencies of life, that they keep their ash-barrels constantly upon their sidewalks, where they stand in long rows,—lines of eloquent monuments —testifying to the absorption of our citizens in purely æsthetic pursuits. When we pass from such streets as these into houses holding the best-dressed men and women in the world, surrounded by every appointment of tasteful luxury,—men and women whose feet press nothing but velvet, and whose eyes see nothing but forms of beauty (except when they happen to look out of the window), we may well point the finger of scorn at those who taunt us with being devoted to the gratification of our senses. New York devoted to the senses! Why, it is not even courteous to the senses: it does not so much as hold its nose!

We might proceed with the illustrations of our point, but they would be interminable. We might show how we have so left out of consideration the matter of utility in the erection of beautiful churches that we have spent all our available money without giving half our people sittings, and in doing so have made the sittings so expensive that not half of them are occupied. There is money enough invested in churches in New York to give every man and woman a sitting, and support the ministers, without costing a poor man a cent. Can this justly be called supreme devotion to practical affairs? Our love of fine architecture has even led us to forget our religion; and yet we are accused of having no love of art! Let us comfort ourselves with the consciousness that we have arrived at that pitch of civilization which enables us to hold an even head with Rome, whose atmosphere of art is malaria, or with old Cologne, whose exquisite cathedral bathes its feet in gutters that reek with the vapors of disease, and the nastinesses of a people absorbed in making Cologne water, and in the worship of eleven thousand virgins, none of whom are living.

The Conservative Resources of American Life.

We are witnessing, in these passing days, new demonstrations of the Conservative influences and resources of American life. Reflecting persons are sometimes scared by the liberty and latitude which our institutions confer upon every kind and class of men, and are filled with the gravest apprehensions while contemplating the tendencies of society to corruption and extravagance, or other forms of vice and folly. With a press whose liberty is absolutely unbridled; with the privilege of universal self-direction and self-service unwatched and untouched by the police; with a freedom of speech and movement that more frequently forgets than remembers that there is such a thing as law, and with an underlying conviction and consciousness that human nature is selfish, and that great masses of society are almost hopelessly degraded, it is not wonderful that there are thinking men who look despondingly into the future, and who load their lips with prophecies of evil.

A gentleman who had been at both the sieges of Paris, and who had spent much time in Europe, was present during the late Orange riot in New York, and witnessed its suppression. He was filled with wonder at the ease with which it was handled, the lack of all apprehension of a dangerous outbreak on the part of the people of the city, and with the fact that everybody went to bed on the night of the riot and slept soundly, in the confident expectation of finding the city in perfect peace the next morning. Such an event in any capital of Europe would have aroused the intensest suspicions on the part of the government, and led to the most jealous and efficient precautions, while the people, greedy for change and ready for anything that would give them liberty, if only for a day, would have been roused into a fury of sleepless excitement. In Paris, it would have been the signal for a revolution. In New York, opposed by a militia called out from among the people themselves, it never had the chance to do any damage except to the misguided men who were engaged in it.

Not long ago New York City was in the hands of a gang of such gigantic thieves as the world has rarely produced, in all its centuries of fruitful wickedness. There was no ingenuity of corrupt expedient that had been left untried, in the achievement and retention of power. There was no scheme of plunder too bold and shameless for them to undertake. They had suborned judges, and bribed legislators, and tampered with administration. Their tools and servants were in offices of trust. Their paid bullies were a terror at every polling-place. Surrounded by every appointment and feasted by every ministry of luxury, they defied public sentiment and public punishment, and laid their plans for the future with the confidence of integrity, and half deceived themselves with the thought that they were gentlemen. But the press, in its fearless liberty, laid hold of them, dragged them forth from their strongholds of crime and shame, and exposed them to the execration of the men they had wronged and robbed. The sceptre dropped from their hands, and, in a few brief months, the whole infamous gang became fugitives from justice.

No scheme of iniquity can stand under the exposure of a faithful press. The little pencil of Nast alone, when employed in a thoroughly righteous cause, is more powerful than armies of men and millions of money. It is the habit of some good men to bemoan the licentiousness of the press, and its undignified and often disgraceful quarrels and personalities; but, with all its faults it is the very bulwark of the public safety. Without the press, the great metropolis would be to-day in the hands of the Ring. Indeed, without the press—perfectly untrammeled—there can be no hope of the perpetuation of the liberties of the country. That power which kings and emperors fear, and seek to regulate and control, is the power which alone can preserve the republic. Monarchs recognize its voice as the voice of the people, and the republic that fails to do the same becomes its own enemy.

In contemplating society, we easily detect certain tendencies that seem to have no end except in disaster or destruction. "Whither are we drifting?" is the questioning cry. There is prevailing and increasing infidelity to the marital vow; there is growing of lavish luxury; there is deepening and spreading corruption in high places; there is augmentation of desire to win wealth without work; there is a fiercer burning of the fever of speculation; there is a lengthening reach and strengthening grasp upon power on the part of great corporations, whose effect is to limit the liberty and diminish the prosperity of the people. We mark these tendencies to enormous and disastrous evil, and it seems as if nothing could avert its near or distant coming; but, at last, the people turn their eyes upon the disease that threatens greatest danger, the press in tones of thunder speaks the voice of the popular conviction and reprehension, and all in good time the wrong is righted, the drift toward destruction is arrested, and the agents of mischief are reformed or rendered powerless. This is the lesson of the last ten years of American life, and it is full of hope and promise. We are not likely to encounter anything more terrible in the future than those evils—political and social—which this conservative power has arrested in their course, or expelled. We drift toward a precipice, but when the waters quicken, and we feel ourselves tossing among the rapids, we spring to the oars, and with free, strong arms we row back to broader waters and sweeter and safer shores. We have the strongest faith in the conservative power of our free American life, and, with all our tendencies to evil, we firmly believe that we have the strongest government and the safest society of any great people whose life helps to weave the current history of Christendom.

Living with Windows Open.

More than any other people in the world, Americans live with their windows open. Less than any people who have homes do they regard their homes as sacredly private. Every family knows its neighbor's affairs; and nothing transpires concerning the most private relations that is not immediately noised abroad, discussed, and judged by meddling and gossiping communities. Homes that should be guarded with the most jealous care are of easy access to strangers, who come with the flimsiest credentials, or with none at all; and every year produces its crop of personal and social disasters which this unwise exposure of the soil gives to reckless or villainous sowing. If a man should wish to see how Americans differ in this thing from other nations, let him try to get into a German or an English family, or even into a French family, abroad. He will at once discover that he has undertaken to do a very difficult thing. No man can obtain an inside view of the economies and habits of a foreign home, and share in its communion, who does not enter it with a record or an introduction and indorsement which place him above suspicion. Students who go to continental Europe to study language, with the natural expectation to accomplish their purpose by entering a French or a German family, find, to their surprise, that nothing but necessity will induce any family to open its sanctities to them.

It will naturally be said that old or mature communities are conservative in this, as in other matters; but we do not see that, as America grows older, it mends in this respect. Indeed, it is certainly and swiftly growing worse. The greed for personalities—the taste for everything relating to the life of individuals—and the base desire to be talked about, were never more prevalent than now. We have only to take up a fashionable paper to learn who has had parties, who attended the parties, who were the belles of the parties, and how they were dressed; and we know while we read that the ladies who gave the parties gave also the information concerning them, and were glad to see the reports in print. Weddings, which should be sacred to kindred and closest friends, are turned into public shows; and trousseaus are inventoried by the daily prints and spread before the country. It is not enough that one's marriage be published when it takes place, but the engagement must be bruited in *Jenkins's Journal*, Jenkins having previously been assured that the announcement would not be offensive, and subsequently repaid by an order for extra papers. The inanities of the Court Journal, over which Americans were in the habit of laughing a dozen years ago, are more than matched by the daily report of the movements of every man of title, or place, or notoriety. When a woman lectures, the reporters understand that the first thing people wish to learn about her relates to her face, figure, and dress; and that is the first thing they write about. The women of the platform—being all very sensible women, and too wise to be vain—are of course offended by this treatment; but it somehow happens that the reports are generally of a flattering character.

It would be possible to get along with all this. A man may become used to smothering his sense of humiliation and disgust when reading the public record of private life, so long as that record is made with the consent, or at the wish, of those to whom it relates; but it happens that we have in America now a prowling, prying, far-seeing, vivacious, loquacious, voracious being known as the Local Editor, who must get a living, and who lives only upon items. If a man sneeze twice in his presence, the local column of the morning paper will contain the anouncement that "our esteemed fellow-citizen" is suffering from a severe cold. If a man lose his hat in a high wind, it excites the mirth of the local editor to the extent of a dozen lines. He amplifies an accident that kills, or a scandal that ruins, with marvelous minuteness of detail. His eye is at every man's back door, to see and report who and what go and come. There is nothing safe from his pen. All the private affairs of the community for which he writes are published to that community every day. If a man shoots a dog, or catches a string of trout, or rides out for his health, or is seen mysteriously leaving town on an evening train, or sells a horse, or buys a cow, or gives a dinner-party, or looks sallow, or grows fat, or smiles upon a widow, or renews the wall-paper of his house, he gives the local editor an item. The local editor turns the houses of the community inside out every day, and keeps the windows open by which the secrets and sanctities of every home are exposed to public view.

The local editor is, we regret to say, not without excuse. Occasionally some indignant victim of his prying and publishing propensities scourges or scolds him; but it must be confessed, with sorrow and shame, that his local column finds a greedy market. Instead of frowning upon the liberty he takes with persons and homes, and the details of individual private life, the multitude read his column first of all. That its results are mischievous and demoralizing in their ministry to neighborhood gossip and scandal, there is no doubt. Among its worst results is the destruction of all reverence for the right of every private man to live privately, and of every home to live with its windows closed. There is unquestionably a desire in a certain sort of private life to get into the papers—a desire to spread all the details of its doings before the world. This life may be "high" or low, fashionable or unfashionable, but it is irredeemably vulgar, and can only disgust every self-respectful and dignified man and woman. Let us protest on behalf of decency against the familiar treatment which the retiring and the unwilling receive in the local column, and in the more ambitious performances of the omnipresent Jenkins. Let us at least have the privilege of repeating the cry of Betsy Trotwood, when her little patch of green was invaded, "Janet! donkeys!"

THE CURE FOR GOSSIP.

Everybody must talk about something. The poor fellow who was told not to talk for the fear that people would find out that he was a fool, made nothing by the experiment. He was considered a fool because he did not talk. On some subject or another, everybody must have something to say, or give up society. Of course, the topics of conversation will relate to the subjects of knowledge. If a man is interested in science, he will talk about science. If he is an enthusiast in art, he will talk about art. If he is familiar with literature, and is an intelligent and persistent reader, he will naturally put forward literary topics in his conversation. So with social questions, political questions, religious questions. Out of the abundance of the heart the mouth speaketh. That of which the mind is full —that with which it is furnished—will come out in expression.

The very simple reason why the world is full of gossip, is, that those who indulge in it have nothing else in them. They must interest themselves in something. They know nothing but what they learn from day to day, in intercourse with, and observation of, their neighbors. What these neighbors do,—what they say,—what happens to them in their social and business affairs,—what they wear,—these become the questions of supreme interest. The personal and social life around them—this is the book under constant perusal, and out of this comes that pestiferous conversation which we call gossip. The world is full of it; and in a million houses, all over this country, nothing is talked of but the personal affairs of neighbors. All personal and social movements and concerns are arraigned before this high court of gossip, are retailed at every fireside, are sweetened with approval or embittered by spite, and are gathered up as the common stock of conversation by the bankrupt brains that have nothing to busy themselves with but tittle-tattle.

The moral aspects of gossip are bad enough. It is a constant infraction of the Golden Rule; it is full of all uncharitableness. No man or woman of sensibility likes to have his or her personal concerns hawked about and talked about; and those who engage in this work are meddlers and busybodies who are not only doing damage to others—are not only engaged in a most unneighborly office—but are inflicting a great damage upon themselves. They sow the seeds of anger and animosity and social discord. Not one good moral result ever comes out of it. It is a thoroughly immoral practice, and what is worst and most hopeless about it is, that those who are engaged in it do not see that it is immoral and detestable. To go into a man's house, stealthily, when he is away from home, and overhaul his papers, or into a lady's wardrobe and examine her dresses, would be deemed a very dishonorable thing; but to take up a man's or a woman's name, and smirch it all over with gossip—to handle the private affairs of a neighbor around a hundred firesides—why this is nothing! It makes conversation. It furnishes a topic. It keeps the wheels of society going.

Unhappily for public morals, the greed for personal gossip has been seized upon as the basis of a thrifty traffic. There are newspapers that spring to meet every popular demand. We have agricultural papers, scientific papers, literary papers, sporting papers, religious papers, political papers, and papers devoted to every special interest, great and small, that can be named, and, among them, papers devoted to personal gossip. The way in which the names of private men and women are handled by caterers for the public press—the way in which their movements and affairs are heralded and discussed—would be supremely disgusting were it not more disgusting that these papers find greedy readers enough to make the traffic profitable. The redeeming thing about these papers is, that they are rarely malicious except when they are very low down—that they season their doses with flattery. They find their reward in ministering to personal vanity.

What is the cure for gossip? Simply, culture. There is a great deal of gossip that has no malignity in it. Good-natured people talk about their neighbors because, and only because, they have nothing else to talk about. As we write, there comes to us the picture of a family of young ladies. We have seen them at home, we have met them in galleries of art, we have caught glimpses of them going from a bookstore, or a library, with a fresh volume in their hands. When we meet them, they are full of what they have seen and read. They are brimming with questions. One topic of conversation is dropped only to give place to another, in which they are interested. We have left them, after a delightful hour, stimulated and refreshed; and during the whole hour not a neighbor's garment was soiled by so much as a touch. They had something to talk about. They knew something, and wanted to know more. They could listen as well as they could talk. To speak freely of a neighbor's doings and belongings would have seemed an impertinence to them, and, of course, an impropriety. They had no temptation to gossip, because the doings of their neighbors formed a subject very much less interesting than those which grew out of their knowledge and their culture.

And this tells the whole story. The confirmed gossip is always either malicious or ignorant. The one variety needs a change of heart and the other a change of pasture. Gossip is always a personal confession either of malice or imbecility, and the young should not only shun it, but by the most thorough culture relieve themselves from all temptation to indulge in it. It is a low, frivolous, and too often a dirty business. There are country neighborhoods in which it rages like a pest. Churches are split in pieces by it. Neighbors are made enemies by it for life. In many persons it degenerates into a chronic disease, which is practically incurable. Let the young cure it while they may.

American Incivility.

There is, undoubtedly, something in the political equality established by American institutions which interferes with the development of civility among those who occupy what are denominated the lower walks of life. It is hard to see why this should be so. One would naturally suppose that political equality would breed reciprocal respect among all classes and individuals, no less than self-respect. Certainly there could hardly be a better basis of good manners than self-respect and respect for others; yet, with everything in our institutions to devolop these, together with a respect for woman which is entertained in no other country with which we are acquainted, it is not to be denied that among the workers of the nation politeness is little known and less practiced. A man who steps into Washington Market, with a good coat on, looking for his dinner, will receive the utmost politeness of which the stall-keeper is capable, and this will consist in calling him "boss"—a boorish concession to civility for the sake of trade. The courteous greeting, the "Sir," and the "Madam," the civil answer, the thousand indescribable deferences and attentions, equally without servility or arrogance, which reveal good manners, are wanting.

It all comes, we suppose, of the fear of those who find themselves engaged in humble employments, that they shall virtually concede that somebody somewhere is better than themselves. It is singular that they should voluntarily take a course that proves the fact that they are so unwilling to admit to themselves and others. The man who undertakes to prove that he is as good as a gentleman, by behaving like a boor, volunteers a decision against himself; while he who treats all men politely builds for himself a position which secures the respect of all whose conduct is not condemned by his own. The American is a kinder man than the Frenchman, and better-natured than the Englishman, but the humble American is less polite than either. One of the charms of Paris to the traveling American grows out of the fact that it is one of the first places he visits, and that then, for the first time in his life, he comes into contact with a class of humble people who have thoroughly good manners. He is not called "boss," or "hoss." He is himself put upon his good behavior, by the thoroughly courteous treatment he receives among railway officials, shop-keepers, waiters at café and hotel, cab-drivers, etc. The "bien! Monsieur," and "bien! Madame," which responds to one's requests in Paris, is certainly very sweet and satisfactory after: "all right, boss; you can bet on't."

Where the cure for our National trouble is coming from, it is hard to tell. There was a time, fifty years ago, when there was a degree of reverence in American children, and at least a show of good manners. Great respect to those of superior age and culture was then inculcated, and at least formal courtesy exacted. Certainly much of this training is done with. Even the men and women—fathers, mothers, and teachers of fifty years ago, had receded from the courteous habits of previous generations. In the old colonial, and even later days, great respect was paid to dignities. The clergymen was reverenced because he was a clergyman, and occupied the supreme position of teacher of the people. He was reverenced not only because of his holy calling, but because he was a scholar. All this has gone by. The clergyman, if he is a good fellow, is very much liked and petted, but the old reverence for him, and universal courtesy toward him, are unknown.

Are the people any better for all this change? We think not, and we do not doubt that the change itself has much to do with the habits of incivility of which we complain. Men must have some principle of reverence in them, as a basis of good manners, and this principle of reverence in the modern American child has very little development. He comes forward early, and the first thing he does in multitudes of instances is to lose his respect for his parents. Poor men and women try to give their children better chances than they had themselves, and the children grow up with contempt for those whose sacrifices have raised them to a higher plane of culture. They call the teacher "Old Snooks," or "Old Bumble," or whatever his name may happen to be. It is not unjust to declare that there is in America to-day no attempt, distinctly and definitely made, to cultivate a spirit of reverence in children.

We acknowledge that we have no faith in any attempt to reform the manners of the adult population of the country. Our efforts to make sober men out of drunkards, and total-abstinence men out of moderate drinkers, are failures. Our temperance armies are to be made entirely out of children. We can raise more Christians by juvenile Christian culture, than by adult conversion, a thousand to one. So it will be in this matter of National politeness. The parents and teachers of the country can give us a polite people, and this by the cultivation of the principle of reverence not only, but by instruction in all the forms of polite address. With a number of things greatly needed to-day in home culture and school study, this matter of training in good manners is not the least. Indeed we are inclined to think it is of paramount importance. It should become a matter of text-books at once. A thorough gentleman or lady, who has brains enough to comprehend principles, while proficient in practice, could hardly do a better service to the country than by preparing a book for parents and teachers, as at once a guide to them and to those who are under them. Children must be trained to politeness, or they will never be polite. They must drink politeness in with their mother's milk; it must be exacted in the family and neighborhood relations; and boys and girls must grow up gentlemen and ladies in their deportment, or our nation can never be a thoroughly polite one—polite in soul as well as in ceremony, and kind in manner as well as kind in heart.

Where are the Young Men?

There are curious facts, noticeable in the Eastern States, to which occasional allusion is made in conversation and the newspapers—facts which illustrate the scarcity of young men of a certain class. At every fashionable summer resort, the small number of young men and the comparative plentifulness of young women are matters of notoriety. If there should happen to be, in such a gathering as this, half a dozen young men, of unexceptionable position, to six times that number of young women in a corresponding position, the thirty-six women would account themselves peculiarly fortunate. In a hotel "hop," one will see half the girls with partners of their own sex. The ladies of a traveling party in Europe are, as a rule, in an overwhelming majority. The fact that beaux are scarce in all public places, is one with which the young women of the Eastern States are painfully familiar. There are many good reasons to be offered for this disproportion of the sexes in such places—the pressure of work or of study upon the men, at a period of life when their time is not wholly at their disposal, being the principal one.

If it were only in the resorts for summer recreation that young men are scarce, the fact would not be noteworthy particularly. They ought to have something to do, and enough to do to keep them from spending a great deal of time in the pursuit of pleasure. It is a startling fact, however, that the young men of the first class or those regarded as belonging to the first class, are as scarce in the towns as they are at the summer hotels. The marriageable girls among Eastern families of the best position are in overwhelmingly larger numbers than are the marriageable young men in the same position. Something of this is due to the ravages made by the late war among the ranks of the young men. Something more is due to the emigration westward of great numbers of them, so that, in some of the Western States, the men outnumber the women. Whatever the causes may be, they are sufficient to establish a marked inequality in the number of the sexes in the class to which we allude. There are many social circles, in every Eastern city and considerable town, embracing great numbers of beautiful and well-educated young women, in which there cannot be found a brilliant or even particularly desirable match among the men. Two or three hackneyed beaux, whose hair remains black by reason of the barber, and whose teeth are sound by reason of the dentist, do the polite for two or three generations of beauties, and are so busy in the service that they forget to marry, and so pass away; while, shrinking into a thriftless maidenhood, with hearts unwon and charms unappropriated, the sweet life of the women dries up, and sinks to the dust from which it rose.

Now to us this is one of the most sad and serious things connected with our social condition; and it has a world to do with the uneasiness of women, manifested in various ways,—the universal seeking for something with which to fill up life, and make it significant.

But we have a practical reason for calling attention to this matter; and this we propose to present in a statement relating to a large number of young men, usually assigned to the second class in society. While our fine girls are bemoaning the lack of young men, and the scarcity of beaux who are marriageable and who mean marriage, there is a class of young men whom they do not recognize at all, yet who will furnish to the next generation its men of enterprise, of power, of position, and of wealth. It is not the sons of the rich who will, as a rule, remain rich. The sons of the poor will get rich; and there are to-day, drudging in offices, and counting-rooms, and store-houses, and machine-shops, and printing establishments, the men who, in twenty-five years, will control the nation socially, politically, and financially. Every man of them means to be married; they will, as a rule, make excellent husbands; they are all at work trying to win success. They are men who would be easily improved by recognition, and by bringing them into good, intelligent society; yet they are as little noticed as if they were so many dogs. Virtuous young men from the country go into the city, and live for years without any society, and are regarded by the fashionable young women with indifference or contempt; but those young men have a hold upon the future; and when their success is won, in whatever field of enterprise it may be, the fashionable will be glad to claim them as belonging to their own number. We regret to say that, as a rule, the young men for whom a position has been won by virtuous and enterprising fathers amount to but little in the world; and we rejoice to say that companions chosen from those who have their fortunes to make and their position to win, are those to whom a well-bred woman can generally with safety intrust her happiness and herself.

If there is anything in all these facts, thus brought into association, which points out a duty to "our best society," and urges its performance, even by selfish motives, it will be readily perceived. The hope of the country is in this second grade of young men. They ought to have better social privileges. What better capital can a man have than youth, virtue, intelligence, health, and enterprise? What better claim than these can any man present for admission into good society? To young men of this class, now almost wholly neglected, the society of educated and accomplished women would be a rare and fruitful privilege—fruitful to themselves, and quite as fruitful to those whose courtesies they receive.

The American Restaurant.

The typical American restaurant is an establishment quite as well individualized, and quite as characteristic, as anything of the kind to be found in the world. The French *café*, the German beer-garden, and the English chop-house, all have their characteristic habits, appearance, and manners; but the American restaurant is like neither of them. It can only be conducted by an American, and, we regret to say, it can only be frequented and enjoyed by Americans of the second and lower grades. The aim of the conductor seems to be to sell the greatest amount of food in the shortest possible time—an aim which the guests invariably second, by eating as rapidly as possible. We have seen, in a Broadway restaurant, a table surrounded by men, all eating their dinners with their hats on, while genuine ladies, elegantly dressed, occupied the next table, within three feet of them. In this restaurant there was as much din in the ordering of dishes and the clash of plates and knives and forks, as if a brass band had been in full blast. Every dish was placed before the guests with a bang. The noise, the bustle, the hurry, in such a place, at dinner time, can only be compared to that which occurs when the animals are fed in Barnum's caravan. We do not exaggerate at all when we say that the American restaurant is the worst-mannered place ever visited by decent people. No decent American ever goes into one when he can help it, and comparatively few decent people know how very indecent it is.

Our best hotels have no equals in the world, and, in asserting this, we know what we say, and "speak by the card." Our best restaurants are mainly kept by foreigners, or, if not, are modeled upon the French type. Nowhere in the world can there be found better cooking, more quiet and leisurely manners, or better service, than in the restaurants of the hotels above alluded to, or the best class of eating-houses. These, however, are direct or indirect importations; while the American restaurant, pure and proper, serves the needs of the great multitude of business men—clerks, porters, and upper-class laborers generally. These do not eat—they feed. Thousands of them would regard it as an affectation of gentility to remove their hats while feeding; and they sit down, order their dinner, which,—pudding, pastry, vegetables, and meat,—is all placed before them in one batch, and then "pitch in." The lack of courtesy, of dignity, of ordinary tokens even of self-respect, would be amusing if it were not so humiliating.

It is useless for the incredulous American to ask the question, "where have you been?" When in a second-rate restaurant a guest asks for fish-balls and hears his order repeated to the cook by the colored waiter as "sleeve-buttons for one!" and hears his neighbor's order for pork and beans transformed into "stars and stripes," he begins to wonder, indeed, whether "civilization" is not "a failure," and whether "the Caucasian" is not "played out." The average American, in the average American restaurant, eats his dinner in the average time of six minutes and forty-five seconds. He bolts into the door, bolts his dinner, and then bolts out. There is no thought of those around him, no courtesy to a neighbor, no pleasant word or motion of politeness to the man or the woman who receives his money—nothing but a fearful taking in of ammunition—the feeding of a devouring furnace—and then a desperate dash into the open air, as if he were conscious he had swallowed poison, and must find a doctor and a stomach-pump, or die. A favorite method of devouring oysters is to stand, or to sit on a high stool, always with the hat on;—oysters on the half-shell and the eater under a half-shell. There may be something in the position that favors deglutition: we don't know.

The penalty a man pays for getting his lunch or his dinner at a reasonable price is to encounter the offensive scenes we have described. The penalty he pays for eating where he finds the manners of civilization is an unreasonable price. When a man pays half a dollar for a bit of cold meat, or seventy-five cents for a steak, or a quarter of a dollar for a couple of boiled eggs, he recalls sorrowfully and wonderingly,—if he has ever traveled,—the nice little breakfasts he used to get at Madame Dijon's in Paris for two francs, his dinners in the *Palais Royal* for three, his daily board, with rooms, at the *Pension Picard*, in Geneva, for five, and his luxurious apartments with an elaborate *table d'hôte* at all the principal hotels of the Continent for ten. Is there any necessity for such prices as we are obliged to pay at the best restaurants—or any apology for them? Any man who keeps house, and does his own marketing, knows the first cost of the expensive dishes placed before him in these restaurants, and he knows there is no just relation between the cost and the price charged, after all allowance has been made for cooking, service, rent, etc.

Sometime or other there will be a change, we suppose. When the times of inflation are gone by, when on one side men will content themselves with reasonable profits, and on the other, money comes harder and slower, we shall have a reform of prices in the better class of eating-houses. Our expectations in regard to the second-rate places are more indefinite. It takes several generations to train a people to ideas of refinement and good manners at the table. The average German has nothing to boast of yet in this respect, and we can only hope that the American, with his greater sensitiveness and quicker instincts, will reach the desired point before him.

The Common Schools.

It seems rather late in our history as a nation to be discussing the question whether the State is transcending its legitimate functions in educating its children; yet, by the letters which we read in the newspapers, it appears that there are people who entertain the question in its affirmative phase, and who declare that the duty of education attaches only to the parent. In what interest these men write we do not know,—whether in the interest of their pockets or their religious party. It is exceedingly hard to give them credit for either intelligence or candor. The lessons of history are so plain, the results of universal education have been so beneficent, the ignorance that dwells everywhere where education has been left to the parent and the church is so patent and so lamentable in every aspect and result, that it seems as if no man could rationally and candidly come to a conclusion adverse to the American policy in this matter. The simple fact that we are obliged to pass laws to keep young children out of factories and bring them to the free schools, shows how utterly indifferent multitudes of parents are concerning the education of their children, and how soon the American nation would sink back into the popular apathy and ignorance which characterize some of the older peoples of the world.

A State is a great, vital organization, endowed by the popular mind with a reason for being, and by the popular will with a policy for self-preservation. This policy takes in a great variety of details. It protects commerce by the establishment of light-houses, the deepening of channels, the establishment of storm-signals, etc. It ministers in many ways to the development of the country's internal resources. It fosters agriculture. It is careful of all its prosperities and sources of prosperity. It establishes a currency. It organizes and superintends an elaborate postal service. It carries on all the processes of a grand organic life. Our own nation governs itself, and one of the conditions of all good government is intelligence at the basis of its policy. An ignorant people cannot, of course, govern themselves intelligently; and the State, endowed with its instinct, or its policy, of self-preservation, is, and ought to be, more sensitive at this point than at any other. In the minds of the people, the State has the sources of its life; and to those sources, by unerring instinct, our own country has, from the first, looked for its perpetuity.

There is no organization of life, individual and simple, or associated and complex, in which the instinct, impulse, or principle of self-preservation is not the predominant one. We fought the war of the Revolution to establish our nationality, and the war of the Rebellion to maintain it. We have spent, first and last, incalculable blood and treasure to establish and keep our national life intact, and the national policy with relation to public schools is part and parcel of that all-subordinating determination to secure the perpetuity of the State. Men make better citizens for being educated. The higher the popular intellect is raised, the more intelligent and independent will be its vote. The stronger the sources of government, the stronger the government. If the "bayonets that think" are the most potent, the ballots that think are the most beneficent.

The question, then, which has been raised, touching the duty of the State in the matter of popular education, is a question which concerns the life and perpetuity of the State, and is a question, not for a church, not for a parent, or for any subordinate combination of parents, to decide. It is a question for the State to decide,—not, of course, from any humanitarian point of view, but from its own point of view. To put the question into form, that question would read something like this: "Can I, the American State, afford to intrust to heedless or mercenary parents, or to any church organization, which either makes or does not make me subordinate to itself, the education of the children of the nation, when my own existence and best prosperity depend upon the universality and liberality of that education?" There are many other vital questions which the State might ask in this connection,—for patriotism, as a sentiment, grows with the beneficence of the institutions under which it lives. Every victory which our nation has ever won has been a victory of the common school. This has been the nursery, not only of our patriots, but of our soldiers. In the Franco-Prussian war, the universally educated crossed swords with the partially educated, and the latter went to the wall.

This matter of leaving education to parents and to churches is, to use the familiar but expressive slang of the street, "played out." If the advocates of this policy could point to a single well-educated nation on the face of the globe, whose popular intelligence is the result of that policy, they might have some claim to be heard; but no such nation exists. Where priests and parents have had it all their own way for generations and centuries, there is to be found the greatest degree of popular ignorance; and the men whose votes most seriously menace the health and permanence of American institutions and American life are the very men we have imported from those regions. They are the men whom designing demagogues can buy and bribe, and lead whithersoever they will,—men who cannot read the ballots they deposit, and are as ignorant of politics as the horses they drive, or the pigs they feed.

We have not taken up this subject because we consider the common schools in danger. They are not in danger. The State will never relinquish its policy in this matter. The common school, as an American institution, will live while America lives. Not only this, but the signs are unmistakable that it is to be more far-reaching in its efforts and results than it ever has been. Popular education is one of the primary functions of the State's life. No democratic government can long exist without it, and our best people are thoroughly confirmed in this conviction. We have taken up the subject simply to show that the State cannot "go back on" its record without the surrender of the policy which grows out of the instinct of all living organizations for self-protection and self-preservation. To surrender this policy would be, not only foolish, but criminal; and there is not one American institution that American people would sooner fight for and die for, than that which secures an educated and intelligent nationality.

THE END.

www.ingramcontent.com/pod-product-compliance
Lightning Source LLC
LaVergne TN
LVHW020108110826
845151LV00001B/99

* 9 7 8 1 4 2 5 5 4 4 2 7 0 *